THE SOCIETY OF STATES

THE SOCIETY OF STATES

An Introduction to International Politics

Robert Purnell

Lecturer in International Politics
University College of Wales, Aberystwyth

Weidenfeld & Nicolson, London

ISBN 0 297 76644 9

Printed in Great Britain by
Cox & Wyman Ltd,
London, Fakenham and Reading

For Catherine Julia
with love

Contents

Figures

Behold, my son, with how little wisdom the world is governed –
Count Alex Oxenstierna in a letter to his son written in 1648.

To any intelligent young man of twenty the world seems a great
scandal – *Hippolyte Adolphe Taine.*

It is all very well for people to fast who can't eat; and to preach,
who cannot talk or sing; and to walk bare-foot, who cannot ride,
and then think themselves good. Let them learn to master the
world before they abuse it – *John Ruskin.*

The planet is not yet a centre of rational loyalty for all mankind –
Barbara Ward and René Dubos.

Preface

This is not a book for the expert, who in any case, as has been wryly remarked, is not a person who gets it right more often than the layman but who gets it wrong for more sophisticated reasons. *The Society of States* purports to be no more than an introduction to its subject for the general reader with an interest in international relations. They do remain, after all, one of the most pervasive and momentous aspects of human activity.

Introductions to international politics appear fairly often. Each naturally tends to express a distinctive viewpoint and emphasis. The present volume, for example, concentrates almost exclusively on relations between *states*, although of course international politics is wider than this. I have also avoided touching on the methodology of the subject. Theoretical approaches to it have long been developed in the United States, where they have attained a high level of generality and abstraction. Behavioural and other theorists, for example, are now vigorously active in the field both in Britain and on the Continent. I have been content here with a traditional viewpoint.

An 'Introduction' must inevitably be selective rather than attempt to be comprehensive if it is to endeavour to plumb any depth of treatment at all. I certainly do not wish to seem to imply that aspects largely omitted, for instance international economic relations, are less important than those included. However, the aspects dealt with in these pages, necessarily summary though some of the dealings may appear, I believe to be of fundamental importance in any approach towards an understanding of the world of sovereign states and their relationships.

It is a pleasure to acknowledge with deep gratitude the help of my sometime mentors in the Department of International Relations at the London School of Economics and Political Science. In particular I must mention, both for themselves and as representative of their colleagues, Professors C. A. W. Manning, G. L. Goodwin and F. S. Northedge. It was they who led my speculative steps from what Professor Manning has called primitive impres-sionism' towards something I hope a little closer to 'sophisticated realism'. To Laurence W. Martin, Professor of War Studies in King's College, London, I offer warm thanks for friendship and early encouragement. Special thanks too go to Professor Trefor E. Evans, holder of the Woodrow Wilson Chair in International Politics, University College of Wales, Aberystwyth, for his interest, and to my colleagues in that Department. Their geniality, as well as professional insights most generously shared, in the milieu of a busy teaching Department, prove always a very helpful stimulus. Any merit this book may have owes much to them. Its faults and limitations are of course entirely my own. At some risk of seeming invidious I should like particularly to thank John Garnett, whose acuteness of mind provides constant illumination and frequent correctives; Kenneth Booth for similar reasons, John Baylis for his warm and zestful association in a number of academic enterprises, David Steeds for many intra-mural and extra-mural kindnesses, and Brian Porter, the play of whose humorous fancy is an unfailing solace. Especially do I thank Ieuan G. John, who brought his profound knowledge of international institutions to bear on chapter 8, offering a number of corrigenda and other valuable suggestions which I gratefully adopted. I am also indebted to Ronald Barston, of the Department of Politics, University of Lancaster, who kindly allowed me to see an article on the external relations of small states which he was preparing for the press. Further, I acknowledge the permission of the Editorial Board of *Interstate* to adapt a small amount of material from articles contri-buted to that journal to provide parts of sections of chapters 3 and 5. Not least, I thank my students, from whom one so often learns. I am deeply grateful to Mrs Hilary Walford, of Messrs Weidenfeld & Nicolson, for the patient expertise and forebearance with which she has seen my text through the press. I am also indebted to Michael Clarke, Research Assistant in the Department of Inter-national Politics, UCW, for all his kind help in preparing the index. Lastly I thank my wife Hazel for help that was at once continuous and essential.

R.P.

I

The nature of international politics: the centrality of interests

States exist like hedgehogs in a bag – *Arthur Schopenhauer.*

There's no politics on this council; we're all good Conservatives here – *West Country local councillor.*

Not all nations pursue policies that can be classified as lions' roars; but assumed or actual hostility on the part of other nations have prevented any nation, big or small, from lying down like an innocent, unconcerned, and passive lamb. Constant activity and vigilance are the corollaries of the principles of national self-determination and self-preservation – *Ivo D. Duchacek.*

What politics is

Political situations, it has been said,[1] arise out of disagreement. This may occur over anything of concern to more than one person. Where it does, and where a means is sought of ending the disagreement, either by causing one will to prevail over another, or by both wills deciding on a compromise outcome, political action is taking place. More particularly, politics is that activity in which *disagreements over what to do with available resources arise.* The word 'resources' should be understood here in a broad sense. Resources include anything which is an object of desire or need. Examples are food, raw materials, monetary wealth, territory. We require resources to achieve our purposes. Among these is likely to be the acquisition of further resources. Competition and dispute occur because frequently resources are insufficient to meet all the demands of all the claimants to them. No one would be likely to

---

[1] Notably by Professor J. D. B. Miller, in *The Nature of Politics*, Duckworth, London, 1962.

deny that argument about the allocation of government revenues between defence spending and the social services is political. But while we may not normally think, say, of family relationships in this way yet they too may have their political side. Family politics may be sharply reminiscent of what takes place between rival party leaders in Parliament, or between the statesmen of different countries. For instance, when a husband and wife 'negotiate' over the use of the single family car when both want it at the same time to make separate journeys a political situation exists. There is disagreement and debate about the allocation of limited resources for particular purposes which may not be reconcilable. Of course one hopes that in this case a settlement can be reached which is not too unsatisfactory for either party.

The point to notice about politics from this not wholly frivolous example is its universal nature. Disagreement about policy – about 'what to do' and about the attempted fulfilment of wishes which may be mutually exclusive, or at least not all completely attainable – is always liable to occur, at all levels of society. Changes in the existing condition of things, major or minor, will everywhere be sought by somebody and nearly always resisted by somebody else. Outcomes to the disagreement will sometimes favour change, sometimes represent successful opposition to change or very often take the form of a more or less acceptable compromise. Each outcome itself represents the raw material, so to speak, on which future political activity will operate. Moreover, much of this political activity cannot be isolated in its effects. Disagreements at the level of government may directly affect individuals. Disagreement at a very local level may ultimately involve government decision-making. The public urinal at Clochemerle is a justly celebrated case in a French novel which has the merits of an acute political fable.

Now international politics is simply (though not itself a simple matter) that aspect of politics concerned with disagreement, competition, rival claims and various outcomes arising from a desire for change and resistance to change, in the relations of those special collective entities we call states. International politics is neither more nor less politics than other forms of political activity. But it is endowed with certain special features. These give it a unique quality. Within a state there is normally one legitimate executive authority which decides national policy in relation to its political community and to other states. This authority, if we take the field of foreign policy alone, *adjudicates* in effect between the various rival claims made by sections of the national society for consideration. This adjudication takes the form of the allocation of resources, the granting of facilities, etc. Simple examples would be the channelling of scarce raw materials or the granting of special tax concessions to firms concentrating on exports. Such recipients of government consideration represent the so-called 'sectional interests'. There is nothing improper about them as such. However, their capacity to have their own way is limited in general both by their intrinsic support and by the fact that they function within a situation where a final arbiter also operates, namely the government. That government may be highly unstable. It may lose its legitimacy. This involves its *implicit* mandate to rule, as in a revolutionary situation. Otherwise it will in general function effectively as the arbitrator of claims and as the decider of policy. No doubt it will be grumbled at by the disappointed or the disaffected but it will generally have its will.

The 'international anarchy'

In international society there is no such arbitrator. States are obliged to pursue, broadly speaking unaided, their own conceived interests. They must do this in a world where, for the most part, no one else will do it for them. If he does it, he will do so in pursuit of some interest of his own. It would be a gross oversimplification to say that states must rely for survival on their own 'strong right arms'. Many states have no strong right arm to speak of. But it remains true that each state must do the best it can for itself. There may be appeal to a vaguely defined 'world opinion' on some issue of moment to the state concerned. But there is at this epoch in history no world adjudicator to choose between claims or to settle disputes. There seems little sign that such a body, assuming many or all of the powers of a world government, is likely to come into existence within the foreseeable future.[2] People who simply describe the absence of a world government as 'the international

[2] The reader might suggest that the United Nations Organization is such a body. There is no space to discuss that suggestion here, but there are good grounds for doubting whether in view of its structure and history the UNO has even the potentiality of acting as a form of world government. This point is dealt with in chapter 8.

anarchy, tend implicitly and often explicitly to disapprove of the existing situation. It is true that in international society as constituted at present there is a strong tendency for the will of the stronger to prevail, irrespective of the merit of the claims of either the strong or the weak. International anarchy is formally the case. Anarchy means strictly the absence of a ruler: the *arche*. But international society is not merely in a condition of disorder. It is in fact ordered in all sorts of ways. Hence we may quite accurately talk of the *structure* of international society, or of an *international system*. The collection of sovereign states which exists, and whose members are so various in their size, power, stability and political style, is to an extent regulated. This characteristic gives rise to a structure of relationships into which states fit. The ordering of international society also helps to guarantee the continued existence of even the smallest and weakest states.[3] Further, it provides for the coming into being of new states. In fact the number of sovereign members of international society has about trebled since 1939. The regulation of international society concerns the spheres of international law, the norms of international behaviour, the complex machinery of international communication. These are discussed later in this book. Moreover, international order, limited and fragile as it admittedly remains, does make possible the intangible but often vital advantage which all states, from the greatest to the least, derive from the fact that for a good deal of the time their mutual expectations about each other's conduct are more likely than not to be more or less fulfilled.

In short, there is the absence of an international ruler but not of rules. And these are, in very general terms, observed. Breaches of observance nearly always occur because in particular situations the statesmen concerned reluctantly conclude that insistent and perhaps vital national interests require the breaking of undertakings or understandings between their own countries and others. Very rarely indeed do they embark on such action without regret and feelings of apprehension. And it is noticeable that they will usually go to great lengths to offer justifications for their actions, and to put upon them an interpretation which minimizes the appearance of deceit, betrayal or dishonour. There is in international society, then, anarchy, but by no means merely chaos. Nor does the battle simply or necessarily always go to the strong. "'Everyman for

[3] The role of such states in the international system is discussed in chapter 3.

4

himself", as the elephant said when he danced among the chickens.'
But in the dance of international society the elephant is often
obliged to tread carefully, or even to change its ground, given the
influence of an adequate number of sufficiently determined
chickens.

Put differently, whole areas of a great power's foreign policy may
be modified, to that power's advantage or otherwise, by the actions
– or even sometimes the sheer vulnerability – of a small power.
The American involvement in Vietnam, and the British response to
the German violation of Belgian neutrality in 1914, are but two
examples. This adds of course to the complexity of international
politics and of its analysis. However, it also serves to remind us that
even in this 'anarchic' situation the will of the mighty does not
automatically prevail.

We see then that international society is not an anarchy except in
the special sense already mentioned. It forms in fact a *system*. In
this system the interactions between the members comprising it
are subject to a considerable measure of regularity and indeed of
regulation. Not only the continuation of relationships but even
their disruption are normally expressed in diplomatic terms, and
by modes of international communication which are generally
acknowledged and understood.

What remains essential for international politics to occur is the
persistence of those elements common to all politics. There needs
to be both the component of disagreement and the component of
competition. As in domestic politics there may be disagreement
either about the best way to pursue agreed ends or about the ends
themselves. In the former case there will normally be argument
about the best methods of marshalling and allocating available
resources. In the latter there will be competition for them.
Another requirement is that there shall be some established
means of determining the dispute. In internal politics this is
customarily done by canvassing rival political programmes both
within political parties or groups and between them. Political
programmes need to be 'hammered out' within parties until broad
agreement is reached on the basis of which political agitation on
behalf of the programme can be carried on. In single-party systems
such as prevail in many parts of the world, particularly in certain
African countries and among the communist states, the politicking
that goes on is almost exclusively of this kind. Members compete

5

for power, influence and office, and for the promotion of their particular policy preferences, within the structure of the one authorized party, the sole legitimate instrument of decision-making within the political community concerned. In the so-called 'pluralistic' political systems this competition is both accompanied and followed by competition for executive power, or at least a measure of public influence, between rival parties themselves. Normally all this activity takes place within a legitimate constitutional framework, and will generally receive popular support or endure popular rejection by means of a process of electoral decision. At times, of course, internal policy preferences may be successfully urged by means of illegal challenge such as insurgency or civil war. In international politics the political process is carried on by means of diplomatic negotiation and frequent agreement between the members of international society, though there may be resort to the use of that special political instrument of organized armed violence called war. And both in domestic and international politics unsettled disputes may continue for many years without any agreed or imposed resolution being achieved at all.

Society and community

In the preceding pages we have used the terms 'political community' and 'international society'. It would be well before going further to look at some of the implications flowing from the use of these phrases in order to assist our understanding of the nature of international politics.

From earliest times human beings have formed societies. For many thousands of years they were probably rarely larger than family groups, hunting and food-gathering. Surviving bushman *bands* perhaps best represent today this level of human social organization. Until relatively recently quite extensive and elaborately ordered societies could develop in virtually total isolation from each other. More typically, however, comparatively homogeneous societies have been in more or less continuous contact with others. Where societies touch at the edges, so to speak, conditions exist for the growth of political relations between them. Indeed the circumstances virtually ensure that such relations will develop. For contiguous societies will tend to find, probably sooner rather than later, that the collective interests of each will affect those of the other. In view of what has been said above about disagreement and competition we should bear in mind that of course such contacts will very often prove mutually advantageous, as for example when they take the form of economic exchange. Still, interests will also tend to be pursued by each partner in the relationship in ways which are likely sooner or later to guarantee competition. If the interests are important enough their rivalry or incompatibility may give rise to a relationship less cooperative than hostile, and this in turn may be expressed by the violent assertion of the claims of each side. The fact remains that the basic ingredients of international politics are present where societies, however simple their organization and style of collective life, have cause, through such determinants as locality, contiguity and economic need, to pursue relations with each other.

Modern sovereign states, whether they comprise homogeneous nations or are multi-national, form a complex international society. The relations between its members are in general elaborate, many-faceted and fully institutionalized. However, this international society, now virtually worldwide, differs in complexity, not in kind, from the simple model outlined above. An inter-tribal relationship, whether cordial or hostile, in its motivation through the assertion by its constituent members of claims and interests, complementary, mutually exclusive or (as often) a combination of both, remains political in precisely the same way as is a fully diplomatized relationship between two modern sovereign states.

Is there, meanwhile, any value in distinguishing between 'society' and 'community'? In discussions on international affairs the two words are sometimes used interchangeably, but a distinction seems to be useful. Mainly this concerns a difference in the degree of closeness and intensity in the relations binding together the units comprising the collectivity whose nature we wish to analyse. The essence of a society is that there are significant relations between its members. Thus we speak of social animals. These are the species which herd or flock together and derive biological advantage from their mutually interdependent association. The needs of man are so various and complex that his societies are correspondingly elaborate. Where a human society is characterized by a high degree of homogeneity, in language, social custom, legal norms, habit of collective life, or a combination of any of these, we are justified in

7

describing it as a community. Since most nation-states, for instance, for relatively long periods of their history, tend to develop a national homogeneity it is valid to refer to such social units as 'political communities'. Indeed, as we shall notice later, linguistic and cultural homogeneity is widely regarded as a defining characteristic of nations. Further, the notion of community is reinforced by the sense of a generally observed common obedience to legitimate authorities within the national society. It is precisely such an over-arching authority which we have noticed as being absent in international society. Finally, there is also a certain connotation in the word community, a suggestion of intimate goodwill. This may be evident among individuals, and even at the level of localities and districts. Pressing the idea rather far, we might apply the suggestion to the nation itself, though here it proves very variable. But a question follows: do the one hundred and forty or so sovereign states at present in existence comprise an international community? We may well feel, hardly yet, and perhaps never. International relations are clearly often intense. During an international crisis diplomatic contact between the states concerned is apt to become virtually continuous, both day and night. Again, groups of sovereign states may develop such close political and economic ties as to become an association approaching a confederal or federal status. There is thus much reason in devising the term 'European Community' to denote those countries of Western Europe who have bound themselves together in the so-called Common Market, with its far-reaching and deliberately envisaged political implications. But, of course, mere intensity of international relationship may be destructive of community. War represents an extremely intimate form of relationship between the states engaged in it. Such intimacy is sometimes symbolized by the use of suggestive phrases: the 'rape of Belgium' by Germany in 1914, or of Czechoslovakia by the Soviet Union and other members of the Warsaw Pact in 1968. Invasion does, after all, represent a form of physical possession of the 'body' of the country invaded.

In any case, over the whole spectrum of international relations we may well feel unjustified in regarding either the level of contact or the degree of common interest prevailing among these one hundred and forty-five or so sovereign states as characterizing an international community. Clearly, however, there does exist an international society. It remains to be seen whether increasing economic interpenetration between states, the further development of worldwide communications, and a growing role played by international institutions, will come at length to create conditions that might seem best described as those characteristic of a global international community. For the present we may decide that what we live in is an international *society* of states. Their relations (which cause them to form a society) are complex and variegated. But these all, economic, military, cultural relations as well as strictly diplomatic ones, have strong *political* connotations, in the sense of political as discussed at the beginning of this chapter.

International society and personality

Today all men live in states, whether or not as citizens of the states they live in, or, in relatively few cases, in territories which are dependencies of states. International society, and hence international politics, are thus truly global in the modern world. Any society, obviously, consists of its members. But the members of a society, endowed with a capacity to act, and pursuing relations with each other, are evidently *persons*. A moment's reflection will suggest to us that we need to think in terms of two kinds of person. There is the individual person – you or I – and the collective or institutional person. The latter is a person by virtue of its ('his') active membership of the society in question. This exists because its constituent members comprise it, and they are persons because they comprise a society. Now a society functions by means of the application of rules which are binding upon its members. These rules both recognize the personality of the members of the society, impose duties upon them, and guarantee rights to them in terms of the purposes for which the society exists. The 'personality-conferring' function of rules in a society is illustrated by the use of the phrase 'legal personality' as applying, for example, to a firm, or a club, or a learned association, each of which is endowed with rights and obligations in relation to which it may, for instance, sue or be sued. International society, we have seen, consists essentially of states.[4] Inasmuch as they comprise a society they have personality attributed to them. They are 'international persons'. Individual

---

[4] An exception is the United Nations Organization: not a state, it has by international agreement been endowed for legal purposes with a measure of international personality.

men and women are not. Though they too of course comprise another global society – the worldwide society of mankind, numbering now perhaps four thousand million.

It is important to note here that we are not making an analogy. We are not saying that states are something like persons, or may be regarded as behaving – figuratively – in personal ways. We are saying that states *are* persons, in fact and in deed, in what Professor C. A. W. Manning[5] calls 'the theory of diplomatics'. International society, being a society, consists of persons; international persons, which is to say, states. How, we may ask, does an international person 'come to birth'? The short answer is, by the process of diplomatic recognition. Such recognition does not have to be universal. But it does have to be substantial. Any state may grant diplomatic recognition to, or withhold or withdraw diplomatic recognition from, any other. What matters is that in a given case there shall be seen to be a wide enough measure of international recognition to enable the state concerned to function as a member of international society. No hard or fast line can therefore be drawn. At any particular epoch a few states may be in process of losing or of acquiring full international personality. At the time of writing Bangladesh seems to be well on the way to the attainment of full statehood and membership of international society, Taiwan to be in the process (which may be prolonged) of losing them. The vital point is that if in any meaningful sense international society exists, international persons – its members – exist also.

Individual persons – you and I – use various means to communicate with other persons: speech, touch, expression, the written word, etc. States too use instruments of communication in their relations with each other. These instruments include, typically, those parts of the machinery of government concerned primarily with diplomatic procedure. But supremely the means of inter-state communication are human beings themselves. At one level relations between states are relations between people – heads of state, their accredited representatives, statesmen, officials of all kinds, even private citizens who visit other countries and do business in them. At another level the relations are between the states themselves which are consequently deemed to possess personalities, desires and wills. Rulers, statesmen and diplomats represent and

[5] The discussion in this section owes much to C. A. W. Manning, *The Nature of International Society*, Bell, London, 1962.

act on behalf of their states which choose, will and act through them. This 'organic' relationship between the state and those men and women whose role is to represent it and perform its actions may seem an obvious one, but its implications are important, as we shall see when we come to consider, for example, problems of the nature and scope of international morality.

The processes of international politics are often likened to a game, defined by certain rules and procedures without which the game could not exist or be carried on. This game men implicitly choose to play. 'Let us play sovereign states.' Among the agreed conventions for playing this important game is the one that states shall be regarded as persons. International personality then becomes a specific concept of great – indeed of fundamental – importance in that set of regulations for the game that we call International Law. We remind ourselves once more that it is because states are *notionally* persons that they can have relations with each other and so form a society.

In 1962 the Franco-German Treaty of Friendship was nego- tiated by the late President de Gaulle and the late Dr Adenauer. They worked in collaboration with their political and diplomatic advisers. The documents concerned were drafted by high officials in each country. These documents were then duly initialled and ultimately signed by the representatives of each state and ratified by the respective legislatures. All quite straightforward, as well as being of considerable political importance to the two countries concerned, and indeed to their allies. It is equally true, and neces- sarily true, to say that *France* and *Federal Germany* had agreed a treaty between them, and undertaken thereby certain mutual obligations. Both in law and in diplomatic fact those two notional national group persons, France and Federal Germany, willed and performed a joint act.

It is worth noticing that we cannot correctly speak in this con- nection of 'Germany' as we can of 'France', or as we could of the former if referring for instance to Stalin's pact with Hitler in August 1939. For then 'Germany' was broadly co-extensive with the German state. Now there is a German nation or *volk* divided into two states, the *Bundesrepublik*, or Federal Germany, and the *Deutsche Demokratische Republik*, often loosely and inaccurately referred to as 'East Germany'. So here there are two notional facts co-existing: the notion of Germany the nation, and of two international German persons; two states which may or may not one day be reunited into one national German state. Now we should also note that the international personality of the German Democratic Republic is less developed, or less complete, than is that of the Federal German Republic, since it enjoys rather less widespread diplomatic recognition. Such recognition is still the subject of disapproval and diplomatic sanction by Federal Germany against states, other than the Soviet Union.[6] We may say then that the international personality of Federal Germany is at the present time more secure than that of the GDR. On the other hand, a state player in the 'game' of international politics exists if his claim to do so is conceded by a sufficient number of other players. What constitutes a sufficient number may vary with circumstances and must be a matter of general judgement and tacit admission in any given case. So far as the GDR is concerned its status as a full member of the Warsaw Pact, and hence of the 'socialist camp', and its career as a *de facto* international political entity for some two decades, would make a denial of its effective international personality both pedantic and eccentric. As we shall notice more than once in the course of our discussion in this book, things exist if they are deemed to exist. Much of international politics is 'in the mind'. An interesting point about 'East Germany', which at least until very recently was known officially in Federal Germany as 'the Soviet Zone', is how far its *de facto* political separation from the rest of Germany for so long will give rise to that complex of collective feelings, attitudes, beliefs, claims and interests which together constitute so much of the substance of a 'nation'. Different political systems, reinforcing and reinforced by divergent ways of life, might, if the separation continues long enough, lead to the evident existence of two perceptibly distinct German nations. We need not suppose that this *will* happen. But the processes at work within the 'two Germanies', touching collective life at so many points, are among those which can bring new nations into being.[7]

Niceties of diplomatic recognition often have very important consequences. However, we must not suppose that outside the strict rules of the game statesmen fail to shape their policies with the facts of actual political power in mind. Take for example the

---

[6] The 'Hallstein Doctrine', now (1973) substantially modified.
[7] The relationship between state and nation is discussed in chapter 4.

twenty-two years between the communist victory in the Chinese civil war in 1949 and the visit of President Nixon to Peking in February 1972. For the whole of that time the People's Republic of China was diplomatically invisible to the United States.[8] But this did not mean, and could not mean, that the United States behaved as if mainland China did not exist. The rules of the game allowed for discreet official contact – or, more strictly, discreet contact between officials – to take place between both countries through the good offices of a third party, in this case the People's Republic of Poland, which enjoys diplomatic relations with both the United States and the People's Republic of China. Where interests dictate, ways of useful mutual consultation or the exchange of information can always be found. In this case the international person Poland placed certain facilities at the disposal of America and China, and no doubt received suitable acknowledgement from both of 'her' helpfulness.

Let us take another example. The statement, 'at Easter 1939 Italy invaded Albania' is historically correct. That is to say, it is a verifiable event in modern European history. But what 'really' happened? Clearly a number of diverse but closely connected events took place, all amounting to the fact that Italy invaded Albania. Among them we may note the following: Benito Mussolini, the Italian *duce*, no doubt after asking for and receiving advice, took certain decisions. His army, navy and air force commanders were briefed. Logistical preparations were set in hand. At the Easter weekend contingents of Italian troops were conveyed to Albanian territory, which they advanced into, ready to oppose with force of arms any resistance they might encounter. Here were individual men, some deciding and giving orders, some fighting in their units, all acting in concert. But not Mussolini, nor King Victor Emmanuel III (subsequently proclaimed King of Albania), nor the Italian forces, were 'Italy'. They all represented that forceful international person called Italy, who had decided to attack the much smaller and weaker international person called Albania. And when the sporadic resistance was speedily overcome, and King Zogu Ahmed of Albania fled the country, it was Albania the international person who, grudgingly or otherwise, acquiesced in her conquest at the hands of her mightier neighbour, and in that loss of

---

[8] At the time of writing normal diplomatic relations have not been entered upon between the United States and Mao Tse-tung's China.

her international personality and identity implied in her incorporation into the expanding Italian Empire. The international personality of Albania was to some extent revived when, early in the second world war, King Zog set up a government in exile, enjoying allied recognition, in a London hotel.

A last example of the game of sovereign states in progress, which also happens to involve both China and Albania: in the 1960s, for diplomatic and ideological reasons of her own, the People's Republic of China developed a close friendship with the People's Republic of Albania. The Albanian leadership had grown increasingly at odds with the Soviet leadership, and with many aspects of the Soviet Union's policy towards its partners in the Warsaw Pact. There is no need to enter here into the obscure if embittered ideological wrangle between the Russians and the Chinese, only to notice that the Albanians took the Chinese side. They claimed that Peking and not Moscow was in the right so far as a 'correct' interpretation and implementation of Marxist-Leninism was concerned. Now what matters for our present purpose is to appreciate, what ardent nationalists everywhere tend to see so clearly, how much value there is in being a state. The real importance to communist China of Albania's friendship is not that the 800 million or so Chinese enjoy the approval and support of about one and a half million hardy mountaineers dwelling in a corner of southern Europe but that Albania is a state, an international person, a member of the United Nations, possessing the symbols and reality of sovereignty, and having an audible, even strident, voice to be heard both amidst the diplomatic chatter and clamour of international politics generally and in the doctrinal disputations of the communist world. It is, in short, in terms of the game of sovereign states that Albania matters to China, irritates Soviet Russia, and acts as a factor of influence in the issues that divide the two.

Society and system

We have tried to show that the sovereign states of the world comprise an international society. Now we can go on to suggest that the relations between them are ordered and structured in such a way that we are justified in talking of an *international system*. The elements in this structure we have noticed already. They include the whole elaborate machinery of diplomatic negotiation, the relationship between governments and their agents in the field of foreign affairs, the observance most of the time by most members of international society of the rules of international law, and the whole complex of contacts between states and their peoples arising from mutual claims and interests of all kinds. Little if any of this welter of activity goes unregulated. Difficulties constantly occur in the working of all sectors of international relations. When these arise governments tend to be involved at an early stage and often at the highest level. Policies are formulated and decisions taken in response to the new situation. Such policies may be well founded or not. They may be based on inadequate information or faulty judgement. They may reflect weaknesses in the machinery or in the men. Statesmen need a fair measure of luck as well as flair. But successful or not, the decision-making function of those representing the eyes, ears and above all brains of states both reflects the operation of an international system and ensures its continuance.

What we call the international system, then, comprises the more or less agreed and more or less observed *methods* by which relationships between states are carried on. These relationships are organized. They are subject to generally recognized procedures. These make for more efficiency and somewhat reduce risks of possible misinterpretation of intention and the sheer unpredictability of international behaviour.

An obvious but important aspect of the structure of international society is the great diversity in the size and resources and therefore in the power of its members, some implications of which we consider in chapter 3. Let it be said now that the international system necessarily reflects this. The United States, for instance, maintains an elaborate network of officials and agencies which spreads to almost every country in the world, as well as within the main international organizations. This practically universal American interest in international society as a whole is a consequence of the superpower status of the United States. It is to be remembered that such status was assumed by the United States with a good deal of misgiving on the part of many Americans. President Truman's initiative in the famous 'fifteen weeks' in the first half of 1947 in deciding to undertake the containment of communism, and to assist the economic revival of Western Europe, represents one of the most momentous responses by any state to perceived dangers and needs confronting international society in modern times. It ensured among other things that American interests would become global in scope. Only some quarter of a century later did the 'head of steam' behind those decisions appear to be running down, and the United States seem bent on a measure of revision of her commitments, implying both changes in international society itself and in American perceptions of the dangers and opportunities which it presents. At the other end of the scale, yet still part of the system, San Marino, the 'Serene Republic', retains what has been called its 'ceremonial independence' and impinges upon international society with the minuscule effect of consular relations with Italy and diplomatic representation at the Holy See. So variegated are the components that make up the worldwide international system.

Another feature of this system to be taken into account is the way in which states develop far more intense contacts with some states than with others. These variations may be the result of geography, ideology, strategic necessity or political history. Clearly these determinants are likely in practice to overlap. It is no accident that certain traditions in political doctrine and method should distinguish at the present day the countries of Western Europe, whose geographical closeness to each other ensured a large degree of shared history. Again, world communism as a doctrine and a movement explains the development of special links between communist states everywhere. This does not necessarily imply cordiality between them. The Sino-Soviet dispute, on its doctrinal side as distinct from its power-political side, has proved so embittered and intractable precisely because ideology plays outwardly at least so large a part in the political style and image of the two countries, and represents so high a stake for each to play for, in terms of the desire of the governing elite in each to influence and direct the interests and aspirations of world communism.

Where circumstances give rise to this special closeness of relationship between states and groups of states we may define important *sub-systems* within the international system as a whole. Sub-systems are defined and studied in order to make the task of analysing international politics more manageable. The data of the subject are so numerous and various as to become easily bewildering. And so we try to isolate significant relationships between certain members of international society, to explain why they have arisen, and to fit them into the overall pattern of international relations as a whole, remembering also that the special relationships between the members of an international sub-system are likely to influence the relations of each with other members of international society outside it. A simple diagram (Fig. 1) illustrates this point. The arrows indicate interactions between each member of the sub-system and between the sub-system and the international system as a whole.

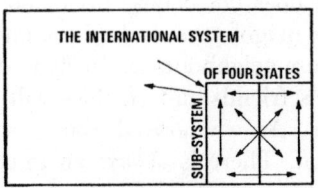

Fig. 1. The interaction of the international system and a sub-system

Let us take by way of example relations which we will assume between two states, of which one feels bound to say that if they have never existed it seems a pity. They are Ruritania, immortalized by Anthony Hope Hawkins, a vaguely central south-east European kingdom which doubtless became a People's Republic after 1945, and Barataria, complete with canals, celebrated by Gilbert and Sullivan. Where the international behaviour of Ruritania is critically affected by Barataria, and vice versa, so that whole areas of the activity of each are determined by her relationship with the other, we may speak of the existence of a binary international sub-system comprising Barataria and Ruritania. The model can be varied. The degree of mutual impact may not be fully reciprocal. Ruritania is perhaps a major power with wide-ranging interests while Barataria is a small principality on her border whose international concerns are almost wholly involved with her relationship with Ruritania. Switzerland and Liechtenstein (between whom a customs union exists) may be taken as another example. It is fair to say that the foreign policy of the Irish Republic, though not exclusively preoccupied with her relations with the United Kingdom, has been dominated by them.

The international politics of south and south-east Asia provides an example of an important sub-system of a regional type. Relationships, whether friendly or hostile, tend to be peculiarly close.

The behaviour of Pakistan must inevitably be a matter of acute concern to India and of India to Pakistan. Malaysia will always observe with particular and perhaps anxious care the foreign policy initiatives and responses of Indonesia. Thailand can never be indifferent to what occurs in the states of Indo-China. Such examples may remind us how many of a state's attitudes and aspirations in international society are conditioned by given circumstances it did not choose and may scarcely be able to change. As a human being does not choose his blood relations, so states cannot choose their neighbours. Indeed the interests, expectations and demands of those neighbours are likely to determine to a great extent who a state's friends and enemies will be in international society as a whole. As we noticed above, sub-systems do not function in isolation. There is always an interplay, more or less significant, between the working of any sub-system and that of the international system at large. In many cases what happens to members of a sub-system may be of as acute concern to the world as to those states themselves. Any outbreak of war between Israel and her Arab neighbours is immediately a matter of urgent consultation within the United Nations and between the superpowers. This is so in large part because the affairs of the Middle East in the second half of the twentieth century became of great – perhaps vital – moment to both the United States and the Soviet Union. Each had developed political commitments to Israel and the Arab states respectively. These commitments carried very important military implications. Hence war between Israel and the Arab states carried the danger of bringing the superpowers into direct and inevitably dangerous confrontation. Such considerations make the study of the Middle East sub-system a matter of high concern. This is true both for statesmen and for political observers. The latter will hope to develop certain insights that may at least enhance general understanding of the predicaments facing the former in the area. In the shape of informed and official advice such analysis may also influence actual policy.

Another sub-system of considerable importance in contemporary international politics exists in the western hemisphere. The salient political fact there is the dominant role of the United States. Of the twenty-five sovereign states in the New World, excluding the United States, a majority have characteristically close relations with the dominating power, and all have to pursue policies which take that dominance into account. The relations between the United States and most of the Central and South American republics comprises a working sub-system symbolized by the Organization of American States. This is an alliance system having both strategic and economic purposes. Within it the United States has taken pains to minimize the element of clientship in the relations of her partners to herself. The security of the United States has traditionally been set by Americans in the context of the security of the western hemisphere as a whole. In 1823 President Monroe promulgated the Monroe Doctrine. This informed the world that for the future the United States would resist any territorial aggrandizement in the New World by any European power. From this time there developed an international sub-system in the New World, a direct consequence of American foreign policy. The Organization of American States has had as a major objective the strong discouragement of any member state from pursuing policies likely to damage or compromise the interests of fellow-members. In particular this has been linked with the danger of any member falling under the influence or political direction of the communist bloc. On this ground the United States has intervened in the internal affairs at certain critical junctures of both Guatemala and the Dominican Republic. However, neither the United States nor her allies felt able to prevent Fidel Castro in Cuba (whose successful overthrow of the notorious Battista regime was generally welcomed) from following a revolutionary path which brought Soviet influence directly to bear upon Cuban foreign policy. This is a salutary reminder of the restraints that very often exist in practice on the freedom of action of even the greatest powers. On the other hand the outcome of the Cuban missile crisis in October 1962 showed what could be accomplished (in that particular case) by the exercise of political judgement of a high order, patience, firmness and a certain magnanimity, qualities revealed to a striking degree by President Kennedy. At the same time it would be unwise simply to assume that the handling of that crisis by the president and his National Executive Committee represents a model of 'crisis management' which could just be applied to other crises. There are too many imponderables for that. However, we may agree that the more that statesmen are endowed with the above qualities the better.

We noticed earlier in passing that world communism as the

prevailing ideology of a number of countries had given rise to a very significant international sub-system. The shared ideology has both motivated and strengthened important economic and strategic interests held in common by the majority of communist countries. The phrase 'socialist camp' betrays the ideological basis of the relationship. It is also true that the relationship – particularly between the Soviet Union and her Eastern European allies – is motivated by other considerations of power and security which the shared political doctrines to some extent mask. However, communism is a great international movement. It has representative parties in nearly every country in the world. In some of these the party is proscribed, in others minute. In some fourteen countries, located in Europe and Asia with the as yet solitary exception of Cuba in the New World, a communist party is in power, generally alone, occasionally in a coalition with other groups which it dominates. The 'socialist camp' consists of these independent countries. In some cases, notably those of the Democratic Republic of Vietnam, the People's Republic of Korea, and the German Democratic Republic, this independence is to some extent qualified by the limitations of diplomatic status caused by still widespread non-recognition. The close relations between these states, based primarily on their respective communist systems of government, do in any case create an evident international sub-system of great importance in the modern world. Again, we should bear in mind that hostility and protracted dispute may be as intense characters of relationship as cordiality. The one thing this particular sub-system is not is 'monolithic'. For this reason the term 'communist bloc', used very frequently during the acute phases of the cold war, and once in this chapter, conveys what is now an undue suggestion of a 'monolithic' centrality of decision-making within the sub-system, and is better replaced by a phrase connoting something rather looser, such as 'communist world'.

Communist countries, no more and no less than others, try to attain the national objectives of security and prosperity. But they do so in the light of rather specific doctrinal requirements. Doctrine has undoubtedly often inhibited the development of their economic and cultural relations with non-communist countries and intensified those with each other. So we find in this case an ideological sub-system, not primarily regional in scope but potentially at least represented in every part of the world.

As we have seen, much of the relationship binding the components of the sub-system together is concerned with defining the status of the principal members in the light of their custodianship of 'correct' political doctrine. Among questions arising from this are the following: is the Soviet Union to retain the political leadership of the socialist camp as the 'socialist fatherland'? Or is the Maoist road to communism the right one? Or does the future lie with 'polycentrism' – the view that there are a number of 'right roads', determined by particular national historical conditions? Is the 'aggressive Soviet revisionist clique'[9] betraying the cause of the toiling masses throughout the world? Are these traitors to the interests of the world proletariat bent on concluding discreditable deals with the 'American imperialists'? Shrill questions such as these fill the air in communist international gatherings and the columns of some communist journals. The point is that both far-reaching cooperation within the communist world and the conflicts over doctrine which characterize it reflect a closeness of relationship which typifies a significant international sub-system.

Soviet interests in Europe have created what amounts to a special sub-system, regionally defined, within the communist international sub-system as a whole. One of the gravest problems confronting the Soviet leadership since the end of the second world war has been how to maintain the *cordon sanitaire* of communist buffer states in Eastern and Central Europe against what were long perceived as the revisionist threats of a rearmed and economically powerful West Germany, supported by an implacably hostile Western Europe and United States. The objective reality of this threat was irrelevant. What mattered was what the Soviet leaders believed the threat to be. It is of course possible that they themselves privately discounted the threat but used it as a means of retaining their control in Eastern Europe. In any case it is evident that the factors of ideology and security reinforced each other in the minds of Soviet leaders over many years. They certainly had direct effects in maintaining the resolve of those leaders to sustain the *status quo* in Europe.

This Eastern European defence sub-system found its institutional expression in the Warsaw Pact. Created at least in part as a response to the founding of the North Atlantic Treaty Organization, it has been used since both as a strategic instrument against

[9] One of the *Peking Review*'s milder phrases of opprobrium.

any military threat from the West and as a political instrument for ensuring the continuance of Soviet control over the partners[10] of the Soviet Union. No political situation, or political institution, can be static. A good deal of development, not to say restiveness, has characterized the international politics of Warsaw Pact countries over many years. There has been a resurgence of nationalism. This has led to the formulation of closely argued concepts of *national* communism. These have had greater or lesser effects in all of them. The Soviet Union has taken note of all this. A measure of political and economic polycentrism has become evident in several countries in the group. Most notable, perhaps, have been the cases of Hungary and Rumania. But the system has not been allowed to break up. In one remarkable respect it has been reinforced.

In 1968 liberalizing tendencies were at work within the communist regime in Czechoslovakia, promoted, with what real enthusiasm is perhaps still uncertain, by Alexander Dubcek and his colleagues. Such tendencies appeared to the Soviet leaders to pose a real danger to the military security of the Warsaw Pact as a whole, as well as to the doctrinal purity of its members. Or so the outside world gathered. Invasion followed in August. With Czechoslovakia occupied by Soviet troops accompanied by token contingents from most of the other Warsaw Pact countries, political changes were carried through which reversed, if not quite completely, the liberal initiatives. This restored, apparently, the integrity of the socialist camp. But the matter did not, and probably could not, end just there. The forceful Soviet action roused worldwide consternation. Moreover, it could be made to seem of such dubious morality, in terms of the comradely relations deemed to exist between fraternal Socialist states, that a doctrinal justification had to be speedily devised. It was thus that the world learned that members of the socialist camp did not enjoy untrammelled sovereignty. They were obliged to exercise it in ways that would not be judged adversely to affect the interests of their fellow-members or of 'world socialism'. Other fraternal states could determine if and when such adverse effects were in train. Such states then had the right, indistinguishable perhaps from the duty, to impose collective restraints on an erring comrade. This so-called

[10] A neutral term. It is well known in some quarters in the free world that the United States has *allies*, the Soviet Union *satellites*.

Brezhnev Doctrine (proclaimed in the name of the First Secretary of the Communist Party of the Soviet Union) clearly had serious implications for the countries constrained to observe it. What it meant in practice was that the Soviet Union reserved the right, in collaboration with such partners as she could induce to join her, to intervene directly and if necessary forcefully in the internal affairs of any allied socialist country whenever she thought fit. The doctrine, with a simplicity a critical observer might think cynical, insists that the right is reciprocal. However, it appears to have been received in some communist quarters with noteworthy coolness. There are signs that in practice it is likely in future to be applied with a good deal of discretion.

We may, however, conclude from the episode that the Soviet Union retains few inhibitions in promoting what she takes to be her interests, if need be at the expense of a fraternal ally. Fewer, at least, than does the United States. Americans may be supposed to have found the political orientation of Cuba in the 1960s as unwelcome as that of Czechoslovakia was to the Russians. Some would urge that the Bay of Pigs fiasco of 1961 shows that there is not all that much in it. But we may decide all the same that the conclusion suggested above is justified. In any case the matter raises the question of scruple, of moral sensitivity, in the behaviour of states towards each other, in particular of great states towards small ones. This large issue of morality between states is discussed in chapter 6.

The 'socialist camp' sub-system, in principle at least, takes no account of regional limits. Another interesting example, because of its multi-racial composition and worldwide distribution, is the Commonwealth. This remarkable association of states can certainly be regarded as one of the historically most prominent international sub-systems now existing, although its significance has grown less in the period since 1960.

Persistence through change

'System' proves a useful word to apply to that complex of relation-ships and interactions which binds together the units comprising the society of states. This is so because these interactions, though various in kind and degree of intensity, are not random. They are subject to a large measure of regularity. And this of course implies human deliberation and purpose. But we must also remember that in an important sense neither international society nor the international system represent 'the works of man's hands'. Clearly they are essentially human phenomena. They are maintained and modified over time by human decisions – as well as by much human behaviour which is habitual and only implicitly a matter of *decision* at all. But they are not simply created by men. The development of international society is far less a result of specific and deliberate human creation than of political and social evolution. This process has reflected the subtle and complex interplay of human volition, both individual and collective, and the constraining effects of the given conditions which provide the context in which human action must take place. States come into being and pass out of existence. Human activity is decisively involved in both processes. But for most of recorded history (which represents perhaps 1 per cent of the whole history of *homo sapiens* alone, apart from his hominoid ancestors) the great majority of men have simply found themselves living in political communities of various kinds and in some kind of 'international' society. They have not been responsible for setting up either. In fact, the period since 1950 has been one of the busiest in the history of the last thousand years so far as the processes of nation-building and the attainment of statehood are concerned. Even so, these tasks have been primarily assumed by political activists and elites, with the enthusiastic support, the resigned acquiescence or the active opposition of the mass of men. Fundamentally the international system is not a device but a 'happening'. It exists as an abstraction. Men in groups behave in certain ways, staking their claims, defending their interests, pursuing their wills, and we discover and declare that they are participating in and operating a political system.

Next we may notice that, though no doubt all things pass away, both states and the international society they comprise with the system of relationships and reciprocal behaviour that binds them together are characterized by a high degree of *persistence*.

Many states in the modern world have proved to be, so to speak, long-lived creatures. And there seem good grounds for expecting a comparable longevity to apply over time to many if not all of the newer states that have come into existence during the present century. The forces which are making for the obsolescence of the sovereign state in the present age are examined in chapter 8. Here

24

we may take note of the fact that even in times of rapid social and technological change, of which the last half-century has been perhaps the most far-ranging and decisive in human history, states are not readily superseded. Their interactions tend to become more numerous, more complicated, more intimate; they limit and compromise their sovereignty in various ways in relation to each other (such actions themselves representing the exercise of sovereignty), but they persist identifiably and self-consciously as states.

This persistence owes much to human acquiescence and inertia. Just as individuals cannot choose their relations, only their friends, so no man can choose his native state. A small minority of us do make a choice later in life, and become naturalized in another state. But this process itself is more or less beset with difficulty. Some people in times of acute international disturbance, such as war, may lose their membership of a national community altogether and become stateless persons, a position of considerable pathos and disadvantage. In general, however, our status as citizens is something given and very rarely withdrawn. Mainly we are content with this. Often we are proud of it. Pride in this matter is in fact one of the commoner irrationalities. A man can no more help being born an Englishman than he can help being born with brown eyes. Only too frequently such pride may assume a degree of felt superiority, national arrogance and xenophobia that can be a great nuisance to nationals of other states. Far more endearing is simply to acknowledge a sense of good luck in the matter. French civilization is widely agreed to have been one of the supreme achievements of European history. But to be born a Frenchman is not itself creditable, just (no doubt) fortunate. As Lord Melbourne said of the conferment of the Garter, 'there's no damned merit about it'. In any case, most of us identify with our native states to an extent that decisively affects our lives. Such identification enables state authorities of various kinds and differing status to direct and control, with little question or defiance, much of our activity throughout life. Both states themselves and the society of states can only continue to exist and function while this remains so.

A further reason for the tendency of states to persist is the long-term continuity of the purposes they serve. What we may perhaps call the central liberal view of states is that they represent instruments by means of which peoples participate in international life.

The state, on this view, also exists to guarantee as far as possible, in the context of both international and domestic society, the safety and well-being of its members; to help make possible, in short, what Michael Howard[11] has simply called 'the Good Life'. In this conception the state has no inherent rights of its own, as an institution, only such attributed rights as may enable it to discharge its functions effectually. Thus the state has the 'right' to protect itself by all necessary means against external attack and internal subversion, since either, if successful, would destroy the capacity of the state to serve its citizens. It is in consideration of this that the severe restraints placed by the state upon the freedom of action of those same citizens are justified.

This, we have said, represents the liberal tradition. There is of course another. Certain varieties within this tradition may be traced with special emphasis in the writings of a group of mainly nineteenth-century German political theorists. J. G. Fichte was a notable example. These philosophers preoccupied themselves with the claims of the national state over its subjects. In their view men exist to serve the state, not the other way round. The state is the end of men: to its perfection they are the means. The end of the state itself is to *be*, realizing ever more fully through the instrumentality of its individual members the ideal excellence of its own being. Neither the 'liberal' nor the 'totalitarian' tradition embody statements which are in the least susceptible of proof or refutation. They are matters of doctrine; of preferential belief. What is, however, worth noting is that both conceptions, in their different ways, have reinforced the tendency of the state in history to persist.

Add to this that there is to be found in all institutions a certain natural conserving tendency, a resistance to change even in times of rapid change, and we may understand why most statesmen, those representatives and protectors of the interests of states, should in many situations reveal what has been neatly described by Professor F. S. Northedge as 'a *penchant* for the *status quo*'. It also helps to explain the remarkable persistence of most state structures, as well as the evident propensity of the international system itself to last for a long time.

[11] In 'Morality and Force in International Politics', D. M. MacKinnon (ed.), *Making Moral Decisions*, SPCK, London, 1969. Mr Howard's brilliant lecture repays most careful reading and reflection.

Within the inherent dynamism of politics there is always a search for stability and equilibrium. This is shown by the relative rapidity with which, after even revolutionary changes have swept over a political community, new institutions for it are fashioned. They are likely to have different names from those preceding them. They will probably purport to uphold different (and by implication 'better') social and political values. But while the needs of society remain broadly constant the new institutions will endeavour to meet them. Political communities in fact generally survive very heavy material and human losses, and still give rise to new forms of political organization to replace those that have collapsed or been fatally discredited. No defeat in modern war has been more complete than that of Germany in 1945. Yet within hardly more than half a decade two viable states had arisen on the ruins of the Third Reich. In Japan, by interesting contrast, though also totally conquered in the same year, even the traditional institutions triumphantly survived, with some modification, to give the support of their prestige and sanction to the reviving international personality of the Nipponese Empire.

Decision-making capacity, whether concentrated or diffused, highly ceremonialized or rough and ready, has to reside somewhere, and may therefore in principle be located. The acute Lenin said that all political problems could be boiled down to one fundamental question: 'Who – whom?' In international society the *loci* of decision-making remain preeminently the sovereign members composing it. In their functioning too they are essentially both subjects and objects of political action. Of them also, in their innumerable interactions, we need to ask, 'Who – whom?'

Linked with the factor of the persistence of states is that of their relative immobility. Geography remains a major determinant of a state's behaviour in international society. Obviously there often is movement. Many states have swelled and shrunk over periods of their history. A spectacular instance was that of Rumania after the first world war, when she expanded, under the provisions of the postwar peace treaties, to more than double her prewar size. She did so westward at the expense of defeated Hungary and eastward at that of revolutionary Russia, though the province of Bessarabia was reabsorbed by the Soviet Union in 1945. An example of territorial contraction was that of Czechoslovakia at the same date, who lost Ruthenia (Carpatho-Ukraine) also to the Soviet Union.

27

One of the most remarkable instances of the physical shifting of a country across the map in modern times is that of Poland. At the conclusion of the second world war, and with the sanction of the victorious allies, Poland moved, amoeba-like, across part of Eastern Europe, relinquishing a large tract in the east to Byelorussia and Ukraine, flowing west over what had been Eastern Germany (the German Democratic Republic being originally *Mitteldeutschland*), and, as it were, oozing north to absorb the southern part of East Prussia. Yet allowing for all these territorial adjustments, and for the fact that a few states, such as Latvia, Lithuania and Estonia, from time to time disappear altogether as sovereign members of international society, it remains broadly true that states both exist for long periods and stay in one place, having to learn to live as best they can with the given facts, agreeable or otherwise, of their location on the map and of their international neighbours being who they are. It was this consideration which prompted Edward Gibbon, when referring to an Anglo-French trade agreement negotiated by the Younger Pitt, to observe in phrases likely to be approved by very many statesman:

I must rejoice in every agreement that diminishes the separation between neighbouring countries, which softens their prejudices, unites their interests and industry, and renders their future hostilities less frequent and less implacable.[12]

In taking into account the virtual immobility of states we should also bear in mind that modern conditions greatly facilitate the interpenetration of states, economically, technologically and culturally. These penetrations can be of such far-reaching and critical extent as to pose very real political and psychological problems for any state which feels it is being dominated by them.[13]

Before turning from the theme of states' persistence through periods of even radical change, we may notice briefly certain aspects of challenge to this characteristic of states and of the international state system.

We may identify two important sources of rejection. The first is philosophical in origin. *Anarchism* is a theory of politics which prescribes the abolition of the institutions of the state and the

[12] From a letter to Lord Sheffield.
[13] Many Canadians, for example, fear that their national identity may be fatally compromised by the profound economic penetration of their country by American commercial and industrial interests.

system of inter-state relationships. It may do so by advocating revolutionary violence or a more gradual but perceptible process of 'withering away'. Anarchists desire to set up instead a social order providing mutually convenient collective arrangements freely willed by peoples without the sanction of coercive state power. This philosophy of politics and society has enjoyed for a century or so a small if earnest following. In the form of *syndicalism* it became a real force, and remains a living tradition in the political life of Spain. In recent years there has arisen a broadly based political radicalism which is sometimes associated with the student age-group and often with students *as* a group. This mood (it is perhaps as yet hardly sufficiently organized to be properly described as a movement) challenges the necessity as well as the legitimacy of the salient institutions of state power in many parts of the world. The doctrines of this dissent, as articulated by different groups and individuals, may appear sometimes confused and even contradictory. At the level of slogan-making in the late 1960s almost the principal tenet seemed in places to consist of a reiterated belief in the personal immortality of the deceased revolutionary, Che Guevara. But the general drift of the claims often shrilly announced is clear enough. It is that the institutions of most states and the international system as a whole are by their nature oppressive, aggressive, intrusive and irrelevant to the chosen values of common – and sometimes communal – living proclaimed by the radicals. In so far as a slogan much paraded by some among them in recent years – 'Make love not war' – may be taken as representing a major aspect of their prevailing attitudes, we may be inclined to dismiss them as shallow doctrinaires, and to conclude that such an exhortation, as the basis of a programme of action, ignores, where it does not misunderstand, the nature of politics and the realities of international society. Certainly the challenge they claim to represent, if successful, would fatally undermine the whole framework of ideas and practices around which both the internal structure of states and the system of relations between them have been erected through the efforts and with the insights both of statesmen and their publics. However much swayed by political passions or blinded by prejudices governing elites and national populations may be, they are seldom wholly or permanently immune to the influence of reason and common sense. Apart from any other consideration such influence becomes necessary in order that policy-makers may calculate the most effectual methods of pursuing actual interests. We need not attempt to predict here the outcome of this intellectual and ideological challenge to the political *status quo* in the world. But whether prompted to suspect that 'there may be something in it' or not, we shall be wise to note its current pervasiveness, its vociferous character and the implications for the future viability of the existing international order which spring from it.

Secondly, there is the challenge from illicit violence itself. Some of this we may suppose to be caused by criminal and psychopathic elements in national populations, who exploit or are stimulated by real or imagined social and political grievances. Actual imitation by unbalanced or immature persons of terrorist acts committed by extremist groups does not seem to be negligible either. But we may safely assume that the main motive for the practice of 'armed dissent' in various countries spread right across the world, which substantially increased from the early 1960s, is ideological in motivation. Some of it evidently stems from frustrated nationalism among groups feeling themselves to be national in character yet politically deprived. But of course a very important aspect of illicit violence concerns the spread of political radicalism of the kind referred to above. Another component is the 'racial divide' in which resentments expressed by disadvantaged ethnic groups may have explosive effects within racially plural countries and at the level of international relations as well. The fact is that in every continent there has come to exist, somewhere, violent challenges to the established order. At the levels of terrorism, insurgency, guerrilla activity and revolutionary war these challenges have disrupted or threatened to disrupt whole political communities and (as in Indo-China) a whole group of such communities.

A serious development has been the flouting of the accepted norms of international behaviour by dissident movements who impose sanctions upon third parties in disputes, parties who have no responsibility for the condition of things giving rise to the dispute itself. The history of kidnappings and hi-jackings of third parties by extremist organizations carries serious implications for the international system. The threat to international order posed by this practice has been admirably analysed by John C. Garnett. Referring to hi-jacking activities by Palestinian guerrilla groups he wrote:

Those who are dissatisfied with their lot and who have exhausted all constitutional channels for promoting the changes which they desire, are always tempted to use illegal, even violent, methods to achieve their objectives. It is easy to appreciate the difficulties faced by the Fadayeen, but few can approve of its recent hi-jacking activities. Apart from the dubious morality of reprisals against those who cannot be held even remotely responsible for the predicament of the Palestine Arabs, the most important reason why all civilized states are justified in condemning such behaviour is that it threatens the very fabric of the society to which they all belong, and thereby ultimately threatens their interests.

... The rules of state behaviour have evolved over hundreds of years, and are reflected in a complicated web of diplomatic practice and in countless laws, customs and mores. In their own interests, states – and even those groups which aspire to become states – must recognize that if the international system is to provide a sufficiently stable environment for them to carry on normal business dealing with each other, then this minimum code of behaviour must be generally accepted, even when it is inconvenient.

Traditionally, certain things are simply not done in international politics. Diplomats are not kidnapped; embassies are not violated; ambassadors are not assassinated; and aeroplanes are not hi-jacked. If restraints of this kind disappear, then international society is impoverished, and life for the states which belong to it will inevitably become more difficult and more dangerous.[14]

These are wise words. Their general application stands, whatever rejoinder may be offered, so far as the Middle East is concerned. If we examine one rejoinder commonly heard we may agree that even in the particular question at issue Garnett's argument prevails. For the case made was that several major countries, including particularly the United States and Britain, do share a responsibility, by virtue of their policies, for the plight of the Palestinian Arabs. Therefore, the argument ran, if American or British nationals are hi-jacked or otherwise inconvenienced, they should be regarded as the symbolic expiators of the guilt attaching to the governments of their countries. This line might perhaps plausibly be stretched to include the diplomatic representatives of the countries concerned. However, the needs of international order would still deny its validity. But to apply the notion of derivative guilt to, say, a child passenger, or to a national of a country not involved in the decisions giving rise to the grievance, is to expand

[14] In a note to the author.

the idea of responsibility until it loses meaning. Far sounder, we are likely to agree, to insist that dissident organizations which choose recklessly to outrage norms of international behaviour seriously jeopardize international order itself. A consequence of this will almost certainly be to make more difficult and problematic any international action that might be taken to reduce or redress the supposed wrongs of the dissidents. No sane interests, let alone legitimate ones, are served by chaos.

The primacy of national interests

Throughout this chapter passing references have been made to international politics, and it is to the central role of interests that we turn our attention in closing it.

We may say first that there is no such thing as *the national interest*. This is an abstraction. It stands for the whole bundle of interests which are the concern of statesmen. National interests may be complementary to each other; they may conflict; they will almost certainly compete. They often change in relative importance over time. They include such broad public issues as the prosperity and international prestige of the state itself, national security, and the maintenance of cordial and valuable diplomatic relations with other states. They also include those private interests, notably but not exclusively in the field of economic relationships, between commercial enterprises at home and abroad, which both directly affect national well-being and are represented inside the country by interest groups, each claiming the maximum possible share of consideration by policy-makers. In effect the statesman adjudicates between interests, deciding on the degree of support to be given a particular interest at a given time in the light of his understanding of national needs. This understanding in turn will tend to reflect pressures exercised by his own advisers, his colleagues in government, and the media of communication, which will pass upward, so to speak, in one form or another the demands and expectations of the national community.

Interests, we see, are determined by many factors. They are not created by statesmen but recognized by them. States may be said to be 'in business' in international society *in order to* promote and defend interests. As we suggested earlier, states exist to enable peoples to take a collective part in international life. This participation takes the form of pursuing recognized interests. Essentially this process represents an extension to the world at large of what goes on inside national communities. We are reminded once more that politics is ultimately all of a piece.

The paramountcy of interests in international politics has important implications for the statesman. We shall examine the problem of morality in international relations in chapter 6. Here we may just notice a link between national interests and the policy-makers' moral obligations. States do not choose to subordinate their conceived interests to those of other states. They may sometimes be forced to do so, but there is no *moral* quality attaching to an act that one cannot help doing. Broadly speaking, we can say that it becomes the moral duty of states, discharged by the statesmen who act on their behalf, to uphold as best they can their complex of national interests. The fulfilling by a state of its purpose for existing may be regarded as a moral obligation. On this view a state is acting morally, and only then, when it is promoting the national interest. A state in that case which put any interest of any other state above its own would be acting immorally. The supreme obligation of the state is, by this token, to act on behalf of the interests of the community identified with it, that is to say to act from a motive of collective self-regard. That the calculations involved may be hazardous, the interests to be defended vulnerable or perhaps incompatible, and the capacity at hand limited, are just part of the predicament which is inseparable from the role of the statesman. To that predicament we shall have occasion to return several times in succeeding chapters, for it is a fundamental aspect of international politics.

Note on foreign policy
All states will develop a 'foreign policy' of some kind, since they all will have relations with some other state or states. In the modern world the total isolation of a state is probably impossible. Afghanistan in its highland fastnesses has critically important relations with Pakistan, Iran and the Soviet Union. Even the thirty-two square mile Republic of San Marino has diplomatic relations with Italy and the Holy See. (At one period a Samarinese restaurateur in Knightsbridge doubled as the republic's envoy at the Court of St James.) But foreign policy is not a 'thing'. Countries do not start out with a foreign policy, which they take up and apply to the world outside. Thus Peter Calvocoressi can

write: 'No country should be expected to have a foreign policy: the demand for such a thing is absurd and a belief that you have one is always illusory and often dangerous.'[15] Foreign policy is essentially a set of political reactions to what is perceived by policy-makers to be the current reality of the situation in which their country appears to be placed. Even when statesmen take policy *initiatives*, they are still responding to what they conceive to be the needs of the national interest as shaped by external factors. This is the case whether they are attempting to seize an advantage, or reacting to a threat, or pursuing an ideological objective. Foreign policy is bound up with decisions about the deployment of national resources of all kinds, diplomatic, economic or military, on behalf of national interests. Inevitably these decisions will be to a large extent pragmatic and piecemeal. Sir Thomas Brimelowe of the British Foreign Office offers this useful definition: 'Foreign policy at any given time is that bundle of national decisions concerning foreign relations which are held by policy-makers to be in force.'[16] In acting on such decisions, and adding new ones to them, statesmen are essentially concerned with the application of power. Both power and its application are conditioned by what are conventionally recognized as the *determinants* of foreign policy. These include such factors as geography, population, industrial development and not least national history and tradition. All these factors not only help to determine what specific decisions are taken but profoundly influence political *style*, that is, the mode in which decisions are reached and implemented, and the general character of a state's behaviour in international society. The last word may well be left with Ian Stephens, writing as it happens on the history of Pakistan: 'In the last analysis one may say that a country's foreign policy is what enables her to exist: to keep independently in being. It may be shaped and defined with clarity, but it need not. Details can be kept vague. What matters is maintenance of the will, among her leaders and people, that she should survive.'[17]

[15] In an article in *The Times*.
[16] In a private conversation.
[17] In *Pakistan*, Ernest Benn, London, 1963.

2

Some international systems in history

Plus ça change, plus c'est la même chose – *Anon.*

All that real history can do is to note with wonder and reverence the tides which have surged out from the innermost heart of man. . . . Life makes its own great gestures, of which men are the substance. History repeats the gesture, so we live it once more, and are fulfilled in the past – *D. H. Lawrence.*

When we talk about international society we probably think usually of the contemporary worldwide society of states. This society has its roots of course in history. Essentially the modern states' system goes back to the sixteenth century of our era. The germ of it lies farther back still, in the period when the nations of Europe were forming from the tribal societies which both overran the Roman Empire and were partially civilized by it. But during the epoch of European national statehood and before it there have been 'international' systems more or less cohesive and more or less characteristic in their institutions and inter-relationships. Some of these systems are highly instructive both in their similarities to modern international society and in their divergencies from it.

We have noted that such a system, however much it may resemble or differ from any other, comes into existence when significant interactions develop between an assemblage of autonomous political units. If one imagines a spectrum from point A, which indicates units that are entirely separate and autonomous, and have no relations with each other, to point X, where the units actually merge to form one unitary entity (whatever may be the relationship between the constituent parts) we may place international systems on the continuum towards point A, and federal or confederal systems somewhere along the line towards point X. The degree of intensity in the interactions may vary considerably between one system and another. But the requirement stands that the units comprising the system shall both enjoy a significant degree of political autonomy and sustain perceptible relations with each other, which to some extent condition their characteristic behaviour. Similarly, confederal and federal systems require some definable areas of jurisdiction to belong to the constituent units and some to the central body.

In history many examples are found. They change, naturally, over time. They come into being and disappear. They yield a number of striking parallels with contemporary political experience on the international plane. They illustrate varieties of system, including occasionally (as in the case of Rome) the development of a 'world state' embracing in an effectual political union all the diverse cultural, social and political elements of a whole civilization. We will take a (necessarily selective) look at some of them.

The ancient Greek city-states

But first a word about the use of the adjective 'international'. Admittedly its usage has become fairly loose. It is probably better, when referring for example to the city-states of ancient Greece, to speak of 'inter-state' rather than of 'international' relations. One reason for this is that in a number of important respects the Greeks may be regarded as having comprised a nation, whereas it would be straining the sense of words needlessly to speak of the Athenian 'nation' or the 'nations' of Sparta and Corinth, etc. What mattered was that the citizens of Athens, Sparta, Corinth, Thebes, Plateaea, and other cities, formed *states*, the so-called city-states, each genuinely sovereign, being responsible for its internal political arrangements and external relations. An interesting theme in ancient Greek history is in fact the tension between a real collective ethnic sense among the Hellenes and the particularist ardour of the citizens of the respective *poleis* or city-states. (Indeed, group or 'party' particularism within certain cities sometimes threatened the disruption of the state itself.) Some analogy may be found with medieval Europe. Just as the Greeks were bound together by a number of 'national' cults in honour of the principal gods of the Greek pantheon, gods worshipped by all, so European Christendom developed a sense of mutual belonging and even obligation among those who composed it. In neither case, however, did this element of cohesion prevent or apparently significantly inhibit the use of organized armed violence as an appropriate instrument for the staking of claims or the defending of interests.

For the Greeks, part of being Hellene was an acknowledged sense of kinship. The states themselves were in theory, and to some extent in practice, kin-bound. This kin sense derived from a tribal past and a common language, diversified as this was by dialects. Non-Greeks were *barbarians*. Their speech sounded like 'bar-bar-bar' and was unintelligible. Similarly, to medieval Europeans non-Christians were infidels, outside the 'household of the faith' that was at least supposed to bind in certains restraints and reciprocal duties all those within it. Among the Greeks there actually were certain constraints upon their behaviour towards each other, at least until about the fourth century BC. Greeks should not enslave other Greeks. After a battle Greeks should leave each other in peace to bury their dead, and to raise trophies of victory and perhaps commemoration. In a similar spirit a pope of the eleventh century enjoined Christians not to use that frightful weapon, the crossbow, against each other but to reserve its use for battles with the infidels. However, we must not press these moral restraints too far. A common ethnic feeling among the Greeks did not prevent the city-states from engaging in wars with each other so frequently that it has been suggested that warfare constituted the 'natural relationship' between them. A common civilization bound together by the institutions and doctrines of the Christian Church did not prevent the European Middle Ages from being one of the great military epochs of history. The third most honoured status in medieval society, the others being priesthood and kingship, was knighthood. This chivalric order developed in direct response to the pervasiveness as well as the gloriousness of warfare.

Still, the degree of social and political homogeneity among the ancient Greeks led to the development of an inter-state system which is still of some relevance to modern problems of international order. There were some fifteen hundred *poleis* throughout mainland, insular and Ionic Greece (the western coast of Asia Minor) as well as *Graeca Magna* – Greater Greece – so known because of numerous and in some cases important Greek settlements in Sicily and southern Italy. Many of these 'city-states' were little more than fortified villages. But each enjoyed its miniature sovereignty, and assumed the burden of its own defence. A dozen or so great cities became important states, in modern parlance great powers. Such were Athens, Sparta, Thebes and Corinth in mainland Greece, Rhodes and Lesbos among the islands of the Aegean, Miletus in Ionia, Syracuse in Sicily and Capua in Italy. And there were others. The great cities maintained an intricate web of relationships with each other. These included both the linkage of frequent campaigns, and the apparatus of a developed and quite sophisticated diplomacy. In this heralds and embassies, enjoying what we should now call diplomatic immunities, appeared before the assemblies or councils of each other's cities to issue challenges, propose alliances, offer trade agreements and sue for peace.

It will be seen from the foregoing that the Greeks (as well as some other ancient peoples) had developed complex norms of inter-state behaviour, which for at least a few centuries were relatively well observed. Some coarsening of Greek inter-state relations took place in the fourth century, after the great Peloponnesian war which broke out in 431 BC. It is perhaps not too fanciful to regard that fateful date as ancient Greece's 1914. In the subsequent period mercenaries were employed by warring cities on an increasingly large scale. Prosperity in Hellas, always fairly precarious, seems everywhere to have declined in this period. Able-bodied men found a living hard to gain in their own cities, and sold their military skill to other states, sometimes, as in the case of Xenophon and the 'Ten Thousand', seeking service under barbarian kings.

With economic decline went a lowering of political vitality. This was owing in part to the Peloponnesian war. This momentous struggle is of special interest in relation to the processes of international politics. As the American scholar Peter Fliess makes clear in his striking commentary on Thucydides,[1] the Peloponnesian war was essentially an outcome of 'the politics of bipolarity'. In a manner analogous to the pattern of East-West relations between 1945 and the later 1960s, Athens and Sparta, one the supreme maritime power in Greece, the other the major land power, pursued a mutual rivalry based on the promotion of 'world interests' that eventually clashed. Both had shared in the defeat of the Persian Great Kings earlier in the century. Both went on to develop huge alliance systems, in which each superpower enjoyed an almost over-

[1] Peter J. Fliess, *Thucydides and the Politics of Bipolarity*, Louisiana State U.P., 1966.

whelming preponderance of prestige and decision-making capacity. Sparta held down the greater part of the Peloponnesian land mass by military force. Athens dominated a Delian League of mainly island states so decisively that historians call the later League the Athenian Empire. The lines were laid for a great power confrontation, the less avoidable in that the thrusting confidence and ambition of democratic and Periclean Athens, the premier state of mainland Greece, was at least matched by the hostile suspicion of the highly militarized state of Sparta.

War finally broke out over the immediate issue of Athenian aid to Corcyra (modern Corfu) in a revolt against Corinth, of which Corcyra was originally a colony. Corinth was an ally of Sparta. She invoked Spartan aid against Athens. Other, smaller, states were also involved, Megara being subject to acute economic pressure by Athens, and Potidaea, a member of the Delian League but a colony of Corinth, being required by Athens to break with her mother-city. With one uneasy period of truce the war lasted for more than two decades. As the struggle proceeded many states were brought into the conflict, on one side or the other, and the war spread to a northern theatre in Thrace and across the western sea to Syracuse in Sicily. Even a pestilence early in the war did not break either the will or the capacity of Athens to fight, and victory only came to Sparta when she had succeeded in meeting Athens on terms at sea, with considerable Persian aid in gold and kind. Even as late as 406 Athens could still inflict a crippling naval defeat on her great enemy. In 404 the Athenians finally surrendered, undergoing the miseries of revolution and internal strife before finally a Spartan king, Pausanias, imposed a settlement which restored the Athenian democracy. The Peloponnesian war, said Thucydides, its first and finest historian, was the greatest conflict yet known.

That war was in many respects the central episode in the history of classical Greece. It serves perhaps as an instructive reminder that whatever may be the 'lessons of history' it is possibly more useful to note how the present illuminates the past. Every historical event is unique. It is so in its causation, its circumstances and its outcome. Parallels with other events, however striking, can therefore never be more than suggestive approximations. But bearing that necessary qualification in mind, we can notice that remarkable parallels do arise. Following Professor Fliess we have seen the Peloponnesian war as an example of (forceful) bipolar politics.

39

Now it can have this special significance for modern students of history because of the contemporary experience through which they have passed. In this period world politics was largely dominated by the critically important relations between the communist and so-called free worlds.[2] This experience can enable us to interpret the Peloponnesian war, and to assess its significance, in a way that would not have occurred to earlier historians of ancient Greece. Nothing in their experience quickened in their minds such a concept as 'bipolarity' in international politics. The great liberal English historian, George Grote, for instance, in his monumental *History of Greece* naturally gave due place to this war, but not in these terms.

This is really to say in another way what has often been pointed out by writers on history, that every age must interpret for itself. We see the past only in part. We cannot know, let alone describe or analyse, everything that happened. Our selection of what happened that mattered derives from our current predicaments, values, anxieties, hopes. What mattered in the past may differ a great deal from what happened in the past that matters to us. In the case of the Peloponnesian war we may agree with earlier commentators in seeing as its principal outcome an immediate decline in the power of Athens, although she continued to be a major Hellenic state for some three centuries more, and an even more portentous decline in the quality of Greek political life and of inter-state relationships. But we can also contemplate, and apply to the condition of very recent history, the spectacle of a bipolar constellation of power. Then the rivalry of two great states had the effect of ranging beside each of them, often in reluctant alliance or coerced support, the majority of states in the international system of ancient Greece.

A further aspect of the parallel should not be overlooked. The rivalry was indeed for prestige, for security, for military dominance. To adapt the title of A. J. P. Taylor's fine study of nineteenth-century European history, it may indeed be regarded as 'the struggle for mastery in Hellas'. But that struggle was also, and importantly, ideological. There was in the competition between

[2] The word 'free' in this context is doubtless tendentious, and carries ideological overtones, but may stand here for the grouping of those non-communist states which entered into alliance of one form or another with the United States against the threat of a dangerous increase in the power of the Soviet Union and her allies after 1946.

the superpowers of Athens and Sparta a sharp competition between two political value-systems. The principles of democratic and oligarchic government, of broadly and narrowly conceived citizen's rights and duties, were locked in a deadly struggle between two conceptions of civic righteousness. This aspect of the war gives it a special relevance to the international experience of the middle decades of the twentieth century; and of those other epochs in which the clash of values has motivated the clash of arms. A character in one of G. K. Chesterton's novels[3] has this to say. It is, in its way, a classic statement.

Oh, you kings, you kings . . . how humane you are, how tender, how considerate. You will make war for a frontier, or the imports of a foreign harbour; you will shed blood for the precise duty on lace, or the salute to an admiral. But for the things that make life itself worthy or miserable – how humane you are. I say here, and I know well what I speak of, there were never any necessary wars but the religious wars. There were never any just wars but the religious wars. There were never any humane wars but the religious wars. For these men were fighting for something that claimed, at least, to be the happiness of a man, the virtue of a man. A crusader thought, at least, that Islam hurt the soul of every man, king or tinker, that it could really capture.

This book was published in 1904. We have seen since international society divided into embattled systems of political idealism, claiming total allegiance, proclaiming total mutual hostility and held apart only by a prudential assessment of each other's capacity to inflict an intolerable degree of mutual destruction. It is this consideration which limits the applicability of the Greek experience in the Peloponnesian war to the strategic predicament of the middle decades of the twentieth century. It would happily be rash to assume that the lesson of that crucial episode in the history of Greek city-state relations is that there is any inevitable outcome to the development of a bipolar pattern of power in international politics. Nor need we suppose that the outcome of general armed conflict is necessarily the most likely. Already the acute phase of the cold war seems to have passed. Prudential constraints have impelled policy-makers on each side to pursue their rivalry by other means. In ancient Greece competitive co-existence between the rival blocs eventuated in a great and decisive war. In the modern world such co-existence between the communist bloc

[3] *The Napoleon of Notting Hill*, 1st edn 1904; Penguin Books, London, 1946.

and the Western bloc has been both a feature of the cold war and almost its openly acknowledged successor. However, for a sombre reminder of the consequences that are liable to follow a great power struggle reinforced by the justifying role and energizing effects of rival ideologies, we may turn to the searing judgement of Thucydides himself on what the Peloponnesian war brought to Greece as a whole:

One may say, the whole Hellenic world was convulsed; struggles being everywhere made by the popular chiefs to bring in the Athenians, and by the oligarchs to introduce the Lacedaemonians [Spartans]. . . . The sufferings which revolution entailed upon the cities were many and terrible, such as have occurred and always will occur, as long as the nature of mankind remains the same. . . . In peace and prosperity states and individuals have better sentiments, because they do not find themselves suddenly confronted with imperious necessities; but war takes away the easy supply of daily wants, and so . . . brings most men's characters to a level with their fortunes. Revolution thus ran its course from city to city, and the places which it arrived at last, from having heard what had been done before, carried to a still greater excess the refinement of their inventions, as manifested in the cunning of their enterprises and the atrocity of their reprisals. Words had to change their ordinary meaning and to take that which was now given them. Reckless audacity came to be considered the courage of a loyal ally; prudent hesitation, specious cowardice; moderation was held to be a cloak for unmanliness; ability to see all sides of a question, inaptness to act on any. Frantic violence became the attribute of manliness; cautious plotting, a justifiable means of self-defence. The advocate of extreme measures was always trustworthy; his opponent a man to be suspected. . . . In fine . . . even blood became a weaker tie than party . . . for such associations had not in view the blessings derivable from established institutions but were formed by ambitions for their overthrow; and the confidence of their members in each other rested less on any religious sanction than upon complicity in crime. . . . Revenge also was held of more account than self-preservation. . . . The cause of all these evils was the lust for power arising from greed and ambition. . . . The leaders in the cities, each provided with the fairest professions, on the one side with the cry of political equality of the people, on the other of a moderate aristocracy, sought prizes for themselves in those public interests which they pretended to cherish, and, recoiling from no means in their struggle for ascendancy, engaged in the direst excesses; in their acts of vengeance they went to even greater lengths, not stopping at what justice or the good of the state demanded but . . . invoking with equal readiness the condemnation of an unjust verdict or the authority of the strong arm to glut the animosities of the hour. . . . Thus every form of iniquity took root in the Hellenic countries by reason of the troubles. . . .[4]

The indictment is severe, but the subsequent history of the Greek city-states does much to bear it out. Certainly the war became as 'total' as the technological and demographic resources of the age allowed. Thucydides gives grounds for assuming that this total character of the war was stimulated by the 'dumb-bell' conformation of inter-state power in Hellas that had developed in the fifth century, and by the further weighting of the twin poles with ideological passions. Fig. 2 (p. 44) indicates the bipolar aspects of the Peloponnesian war, in a context in which each side sought to influence remaining neutrals and was itself an object of foreign policy to a third Great Power – Persia.

International relations were not, of course, confined to the Greek city-states themselves. They also had very close and often decisive relations with 'the nations around', principally the great kingdoms on the peripheries of the Hellenic world, to whom the Greek cities represented the political periphery. Most notable was Persia in the east, which played an active role in the inter-state politics of the Greeks for several centuries, and the half-Greek, half barbarian kingdom of Macedonia to the north. Two kings of Macedonia, the brilliant if dissipated Philip ii and his son, the astonishing youth Alexander, were in the fourth century to assume the hegemony of all Greece. Alexander the Great went on to fulfil his father's grandiose dream and lead a conquering coalition of Macedonians and Greeks against the Persian Empire.

Alexander of Macedon has special significance. His military achievement transformed the eastern Mediterranean lands from a complex of numerous and for the most part relatively small competing sovereignties to the first of the two great world states of Graeco-Roman civilization. The Alexandrian Empire itself was to prove short-lived. The conqueror died at thirty-three years of age without naming a successor. The story, likely enough to be true, goes that on his untimely death-bed the great king was asked to whom he bequeathed his inheritance. Alexander whispered, 'To

[4] Thucydides, *The History of the Peloponnesian War*, Book III (Richard Crawley's translation), Everyman's Library, Dent, London, 1910.

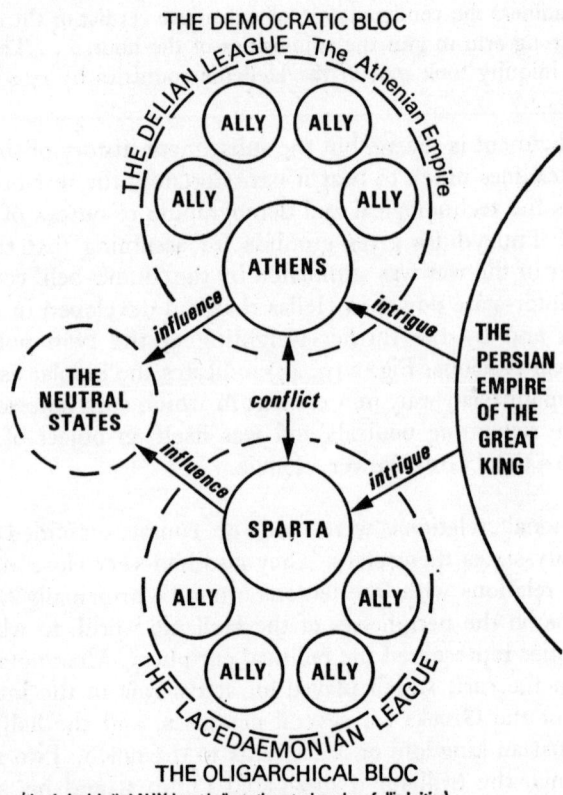

Fig. 2. The Peloponnesian war as an outcome of the bipolarization of international politics

the strongest'. His young son survived a few years, invested with nominal sovereignty, but the Empire, stretching from Macedonia to the borders of India, became the object of competition, and later division, between his marshals. Within some twelve years they carved out great realms for themselves. But the city-states of the Aegean littoral were never the same again. They enjoyed local autonomy for centuries more, but were effectually subservient to one or other of the large Hellenistic kingdoms, the Seleucid Empire in Asia Minor, Macedonia and Egypt, which had divided between them the heritage of Alexander's world state.

This Hellenistic period is in many respects analogous to the

eighteenth century in Europe. International politics was dominated by the relations between a few great powers comprising a
'chandelier'-type of balance of power,[5] diversified by the survival or
coming into existence of a number of smaller states, including both
the relatively important kingdom of Pergamum in north-west
Asia Minor and the old Greek city-states. There never developed a
conscious 'Concert of the powers' as became such a significant
feature of eighteenth- and nineteenth-century European history,
but for much of the period from the death of Alexander the Great
to the Roman hegemony in the eastern Mediterranean in the first
century BC, the rivalries and mutual constraints pursued by
Macedonia, the Seleucid Empire and Egypt achieved a similar
effect.

Fig. 3 shows the pattern of the balance of power in the Hellenistic age as at *c.* 230 BC. This was a chandelier-type balance. The
three great successor realms to Alexander's Empire, the *Diadochi*,
competed with each other for dominance in the eastern Mediterranean area. The comparatively small but rich and culturally
splendid kingdom of Pergamum arose in north-west Asia Minor.
Athens and Sparta, relatively enfeebled, remained independent but

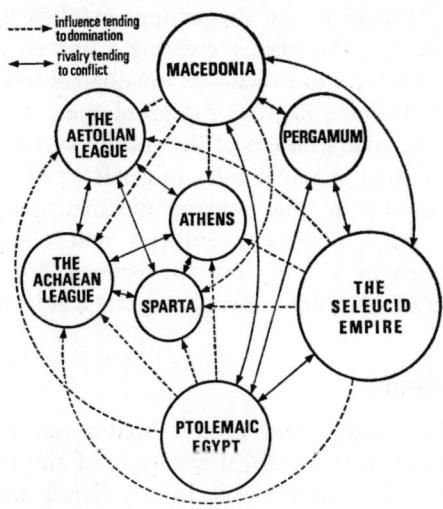

Fig. 3. The balance of power in the Hellenistic Age, *c* 230 BC

[5] See the discussion of the balance of power in chapter 5.

45

upon Macedonian sufferance. The former was already assuming the role of university city she was to maintain for seven centuries. Many Greek states combined in the great leagues. Though represented in the figure as tight federal structures these were fairly lose in their political arrangements, representing for the Greeks the best they could manage in concerted policy making.

The Hellenistic Age was in truth a great one, both politically and culturally. The fluctuating but persistent balance of power was maintained by the extensive use of mercenary armies. On the whole these fought cannily, minimizing casualties, not being inspired by a passion for any cause in which they particularly believed. (The Jews, building up a growing theocratic community round Jerusalem, were an exception.) Prosperity increased. General living standards rose. Commerce burgeoned. The arts flourished, if literature did become less monumental and more personalized than among the greatest Greek writers of the classical age. The splendours and amenities of city life spread far and wide. A diluted Greek culture graced upper-class and urban society from Macedonia to the borders of India. Greek learning was preserved and diffused. The Stoic philosophy held at least an implication for a universalist generosity of thought about the human status. Alexandria and Pergamum established the greatest libraries of antiquity, the former creating a university where the sciences reached a level of excellence unequalled until the seventeenth century. Antioch, *de facto* capital of the Seleucid Empire, became one of the civic wonders of the ancient world. Great kings, worshipped as virtual or actual gods, in general ruled well, experimenting successfully in 'the bureaucratic management of large tracts of territory'.[6] The two centuries that elapsed between Alexander's death in 323 BC and the Roman dominion in the eastern Mediterranean were in many respects a golden age.

The epic of Rome

Turning to the western end of the Mediterranean littoral we observe the remarkable historical spectacle of the rise of Rome. This is not the place to examine in any detail answers to the question why a city-state in the Italian peninsula succeeded in attaining that decisive hegemony which eluded any state in the

[6] J. M. Todd, *The Ancient World*, Hodder & Stoughton, London, 1938.

Greek. Strategically placed midway up the western coast of Italy, with its long-settled communities and good harbours, the fortified settlement of the Romans spread in the fullness of time over the seven hills that dominated the plain of Latium. Between the eighth and the third centuries BC Rome became the greatest power in all Italy. It commanded the centre, then extended first its influence then its control north and south. At last the whole peninsula south of the River Po, including Sicily and Sardinia, represented a great Roman federation of political communities, bound together with the Roman state by bonds of common obligation for mutual defence. The dominating role of Rome herself created an effective *imperium* by 180 BC that we may properly call the Roman Empire. Then ensued a century of grievous crisis. After it the old republican institutions were adapted and transformed, allowing for the rule of an emperor, governing through a centralized bureaucratic machinery. Yet it should be remembered that the Empire never became a 'monolithic' state. Elements of the federal device survived to the last phase of the Empire in the West. So much was this so that it has been said of the Empire in its heyday in the second century AD that it represented a vast federation of city-states, held in union by the consensual operation of imperial administration and military control, for which the emperor was responsible, who in his person and office symbolized the unity and Roman character of the whole political order that arched majestically over three continents.

The Roman Empire was the second and far the greater world state of the Mediterranean basin. At its vastest extent it brought under one international order peoples and their lands from north Britain to Africa, from Spain to Persia, from the Rhine and Danube to southern Egypt. It is true to say that the extent, stability and grandeur of this political structure, supported by the most advanced administrative apparatus and defended by the most efficient military instrument known to the ancient world, has haunted the imagination of Western man during nearly two millennia. For nearly two centuries in the middle period of its five-hundred year course the Empire gave to the whole Mediterranean world its *Pax Romana*, in which one of the greatest of human civilizations took root, flourished, and scattered seeds that were to fructify in later ages and give a special character to the political life of most of Europe, and, through the expansion of Europeanism, to many lands far beyond it. Both in the fields of administration and law, to name but two, the debt of the modern world to the Roman experience is incalculable. Historical Christianity continues to bear upon it the signs of its development in the Graeco-Roman world. This unquestionably shaped and even transmuted the primal Hebraic content. Philosophically the Christian religion came to maturity in the milieu of Graeco-Roman thought. And it was in the context of Roman imperial society that this world religion gained its decisive triumph as a political force. This consideration it was that led the seventeenth-century English philosopher Thomas Hobbes to utter his famous epigram that the Roman Catholic Church was 'no other than the ghost of the deceased Roman Empire, sitting crowned on the grave thereof'.[7]

Indeed, we need not suppose that the Roman experiment was all gain. World states need not, perhaps, be world tyrannies. Yet there is good evidence from later Roman history of a sobering propensity in this direction. 'I have described', remarked the inimitable Gibbon, reflecting upon his monumental *History of the Decline and Fall of the Roman Empire*, 'the triumph of barbarism and religion.' The Roman achievement was great but limited. Even in their heyday the Romans showed nothing comparable to the intellectual brilliance and thrusting speculative enquiry of the Greeks at their best. Romans wrought mightily in law, war, administration and architecture. Their system of communications by land and sea surpassed anything known until the nineteenth century. But their technology remained essentially slave-bound. It made few significant advances on the suggestions thrown out (and also, admittedly, not developed) by the Greek scientists of an earlier age.[8] And it has been cogently argued that one aspect of the imperial 'decline' was in the realm of thought. This lay at the heart of Edward Gibbon's criticism. To him, in the words of G. M. Young, 'the rise of Christianity and the fall of the Empire are parallel effects of a general collapse of the intellect under the pressure of a world tyranny'.[9] We need not be concerned here to enter into the merits of the aristocratic liberal pessimism of Gibbon's eighteenth-century thesis. But it does give rise to rele-

[7] *Leviathan* : the observation represents one of Hobbes's shrewdest insights.

[8] G. Rattray Taylor, the celebrated 'doom-writer', might think this was not to the disadvantage of Graeco-Roman society.

[9] G. M. Young, *Gibbon*, Nelson, London, 1932.

vant reflections about the desirability of a world state in principle. Such desirability has been widely canvassed among liberal internationalists in the present century, who take their stand on a number of idealistic assumptions which may be more readily challenged than many liberals would care to admit. Would a world government, if attainable, really be a 'good thing'? The prospects of this coming about are touched on in chapter 8. Let us just point out now that world states in the past, and perhaps the Roman world state in particular, suggest two sobering considerations that we might bear in mind. First, a world state could impose on the political communities of that world an extremely burdensome and vexatious degree of authoritarian decision, against which there could be by definition no appeal. Either the global tyranny would succeed, or it would be successfully baulked at a regional level. In which case we would be faced by a restoration of something like the present multi-sovereign international system which these idealists deplore. Secondly, an achieved world order seems likely, if it came about at all, to be *somebody's* world order. There was broad peace in the great imperial centuries of Rome. But it was the *Pax Romana*. It was a peace imposed by Roman power and arms on the rest of the Mediterranean world. We have yet to see whether a genuine world order can be created by consent.

However this may be so far as world government as a possibility and a prospect is concerned, we should not on the other hand allow ourselves to be too much influenced by the philosophic liberalism of an earlier, and in many ways favoured, age in judging the Roman achievement. J. C. Stobart[10] remarked that to the Imperial Age the centuries of the Roman Republic, recalled by constitutional liberals of the eighteenth and nineteenth centuries with considerable nostalgia, were a mere preface. The Roman Empire did bestow the blessings of comparative peace and relative prosperity upon vast multitudes of human beings throughout the Mediterranean world for upwards of four centuries. It did so by means of systems of law and administration that revealed a high degree of rationality and a notable minimum of mere arbitrariness in application.

In this achievement the formative role of Octavian, who became Augustus, is a central factor. His great-uncle, Julius Caesar, an

[10] In *The Grandeur that was Rome*, Sidgwick & Jackson, London, revised edition 1933.

opportunitist of genius, lived only long enough, in the months of his legal dictatorship for life, to suggest what might be possible for a ruler who knew his own mind and how to manage men, before the crowd of reactionary republicans hacked him down at the foot of Pompey's statue. For the Empire that lasted till the fifth century AD only came to birth through a collective agony that lasted throughout the last age of the republic, and racked the Roman world with a series of devastating civil wars.

Augustus, as Gibbon acutely pointed out, 'was sensible that mankind are governed by names'. This world ruler with the finely modelled features and indifferent health recognized that the future stability of the New Order he was determined to draw up for the Empire depended upon a proper deference to ancient susceptibilities and current prejudices, both those of the Roman nobility and of the subject peoples throughout the provinces. Thus he publicly and solemnly claimed to have 'restored the republic'. However, he carefully instituted a limited but effectual monarchy. He sanctioned a popular and quasi-religious veneration for his office and person to prevail among the peoples at large, especially beyond Italy, while prudently insisting that he was no more than *Princeps*, Chief Citizen and First Senator, in Rome itself. It was the Romans, grateful for peace and order, who bestowed upon him the mysterious but highly charged personal name of *Augustus*, 'the august one', with its suggestion of a more than merely human sacredness and dignity, and added to it the warm yet noble title, indicative of the loving respect due to him, of *Pater Patriae*, Father of the Country. These honours were deserved. Much was hoped for from Augustus, and for more than forty burdened years he richly fulfilled expectations.

The real guarantee of the system he devised lay in his control of the armies. He established this by a shrewd measure. Augustus associated the senatorial group in government by allotting to their rule the safest and most peaceful provinces. In these an armed presence could be minimal or even merely nominal. The emperor himself governed, through officials directly responsible to him and drawn from the equestrian as much as from the senatorial classes, all those provinces which were newly settled, turbulent or subject to threats from beyond the imperial frontiers. It was in these areas that the main military deployment was required. The legions took a personal oath of loyalty to him, as embodying the claims of the

Roman state upon their devotion.[11] The emperor was responsible for the conduct of foreign relations, and initiated a diplomatic bureaucracy to discharge this responsibility.

Taking his political settlement as a whole, we may fairly say that the conservative Augustus proved himself to be one of the most creative revolutionaries in history. Cold as he personally was, cunning as he had to be, the first and perhaps greatest of the emperors of Rome practised statesmanship of the highest kind. He ensured longed-for peace and a wide possibility of developing prosperity to some eighty millions who dwelt beneath the wings of the imperial eagle.

We have suggested that the Roman peace, while it lasted and where it prevailed (and it was both limited in time and rarely unbroken in extent), was an imposed peace. Men assented to it gladly enough, but cannot really be said to have established it by their own political choice. However, some students of international politics have considered that the Roman experience is relevant to an understanding of the scope of modern international institutions, in particular such an institution as the United Nations Organization, which, in the proclaimed intention of its founders and members at least, exists to regulate the relations of states on behalf of promoting peace, security and general prosperity.

While clearly the Roman Empire was very different in actuality from the United Nations Organization, we may briefly examine the suggestion that there is a likeness in principle. If we admit that the contemporary organization does and should aspire to an executive authority which would enable it to monopolize at least the control of major weapons, and effectively to police the world, as visionaries like Lord Davies of Llandinam conceived a reformed and reinforced League of Nations doing before the second world war, then a parallel with the Empire may be sustained. For all the political communities which constituted that variegated imperial structure shared in the common protection afforded by the imperial armies and generally contributed to their upkeep. Moreover, the Empire was a unifying force. Though local political life was encouraged, it became more and more Roman in style. Provincials gladly identified with Roman character and civilization.

[11] Compare the oath taken by all members of the German forces to the person of the Führer in the Third Reich.

By the third century AD Romanization was so complete (and taxation needs so pressing) that Emperor Caracalla by edict enrolled practically all inhabitants of the Empire as citizens of a common international realm.

For the Roman Empire was essentially multi-national. It comprised an international system in itself. It was a genuine type of world order. As a possible model for a future world government, however, the Empire seems to be open to three major objections. The first of these we have already noticed. The Empire was based on conquest, no less so because many of Rome's successful campaigns were conducted for other reasons than territorial aggrandizement. And diverse as the constituent communities of the Empire were, there was an ascendancy about Roman civilization which ensured its broad adoption throughout all the imperial lands. We cannot so readily conceive the modern world consenting to be Russianized, Americanized or Sinotized even if such a process became practicable.

Secondly, though the Empire may fairly be called a world state, it was always surrounded by other political entities, some, such as the Parthian Empire and the later Empire of the Sassanids, menacingly powerful, and often in a relationship of hostility to Rome. More or less continuously through the history of the Empire either major wars or substantial policing actions were being conducted on or beyond and later increasingly within the Roman frontiers. On the other hand, these outside enemies – until they became overwhelming in the fifth century – probably helped to reinforce the unity and integrity of the Empire itself. It has been suggested that nothing would unify mankind so effectually as a dire threat from those Martians whose existence we have but too good reason to doubt. Still, the Roman Empire was not a total world order. It had always to devote considerable resources, human and material, to the needs of external security.

Thirdly, the Roman world state did in fact frequently pass through grave periods of internal disunity. From time to time provinces revolted against the central authority. Even more serious, the imperial regime never developed a sound and lasting principle of succession. Dynasticism never took root, although some instances of hereditary succession might have seemed encouraging. (Others were disastrous.) Increasingly in the later Empire emperors were the creatures of the army. The imperial purple became the object of often bitter strife between contending warlords at the head of embattled legions. Through much of imperial history the Roman army remained as magnificent as it was indispensable as an instrument of peace and order in the Roman world. But it was also too often a grievous threat to the unity and tranquillity of that world. As a foreshadowing of an international armed force operating under a world government the multi-national Roman army is not altogether reassuring.

Fig. 4 outlines the structure and processes of the Roman World State during the high noon of the *Pax Romana* from AD 96 to 180, and shows how the imperial order successfully combined the elements of a domestic political system with the character and requirements of an international system.

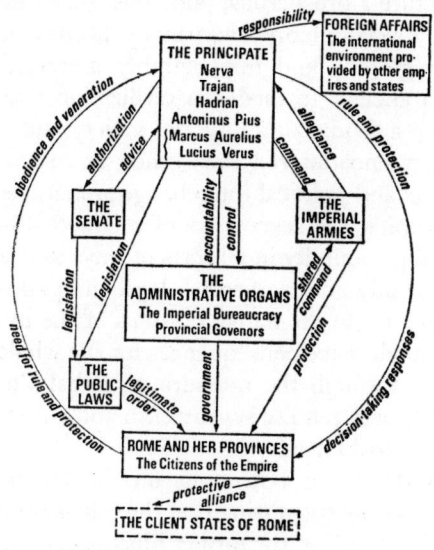

Fig. 4. The Roman Empire, AD 96–180

The world state of the Roman Empire, with its characteristic if changing type of world government, illustrates the limitations upon the capacity of any institution, however prestigious, to 'continue in one stay'. Was there not, uniquely described in the matchless prose of Gibbon, the Decline and Fall? Well, there were processes of decisive change, which may fairly be regarded as a decline, if there was less obviously a 'fall'. The Empire and its complex of inter-related structures were subject to increasing strains. These were partly owing to widespread depopulation. The causes of this are still subject to debate, both as to their nature and degree of effect. The burden of defence and administration became almost intolerably heavy. The economy declined. Trade withered. Self-subsistence at the level of relatively small localities grew common. (Although it is fair to point out that the recorded life of the fifth-century Emperor Avitus at his villa in Gaul reveals how civilized and even luxurious could be the lives of some in the very last age of the Empire in the West.)

Correspondingly, the 'nations around' were increasingly influenced by the vivid collective memories and surviving amenities, as well as by the visual symbols, of the Roman order. It would be quite mistaken to picture a prosperous, populous, sunlit Roman Empire suddenly and unaccountably overrun by hordes of savage barbarians from a gloomy and impenetrably aforested north. The transition from ancient to medieval civilization was gradual and prolonged. Both a feudalizing imperial society and a Romanizing barbarian society encountered each other, so to speak, half way. And this cultural and political interchange guaranteed, on the side of the 'new' peoples, the acceptance of a Graeco-Roman heritage which, modified profoundly in all sorts of ways as it was, prevailed to suggest powerfully norms of social, legal and political procedure that were grafted on to the native customs of the inheritors. This was to have quite decisive consequences for the whole later history of Europe, and, through the measure of global Europeanization which took place between the seventeenth and twentieth centuries of this era, of the world itself.

We may conclude our reflections on the Greek and Roman political experience by suggesting that the relevance of both to our purpose lies in the fact that the former illustrates the vulnerabilities inherent in a persisting system of multiple sovereign units, while the latter makes evident at least some of the limitations that seem perhaps inseparable from the organization of world orders.

Inter-state relations in Renaissance Italy

A further historical international system we will briefly consider is that which developed in Italy of the Renaissance, partly because it produced one of the most seminal of political philosophers. Here a number of republics and principalities, some differing little in scale from the city-states of ancient Greece, pursued their interests with a high degree of political sophistication.

Wars between them were, as we might expect, frequent. But intense policy-making was carried on by other means. These included a remarkable elaboration of intrigue, and a singular refinement of scruple to a point in which any scruples in state behaviour became difficult to detect. It was this vibrant – even febrile – world of Renaissance Italy which gave rise to Niccolò Machiavelli. Cynic or ironist (and so knowing and subtle a man may have been much of both) he expounded a theory of power which specifically subordinated moral considerations to the demands of an unrelenting *realpolitik*. Ironist or not, this Florentine spreads his shadow over the world of today, as Max Lerner[12] has pointed out, for he is 'the man who above all others taught the world to think in terms of cold political power'. Lerner goes on to remark that Machiavelli is one of the rare intellectuals who writes about politics with inside knowledge. Machiavelli has the directness and the assurance of the practitioner who writes about what he knows. He can also give his reader a sense of tingling intellectual excitement at the spectacle of a great philosophic mind cleaving through the illusions, the half-truths, the self-deceptions and conscious hypocrisies with which men obscure from their own knowledge and that of others both their real motives and the compulsions upon them which give rise to political action. To Machiavelli we may turn for the uncomfortable but sometimes needful insistence that politics is not about truth or honesty, but about interests which may clash, and about how to get and keep the power necessary to defend them. Machiavelli's 'grammar of power' has never been superseded because it is concerned with the analysis of some at least of the fundamental constants of human behaviour and human necessity. But we remember that it was a particular experience, at a given historical epoch, in a finite place – Renaissance Italy – which developed insights endowed with a universal validity.

Another feature to be noticed in the working of the international system in the Italy of this age is the role of the great powers on the

---

[12] Niccolò Machiavelli, *The Prince & The Discourses* (introduction by Max Lerner), The Modern Library, New York, 1950.

peripheries. France and Spain sought constantly to enlarge their interests in Italy, both at one another's expense and at that of the Italian states themselves, and then actively and often forcefully to intervene in Italian politics in order to uphold these interests. In this epoch, as so often in European history, dynastic prestige represents in itself a major interest of state to the securing of which policy has to be shaped. The Holy Roman Empire and the Papacy (in its role as a major territorial state) also vied with one another and their French and Spanish rivals in seeking to dominate Italy. The 'fateful game of chessboard diplomacy' was continued until the Italian city-states were overstrained, impoverished and borne down. Machiavelli's Florence, for example, was finally defeated by the mercenaries of the pope, who restored the princely house of the Medici to power, and abrogated the sturdy Florentine republican regime which Machiavelli himself had served. Disgraced, incriminated, tortured and exiled, this brilliantly able man wore out fourteen years of exclusion from the political sphere he so deeply understood, pleading, not very edifyingly, at frequent intervals to be reinstated in a position of influence or at least usefulness. His wish was not granted. But in the history of political thought these years of unwilling absence from the absorbing pursuit of politics were the most important in Machiavelli's life. His masterpieces, *The Prince* and *The Discources*, date from this period, together with *The Art of War,* a *History of Florence* and a quantity of other literary work. His office as secretary to the republican regime in Florence, which he so much valued and desired so deeply to regain, is important to the world as giving him the experience which he interwove into his profound reflections on the nature of politics and the hard necessities of power.

The modern international system

By this necessarily sketchy circle we return to the notion of modern international society, the society of contemporary states. We have noticed that this worldwide order originally developed in its present form in the European state system that arose out of the political institutions and experience of medieval Europe. That is to say that the international system as we know it today is about four centuries old. There were of course 'countries' in medieval times. There were also 'nations', although nationalism of the modern kind, a self-conscious and often highly articulated ideology, was not part of the furniture of the medieval mind. However, its roots were there. The Holy Roman Empire was the 'Holy Roman Empire of the German Nation'. In *Saint Joan* George Bernard Shaw, probably with some justification, makes the Maid of Orleans in the fifteenth century insist that France was for the French. The 'Goddams', i.e. the English troops who were said to swear characteristically in that phrase, should return home to England. There they belonged, and had natural rights of occupation.

We may in fact detect two processes at work in the evolution of the modern nation-state,[13] and of the European state system in which it functioned.

The first was tribalism. This essentially consisted of a sense of folkish homogeneity deriving largely from a shared linguistic heritage, reinforced by customary ways of securing social arrangements. However, powerful though it was, this phenomenon did not reach its greatest psycho-sociological importance until the nineteenth century in Europe. That century witnessed the growth of characteristically modern nationalism. Such modern nationalism was accompanied by, and appears to have been intimately connected with, the gradual politicizing of whole state populations. Notable factors in the process were the spread of enfranchisement, literacy and a popular press.

The second process was that whereby strong dynasties developed around them distinctive state institutions. The peoples came to identify their national societies with these institutions, and, in turn, the dynasts came to base their legitimacy upon them. We can see these developments at work in England and Spain in the fifteenth century, in France and Sweden in the sixteenth and seventeenth, and to a large extent in Russia in the eighteenth. There are other instances. Evidently too the nation-building proclivities of the great dynasties were in turn stimulated by a spontaneous growth of a sense of nationhood in the governed peoples. Shakespeare, in the historical plays of his middle period at least, strikes many times the note of a developed and self-conscious patriotic fervour, which the Tudors, the only successful absolutists in English history, responded to and encouraged.

In the fifteenth century Western Christendom, under papal jurisdiction, had reached a state of severe institutional and spiritual

[13] The ideology of nationalism is discussed in chapter 4.

crisis. Early in the following century a Protestant Reformation inaugurated by Martin Luther changed decisively the political complexion and future history of Europe. One result of this very complex and by no means merely sudden event was a strengthening of the dynastic principle. Religion was pressed into the service of the state in a new way. Insofar as it was accepted that the religion of the ruler was to be the religion of his subjects, and hence of the state he ruled, the state acquired a new authority. No longer merely the 'civil arm' to whom heretics – persons guilty of errors in religious opinion – could be handed over by the Church for punishment, the state itself determined what it was permissible for its subjects to believe. Obviously this determination would differ as between Catholic and Protestant states. The ideal of an overall Christendom, binding together in a universal devotion diverse communities of believers – the Christian peoples – gave way to a concept of a *congeries* of states, Christian certainly, whose individual sovereignty was reinforced by the confessional divisions between them. It was to be some two centuries more before the European states finally relinquished their claim to dictate the spiritual allegiance of their subjects, and conceded that doctrinal dissent in matters of religion was not treason.

The date of the Treaty of Westphalia, 1648, which terminated the long miseries of the thirty years' war, a war which devastated the lands of Germany, is a conventional and convenient point at which to mark the coming of age of the European state system. In Western Europe particularly states had become more secularized. As Sir Herbert Butterfield has put it,[14] 'worldly-minded men' began to argue that though religious persecution might be the ideal, still, 'even for the sake of God, one can hardly go on for ever ravaging a country and committing murder'. Secularism and a growing absolutism in Europe combined to make the state the main focus of the individual's loyalty in his public and even social relations, while his religion, if slowly and patchily, tended to be relegated to the private part of his life, and gradually to be accepted by governments as properly outside the scope of coercive legislation. With generally increasing efficiency states enforced obedience to their laws. But they also conceded more and more widely that those laws should no longer bind consciences in matters of

[14] Sir Herbert Butterfield, *Christianity in European History*, Collins, London, 1952.

religious opinion and belief. It was a very significant development in the secularizing of Christendom when it came to be no longer generally felt that the *security* of a state depended upon the enforced and public observance by all its subjects of the practices of whatever form of Christianity had been embodied in the official ecclesiastical institutions of that state. To suggest a dialectical interpretation, if Roman Catholicism under inalienable papal authority was the thesis, and Protestantism which, in all its ramifications, was defined by a common denial of that authority, stood as the antithesis, the internecine strife between them resulted in the synthesis of a secularized Europe. This Europe still asserted a generalized Christian character, as evident as the Islam of the Ottoman and Mogul Empires, the Hinduism of Indian society under Mogul rule, or the Confucian tradition of imperial China. Most European states insisted upon a state Church. But within the states rival denominations came to co-exist more or less peacefully, until by the second half of the eighteenth century the practice of religious persecution was generally regarded as incompatible with the norms of civilized behaviour which governments were expected to observe. It was fully symbolic of this secularizing trend that the Founding Fathers of the United States should write into the Constitution (Art. VI, para. 3) that 'no religious Test shall ever be required as a Qualification to any Office or public Trust under the United States', and that in the First Amendment (1791) Congress should be expressly denied any right to make provision for an 'establishment of religion', or to prohibit 'the free exercise thereof'.

Another feature of this secularizing European order from the middle of the seventeenth century onwards lay in an increasing degree of sophistication in the conduct of international relations. Europe remained overwhelmingly dynastic. (In 1648 there were only two republican regimes in Europe: the United Provinces of the Dutch and the Swiss Confederation. Of these the former gave a king to England in 1688, who as William III occupied the throne jointly with his wife Mary II, and later itself became monarchical.) The patronymic aspect of state sovereignty, in which the state was regarded as in some sense the private *estate* of the monarch, became in some ways more marked with the development of absolutist principles and notions of benevolent despotism in parts of continental Europe. But diplomatic relations between sovereigns, already highly formalized and elaborate, came to be imbued with elements of real political theory, which in turn influenced the conduct of international affairs. In 1713 the Treaty of Utrecht was signed, which marked the virtual close of the wars of the Spanish succession. In this document explicit mention was made of the balance of power as a principle of foreign policy to be acknowledged by the signatory parties. For the greater part of the ensuing century international relations between the states of Europe, including in general the relationship of war, were conducted with a measure of restraint and high politeness which, even allowing for the occasional savagery of the seven years' war and the ideological passions which were loosed during the French revolutionary wars, made the eighteenth century, at least in respect of international politics, one of the most civilized epochs in the dynamic history of Europe, and, many would be inclined to argue, not in this respect alone. At the Congress of Vienna in 1815, which settled the affairs of Europe following the apocalyptic career of Napoleon 1, the opportunity was taken to overhaul diplomatic protocol and usage, and the apparatus of diplomacy, which, with additional arrangements to take account of changing conditions, prevails today, came into operation.

We have been concerned with the European state system as it developed from the breakdown of the old medieval political synthesis of Christendom which embraced the Church, temporal rulers and their subjects. Now we must consider a most remarkable feature of that European state system, namely, its globalization.

Within the world system of states there exist many deep divergencies between one state and another in terms of internal structure, degree of political cohesion and ideological orientation. But all the hundred and forty-five or so sovereign states in the contemporary world conduct relations with each other through similar institutions and by similar methods. Individual states vary from each other enormously, of course, in respect of the number of multilateral contacts they maintain, of the diplomatic level at which relations are conducted, and most importantly – broadly correlating with the spread of their contacts – of the degree to which their relations affect, for better or worse, the rest of the world. The diplomatic machinery, however, within its different levels of importance and consequent status, is uniform throughout the world. Thus even San Marino, that officially 'Serene' if territorially exiguous republic, maintains consular representation 'abroad', i.e.

in Italy and the Vatican. Thus, too, non-European states through-out Asia and Africa conduct their international relations by means of the ambassadors, ministers, councillors, attachés, the embassies, legations and consulates, the *chargés d'affaires*, which are the creation in their present mode of the European state system as it developed through the period of 'modern' European history.

Whatever may be the future role of Europe, whether institu-tionally united in the ultimate or not, the contribution of its characteristic style and structure of diplomatic representation to the conduct of world politics, together with a very widely adopted type of characteristically European internal political structure of the state, remain a distinctive feature of the contemporary world. International society is, in a real sense, the European state system writ large.

If we ask why this should be so we find ourselves faced with an array of assumptions by way of answer. One such sees the clue in an innate racial superiority enjoyed by Europeans, particularly, it appears, Western Europeans. These supermen in the course of the last two centuries or so parcelled the globe between them. They then went on to impose their typical and uniquely successful patterns of politics and institutions upon the lesser peoples, who adapt them to their needs as best they can. Other countries, as Mr Podsnap judiciously remarked,[15] 'do – I am sorry to be obliged to say it – *as* they do'. Although in its grosser forms this racial explanation has been largely discredited since the high tide of racialist myth-making under the Nazis, at a less fully articulated level the assumptions underlying this interpretation of European history persist. There is no need of a point by point refutation here. One fundamental flaw in the case may, however, easily be detected. It lies in the related assumption that whatever is successful in the sense of becoming dominant is somehow qualitatively the best. The fact that the European state system has become worldwide does not at all prove that that system is qualitatively superior to other forms of human organization. Nor that other conceivable types of political structure might not have served the real needs of mankind better. Unless we take a crudely providential view of the matter we shall not merely suppose that the ultimate victory of Catholics over Arians in the politically reinforced theological struggles of the fourth and fifth centuries itself demonstrated that Catholic doctrine

[15] In *Our Mutual Friend* by Charles Dickens.

is true and Arian doctrine false. 'Great is truth, and will prevail' – how do we know? Is it that truth prevails, or that what prevails is regarded as truth? So far as international politics goes many students of this complex subject incline to the belief that unless the existing institutional form of international society, essentially the European system of sovereign states now developed all over the world, is substantially and rapidly modified it may well prove maladaptive, and lead to a deepening international crisis which could prove catastrophic for the human species. In any case, if we repudiate the doctrine of racial superiority to account for the global adoption of the European state system we must seek a possible answer elsewhere.

It may well be that a large element of chance enters into the explanation. The relationship between technological levels and the nature of societies is a very complex one, that cannot be explored here. However, it is worth remembering that tribal communities in parts of West and Central Africa, for instance, passed into their own Iron Age apparently independently of comparable developments elsewhere. While this technological change undoubtedly had great significance so far as the course of their own civilizations were concerned, it evidently did not result in a dynamic expansion of their political influence in other parts of the world, or in striking new technological achievements. Why not? There is no pat answer. But part of it may simply lie in the particular interplay between social norms and political structure in their societies; an interplay that for some reason tended to inhibit that further exploitation of technical advances which has been such a feature of European society. This would suggest that there may be nothing inevitable about European dynamism, or the European 'success' in the domination of the natural environment and, historically, of non-European societies. What occurred, on this view, was a critical conjuncture between the evolution of a society imbued with a strongly expansionist ethos, and the pretensions of a militant Christendom claiming a divinely ordered imperative to Christianize the world. Granted a certain historical opportunity, a sense of mission which the prevailing religion both justified and fostered, and an absence of culturally determined inhibitions, and the European adventure becomes at least partly explicable. The Chinese discovered the composition of gunpowder, but the norms of *their* civilization happened to inhibit its military application.

Imperial yet insular, they disdained to employ such a device either in fighting each other or in the conquest of barbarians. Europeans of the fifteenth century and later were deterred by no such scruples. Again, granted the development of an efficient merchant marine, itself partly the product of geographical requirements in seaboard Europe and partly of growing commercial rivalry between maritime states, a means existed to subject the New World to European penetration and exploitation, one fateful aspect of which was competition between a group of such states in a massive slave trade at the expense of many peoples in Africa. The combination of an expansionist ideology and impulse, having several strands of justification woven into them, with sufficient technical means, was enough to guarantee the large measure of European domination which manifestly took place.

In this connection we should not overlook a certain stultifying effect which slavery appears to have upon technological innovation. The southern states of the American Union, buttressed alike in their economy, their social structure and their prejudices by 'the peculiar institution', lagged behind the north in technological and industrial development in the decades leading up to the civil war. We have already reminded ourselves that the Greeks and Romans had some remarkable scientific achievements to their credit. But among the Greeks, who had not a world to rule, science remained largely speculative. On the other hand the Romans too, committed to the task of governing the Mediterranean world, seem to have been inhibited from following through the possibilities of their own technology much beyond what had already been achieved in the first century AD in the fields of military equipment and of the magnificent Roman architecture. In large measure the correlation of practical tasks with low social status and the heavy dependence on slave labour, both, so to speak, *given* sociological factors, seem to account for this.

The technological instruments by which Europeans in part at least secured both the degree of world domination which must be conceded to them and the worldwide adoption of their characteristic political institutions, were a remarkable product of a clash of cultures. For 'Western' technology owes far more to the intellectual tools provided by Islamic society, as militant in ethos as Christendom and in many ways more brilliant, than is always remembered. If the literature of Western Europe owes an

63

incalculable debt to the Latin alphabet its mathematics was only possible, indeed literally *conceivable*, by means of Arabic numeration, borrowed by Europeans at an epoch when each civilization seemed almost to be committed to the extirpation of the other. (The Arabs themselves had borrowed from the Greeks; a case of circular cultural diffusion.)

Lastly there is the problem of *intention*. Ends motivate means and means modify ends. We have to ask how far Europeans may be said to have willed their worldwide role. A sense of mission can certainly be detected among some individuals at certain periods. The citizens of 'eternal' Rome became very conscious of this civic pretension. The British, having acquired their Empire if not 'in a fit of absent-mindedness' then at least while attending to legitimate oversea interests that were not in themselves deliberately imperialistic, developed an ideology of empire to account for and justify what had come to be the fact. The career of Cecil Rhodes represented just one of the franker manifestations of this ideology in action. It was to be short-lived. In thirty years the bloom was fading, and in little more than one well-rounded lifetime the whole improbable episode was over.[16] So often do men bring about results vastly different from what they planned. So often do consequences not reflect planning at all, but simply the unexpected. Under a great sovereign of the late Renaissance age, Elizabeth I, a group of remarkable men, half naval officers, half pirates, made England great at sea, but it would almost certainly be misreading history to suppose that this was the conscious intention of her adventurers. Hawkins wished to grow rich on the slave trade, Drake to plunder the Spanish Empire, Elizabeth to contain Spanish pretensions and defend her challenged regal and natal legitimacy. Between them all they changed perceptibly the conformation of European power. Most notably they ensured that their offshore island in the North Atlantic would remain a major factor in that international system which Europeans were already beginning to extend beyond the borders of their native continent.

Our necessarily selective and summary survey of international systems in history may perhaps help us to understand something of the constraints on action which circumstances place around men

[16] For an admirable brief analysis of nineteenth-century European imperialism see M. E. Chamberlain, *The New Imperialism*, The Historical Association, London, 1970.

and which they place around each other. Chance men cannot avoid, conditions they cannot easily alter as they wish, outcomes they cannot foresee – all these elements help to shape the activity and course of politics. In international society the limits on freedom of manoeuvre, on prediction and on the control of events are peculiarly pressing. Human beings are certainly wilful: most suppose that they are in a real sense free. But will and action both exist in a context which conditions them. In the field of international politics we may observe with special clarity the sharp truth of Karl Marx's dictum that freedom lies in the recognition of necessity. History itself, after all, remains a vast prison, of which all men are inmates, some more reconciled to their confinement than others. Yet though none of us, living in our various states, can escape history or break its bars, in trying to understand why the past happened as it did, and in making a related effort to put ourselves imaginatively in the place of those we have cause to fear or occasion to hate, and who perhaps fear or hate us, we may earn a limited parole.

It is now time to turn to the contemporary international system, and to take a closer look at some of its significant diversities.

3
All states great and small: some diversities in the contemporary world

According to Red terminology a member country of SEATO/NATO is not independent, a neutral is semi-independent; those who are Red are the only independents. But according to the Blues, a member of the Warsaw Pact is a satellite, a neutral is a public danger, and a free country is a member of SEATO/NATO – *Prince Sihanouk of Cambodia.*

To this category of unthinkably menacing calamities belongs also the gathering food crisis. . . . Social catastrophes are different from the certainty of death for the individual, as they can and should be avoided. And if we do not use foresight and take measures against them, we will perish and there will be no posterity – *Gunnar Myrdal.*

The stake I play for is immense – I will continue in my own dynasty the family system of the Bourbons, and unite Spain for ever to the destinies of France. Remember that the sun never set on the immense empire of Charles V – *Napoleon I.*

It is the vice of a vulgar mind to be thrilled by bigness, to think that a thousand square miles are a thousand times more wonderful than one square mile, and that a million square miles are almost the same as heaven – *E. M. Forster.*

We had better determine at the outset what we mean by the contemporary international system. The suggestion we will make is that it is to be viewed not only in terms of nearness in time: the international system that evidently exists at the present moment. It is also to be understood as a *unique* international system, more than in the obvious sense in which every period and every object is

66

unique. It possesses, on this view, certain features which mark it out from all previous international systems, whatever genuine parallels and useful analogies we may be able to draw between it and them. For this insight we may feel indebted, among other scholars, to the distinguished historian Professor Geoffrey Barraclough. He has argued powerfully[1] that we are now living not merely and by definition in the most recent period of history but also in a 'new age'. By this he appears to mean that the changes in world politics which he sees as set in train somewhere around 1890 (greater exactness of date being impossible in this context), and which have gathered momentum with scarcely a detectable pause throughout the twentieth century, amount cumulatively and qualitatively to a world in some ways fundamentally different from the world which was characteristic of the pre-contemporary period of history – the period we conventionally call 'modern' – dating from the epoch-making developments of the fifteenth and sixteenth centuries in Europe. That period too was in its own time and its own terms a 'new age'.

It may be timely to quote Professor Barraclough here. He observes:

In the long run contemporary history can only justify its claim to be a serious intellectual discipline and more than a desultory and superficial review of the contemporary scene, if it sets out to clarify the basic structural changes which have shaped the modern world. These changes are fundamental because they fix the skeleton or framework within which political action takes place. Examples of them are the changed position of Europe in the world, the emergence of the United States and the Soviet Union as 'superpowers', the breakdown (or transformation) of old imperialisms, British, French, and Dutch, the resurgence of Asia and Africa, the readjustment of relations between the white and coloured peoples, the strategic or thermonuclear revolution. About all these subjects there is room for differences of opinion; everyone is free to make his own assessment of their significance. But we are justified in describing them as 'objective' trends, in the sense that, taken together, they give contemporary history a distinctive quality which marks it off from the preceding period. Furthermore, all require study and analysis in depth; they are parts of a process which can never be fully intelligible if it is taken out of its historical context.[2]

[1] In *An Introduction to Contemporary History*, Watts, London, 1964.
[2] *Ibid.*, chapter 1.

This overall shaping of the contemporary political world reveals three 'diversities', among others, which we will examine in this chapter. The first is the role of *ideology* in partly accounting for, reinforcing and justifying the division of the world into two great power blocs. These have been loosely known as 'East' and 'West'. The power pattern they express was a dominating factor in international politics for twenty years after 1947, and is still of great importance. It has prevailed in a global context that includes a further category, the so-called 'Third World'. The second diversity is that of *wealth* and *power* between the 'have' and 'have-not' nations. (These two words need qualifications to be attached to them, as both of course are relative.) And the third is the diversity in *size* between the 145 or so independent states that exist in the world today. This last diversity is not only remarkable in itself but one that has all kinds of political implications for the existence of the international order and for the future of the sovereign states that comprise it.

The diversity of ideology

Ideology is most briefly defined as a political value-system. It represents a 'bundle' of more or less comprehensible and more or less coherent political doctrines and traditions that together help to give a characteristic style to the behaviour of a state, both towards its own subjects and towards other states. The doctrines concerned may be strident in their public expression or muted. Political leaders may articulate them very fully and consciously, or they may operate largely by implication. But in every political community they are there. In 'pluralistic' political systems rival ideologies, sometimes basically opposed, sometimes no more than delicately tangential to each other, will compete for popular support and electoral success. Internal stability depends in great part upon current ideologies that compete with each other being, if comparably powerful, not irreconcilable, and if incompatible, not equally strong. In 'Western democracies', as distinct in certain important ways from 'People's democracies', the ideological elements in the rival party programmes are subordinated to the generalized ideology which sanctions the actual political system in which the parties operate. In the major parties, 'the parties of government', this happens because the party ideologies are basically compatible with the ideology of the political system; in minor, 'extremist' parties because these are electorally weak. In any case, ideology influences policy, and at the level of international relations has an effect on foreign policy and the style in which it is pursued. The nature and degree of that effect in a given case provides an important problem in the analysis of state behaviour in the international system.

We have noticed in the case of the Peloponnesian war that ideological factors partly occasioned and to a considerable extent sharpened the actual conflict. From about the middle of 1946 the 'cold war' between two rival power systems, consciously upholding rival sets of political values and policy priorities and goals, divided the society of states. This development among other things gave rise to *neutralism*, a mixture of principles and policies by which certain states, mainly in Asia but also in Africa and elsewhere, sought to maintain their independence of either main power bloc. To some leaders in the West, for example John Foster Dulles, President Eisenhower's secretary of state, neutralism was morally reprehensible. 'Who is not for us is against us.' To communist leaders it tended to seem politically unsound, to buttress 'bourgeois' regimes and to expose their countries to neo-imperialist penetration. However, despite these disapproving views, both East and West came soon to compete with one another in seeking by political pressure and economic and often military aid to influence the neutralists favourably, and so extend their own global areas of political initiative. Rather less urgently, the process continues. However, by the early 1970s it seemed that the competition had become somewhat less a matter of each side seeking to subject the other to political and strategic disadvantage than to attempt to reduce world tension by assisting the economic development of materially deprived countries, thereby rendering the prevalent 'have/have-not' syndrome less acute in world politics. Of probably equal importance was the begrudged cost of aid. Particularly in the United States effective voices came to be raised demanding and obtaining a substantial reduction in the allocation of American resources in direct foreign aid, both on the ground that the political returns represented a poor bargain, and, more disinterestedly, on the ground that foreign aid of this kind was often misapplied by short-sighted or vainglorious recipients, and that it could also actually inhibit the more valuable forms of indigenous economic and social progress. In these years too the moral imperative upon rich countries to assist poor countries in acceptable ways seemed to be more widely acknowledged. The problem was and remains complex. Governments wishing to make aid available had to secure the necessary political assent at home, devise methods and types of aid that would not compromise the often prickly self-esteem of the aided, try to ensure that the best long-term results flowed from the aid, in terms of the general well-being of recipient nations, and seek means of minimizing both immediate and long-term disadvantages to home producers. Increasingly international agencies, such as the World Bank, came to seem the most appropriate instruments for channelling such economic aid as the 'privileged' countries were disposed to make available. However, any sign of a deterioration in relations between East and West tended quickly to invoke a readiness to embark on renewed direct aid. This was overwhelmingly of a military kind. It went in general to Third World countries whose vulnerability was, in the context of the continuing overall objectives of either bloc, a matter of strategic importance. So South Vietnam was assisted and supplied for years by the United States, and North Vietnam was sustained by the limited but positive support of both the Soviet Union and communist China.

Neutralism was a response to the division of much of the world into two power blocs, whose mutual relations were characterized by continuous and sometimes acute hostility. This hostility tended to express itself in charges and counter-charges of bad faith and aggressive intentions. But it also clothed itself in the language of philosophical polemic. Godless communism and capitalist imperialism, in unremitting if variable confrontation, gave one another the worst press they could devise. 'We will bury you!' bawled Mr Khrushchev, not meaning under heaps of radio-active rubble but that Soviet Russia would out-gun, out-produce and out-civilize the West by the 1980s. 'Better dead than Red!' responded someone in the West.[3] 'Kill a Commie for Christ', was a piece of *graffiti* found scrawled on a New York wall. So the two superpowers wrapped themselves round in their own exclusive and implacable aura of self-righteousness. Ideology in action on a world stage!

Several questions suggest themselves. Power is sought to defend and promote interests. Those interests may clash. Could a bipolar

[3] I have been unable to trace this proverbial utterance to any reliable source.

system have developed in world politics in which the relations between its components were not prevailingly hostile? Conceivably, but not in this case. For bipolarity had emerged from a world war in which one at least of the principal victors had urgent and vital interests to protect, arising in part from the war itself. It is likely enough that President Roosevelt and his advisers never fully appreciated the depth of Russian fear and suspicion of a West from which had come hammer blows that had destroyed much of European Russia and rocked the regime. True enough too that Winston Churchill and those representatives of the old European order who thought like him viewed the emergence of a looming and triumphant Soviet power in the East with equal anxiety and mistrust. That both sides had *some* grounds for suspecting the *bona fides* of each towards the other seems undeniable, if only because the existence of the suspicions themselves engendered some will to seek practicable preemptive action against any move by either to gain an undue advantage. So we see that the potentiality for hostility was built into the power situation from its emergence upon the scene of a ruined Europe. It seems likely that this will always be so. The fact that international interests, though often complementary, can rarely if ever be completely harmonized, provides in itself such a potentiality. What can be cautiously hoped, until and unless destruction ensues, is that a sufficient degree of rational prudence will imbue statesmen representing their confronting states, so that their respective strategies, unrelentingly pursued, will not manoeuvre them into a position in which either they or their opponents have no alternative to attempting a first strike, more or less in desperation, except mere surrender, and the consequent abandonment of the goals for which the very capacity to strike was developed. At the time of writing an effective prudential balance has been maintained between the two rival systems.

If, however, more power is sought by each side to make more secure its existing power, by offering the check of parity to the growing power of the other side, what in this situation is the role of ideology? How far are rival value-systems a real cause of a power struggle between states or groups of states, and how far a means of rationalizing both the competition and the hostility it generates? Do I fear and hate your beliefs and ideas because they are a real threat to me, reinforced by such power as you have, or do I hate and fear your real power, reinforced perhaps by your beliefs and ideas which I can identify and react to by making them the *rationale* of my fear and hatred?[4]

It is probably misleading to say simply that ideology masks *real* political objectives. No doubt it does perform a rationalizing function. The invasion of Czechoslovakia in 1968 by Warsaw Pact countries was an action taken – we may plausibly suppose – partly and perhaps largely on security grounds, to be justified at the time and even more strikingly later on doctrinal grounds. But ideology is not really separate from political objectives. It is woven into them. It helps define them. It colours them. To some extent it motivates them. It has a part in directing them. It is an energizing component of political action. In times of rapid change, revolutionary turmoil or post-revolutionary effort, ideology is probably most often at its most specific and articulate. It can in these situations release enormous collective enthusiasm for the attainment of goals which the ideology itself may have largely defined and which draw their legitimacy from it. In these circumstances ruling elites are very often able to impose appalling hardships upon their peoples in pursuit of the authorized goals.[5] The 'head of steam' which an active ideology represents is generated partly by the historical circumstances which give it credibility, partly by the assiduous propagation of the political faith it enshrines, which tends to be received by the masses in the simplified form – 'pre-packaged' so to speak – of slogans. When fully operational such a body of political and social doctrine can carry a whole country through the most decisive changes, often accompanied by the most evident sufferings.

At the same time, this is not the whole story. There are constants of policy that remain through all changes. The search for power as a means of gaining security remains a primary preoccupation of rulers from one age and one regime to another. As superpowers the Soviet Union and the United States have global interests which are certainly coloured by ideological considerations, finding expression internationally in the *odium theologicum* between their rival value-systems, but which also exist as it were in their own right, arising as they do out of the given circumstances of superpower

[4] Victor Hugo has a famous saying that there 'is nothing in the world so powerful as an idea whose hour has come'.

[5] Revolutionary France, Bolshevik Russia, Maoist China and some of the newly independent African states have all been examples.

status. If being a superpower gives a large measure of freedom to act in the world, it equally and correspondingly imposes many restraints, involves heavy obligations and gives rise to burdensome responsibilities. All these too will be very likely to reflect ideological factors. But they clearly exist in themselves. They create the need to formulate policies which may and often do pay scant regard to doctrinal niceties. The compulsion of facts can be very compelling indeed. Granted, for instance, on the part of the Russians, a super-power motive to become influential in the Middle East, massive military and diplomatic support has been forthcoming for Egypt, a Muslim country with no native tenderness towards communist materialism, and which for most of the period of Russian alignment has denied the Egyptian Communist Party any legal status. But in this case an ideological factor obtained. Egypt was at least 'anti-imperialist', that is to say opposed to whatever Egyptians chose to regard as imperialism on the part of the Western powers. Again, the United States has had a close and generally cordial relationship with Falangist Spain for many years. This political friendship was firmly structured into the over-arching American defence system for the free world. Yet General Franco's political doctrines and style had no ideological congruence with the traditions of American pluralistic democracy. Although here too was a common ideological factor. Both countries were strongly anti-communist. World politics, like adversity, can make strange bed-fellows. Yet the strangeness will never, it seems safe to say, be absolute. The coming into existence of shared interests which may bring incongruous international partners together will usually be found to have at least a slight ideological motivation, and to develop, sooner or later, a measure of mutually agreeable doctrinal justification.

When all is said, however, we will still often find power politics being indulged in on behalf of given interests with little overt regard to ideological considerations. As we suggested earlier, some countries are much more openly ideological in their attitude towards the rest of the world and towards their own role in it than others. But all countries have to take account of the facts of inter-national power. The constraints these facts of power impose may bring ideology more to the forefront of policy, but at least as often they are likely to oblige policy-makers to modify their observance of received political doctrines, and even to adapt the doctrines them-

73

selves, in the light of political necessities arising from the conformation of power.

It can hardly be overemphasized that all states have certain basic
and more or less constant interests which may be supported by –
and even to some extent shaped by – the prevailing value-system
but in the pursuit of which ideology may sometimes get in the way.
In the first flush of the successful Bolshevik revolution it seemed to
many influential Russians that the old international order was
damaged beyond repair, and that a world revolution was becoming
historically ripe. Leon Trotsky, warm, volatile, acutely intelligent,
on appointment as first commissar for foreign affairs, declared with
humourous enthusiasm that he would issue a few announcements
and then 'shut up shop'. But the discredited capitalist international order did not collapse after 1919. Patchily, with great
difficulty, profoundly changed as in some ways it was, the old
system survived and recovered. Stalin, wise in his generation,
recognized that world revolution would be postponed indefinitely,
and turned to the consolidation of the revolutionary Soviet state at
home, after his own manner. Within a few years of diplomatic
isolation communist Russia, enfeebled but still essentially a great
power, and committed to her Herculean task of modernization,
quietly rejoined the international system, developing in the process
a set of diplomatic manners that showed a rigid regard for the
punctilios of protocol. Admittedly, Soviet leaders retained an
anxious interest in world communism, analysing its opportunities
and encouraging its adherents or restraining them as and where it
was deemed theoretically correct to do so. But what mattered most
was that an internationalist ideology, which in principle rejected
the whole concept and practice of the traditional international order
of competing sovereign states, was subordinated to the requirements of policy arising from the fact that this order still existed,
could not soon or easily be overthrown, and that the socialist
fatherland had national interests in these circumstances which
could only be served by entering and operating within the prevailing system. More and more, from the end of the 1920s onwards,
Stalin was to sound the note of traditional Russian nationalism,
until in the collective gallantry and misery of the 'Great Patriotic
War' against Nazi Germany the Soviet regime was to be hailed not
primarily as a springboard for world revolution at all but as the
means by which Mother Russia would fulfil her national destiny

among the other nations of the world. And from the way they were carried out it seems evident that direct Soviet expansion in Eastern Europe after 1945, and the setting up of congenial regimes along her Western borders, were processes less concerned with 'exporting revolution' than with seeking to guarantee security.

This vital Russian interest has in fact been served with impressive effectiveness by a combination of continuing political control and growing military capacity. We look at power balances more closely in chapter 5, but may notice here that the cold war between East and West, when both mutually hostile ideologies and rival power interests combined to pose a grave threat of imminent conflict, has by the very reality of the power of each side to inflict intolerable – and perhaps total – damage on the other led to a stability which in turn has made possible the cautious and intermittent search for a *détente*. So far has this search gone that as between the two great defensive alliance systems, and their respective principal members the United States and the Soviet Union, we may speak meaningfully in the early 1970s of the cold war as being at an end. Circumstances could renew it. But from the middle 1960s 'peaceful co-existence', while still dependent upon effective mutual military deterrence, came almost to be taken for granted.[6] This implied a lessening in the relevance of purely ideological considerations in the relationship between the two blocs. As the process developed, the monolithic connotations of the word 'bloc' seemed less appropriate. There was a good deal of loosening of the political cement binding together the members of each bloc. Gaullist France relinquished her military obligations within NATO, and in the Warsaw Pact Poland, Hungary and Rumania in particular discreetly eased themselves into positions in which they could pursue a somewhat more authentic autonomy both in internal policy-making and external relations. These changes did not appear to be significantly compromised by the outcome of the political initiatives taken by the Czechoslovak leadership in 1967 and 1968, although in principle the Brezhnev Doctrine of limited sovereignty which was part of that outcome had very important implications for the future.

[6] Sir Winston Churchill's well-known parliamentary phrase, 'security the sturdy child of terror', while having little application to the unilateral nuclear capacity of the United Kingdom remains highly suggestive of the strategic balance between East and West as a whole.

Another notable example of the interplay between ideology and power politics may be seen in the case of the celebrated 'Sino-Soviet dispute'. Since the middle 1950s the relationship between the Soviet Union and the People's Republic of China has brought into being a whole literature of political disputation between theoreticians and polemicists of both sides, in much of which apparently the bitterness of disagreement has only been matched by the obscurity of doctrine, and a whole library of analysis and commentary by outside observers.

It is evident that from the first decade of Soviet history Russian attitudes towards Chinese communism have been ambivalent. Stalin actively discouraged certain revolutionary initiatives by Mao Tse-tung at this period, apparently on the ground that China had not attained in her political and economic development the 'age of readiness' for a revolution that would establish the dictatorship of the proletariat. Certainly a significant difference between the Russian revolution and the Chinese communist revolution when it occurred lay in the emphasis of the former upon the industrial and urbanized proletariat as the spearhead of revolutionary power, which, fully militarized, was turned against a reluctant and in many places recalcitrant peasantry, and the readiness of Chinese communist leaders to base their strategy from the beginning upon a whole-hearted coalition of workers, peasants, students and intellectuals generally. This agrarian emphasis may have been doctrinally suspect, but it worked. The Soviet Union showed itself curiously slow, however, in offering the newly fledged People's Republic that comradely help that might have been expected. Ideological solidarity was loudly affirmed, supported by some actual trade and cultural exchanges. But essentially the Chinese found themselves obliged to carry through their own industrialization and modernization, processes made peculiarly difficult and hazardous because of internal conditions. In particular, the Russians never gave their Chinese comrades the slightest assistance in attaining that nuclear capacity which has been from the beginning of the postwar era, because of its military implications, so important a symbol of great power status. Then, as noted above, in the mid-1950s the breach between the two major communist states became public and strident.

Why should this have happened? It is difficult to resist the conclusion that behind the clash of doctrinal orthodoxy and heresy, and the vexed question of which is which, there lay – and lies – a conventional power-political rivalry between two great states, each conceiving itself to have a global role to play in international society, each competing for influence and prestige both within world communism and in the world at large, and, on the Chinese side at least, nursing historical grievances. If we are right to assume the central importance of this rivalry of power, we see that the ideological split symbolizes and sharpens it, being an aspect of the competition but not its cause. That both multi-national Russia and relatively homogeneous China should have become communist powers is doubtless one of the most momentous developments in world history. But what may well prove more momentous still is the fact that they are two great states – one a superpower and the other likely to be so within a decade or two – who have power-political interests that clash, and whose shared ideology has been pressed into the service of each set of claims upon the attention of international society. That they should in fact become rivals seems to be an inescapable consequence of their power-political importance. It could not be to the interest of the Soviet Union that a successful challenge should arise to her leadership of the communist world, any more than that her superpower role should be compromised by the emergence of another superpower along her south-eastern frontier.

Thus we see that as between the United States and the Soviet Union a major part played by their respective and mutually hostile ideologies was to justify as well as strengthen their rivalry in the field of power politics. As between the Soviet Union and China a large part played by a shared ideology was to provide an additional arena in which their power-political rivalry could be conducted.

We shall look again at the role of power in international society in chapter 5. Let us close this part of the discussion by suggesting that what is chiefly important in the relations of great powers to each other is not their ideological agreement or alienation but their propensity to compete. This propensity arises from the nature of power politics itself. Ideology has significant political effects but is essentially secondary. Thus we may venture to adapt a famous aphorism[7] and remark that there is more in common between two

---

[7] In the days of the Third Republic Henri de Jouvenel sagely observed that 'there is more in common between two deputies, one of whom is a communist, than between two communists, one of whom is a deputy'.

great powers one of which is a communist state, than between two communist states one of which is a great power.

We referred above yet again to interests as a fundamental concern of states. We may now notice that ideology itself functions as one of the national interests which statesmen must seek to protect. As we saw earlier, ideology plays an important part in both motivating and justifying political action. It therefore represents one of the political resources used by rulers and their agents to promote the well-being of the political system they are charged to uphold and obliged to operate. In the course of political activity this resource is expended and needs to be renewed. This renewal is accomplished by means of political *education* (in the case of political systems we approve of) or of *indoctrination* (in political systems we dislike). Hence all governments, whatever their type and style, make use of official propaganda, whether blatant or subtle, to keep, so to speak, the prevailing ideology green. The value-system of a country is the primary legitimizer of its institutions. It is in turn refreshed and helped to remain potent by the purposeful and entirely proper parade of the symbols of legitimacy – heads of state, national flags, formal openings of Parliament, and the like.

In international relations too ideology is both expended and recouped. Through the international communications media countries denounce their enemies and solicit their friends. Thus an American president will, over the television networks, invite 'free men everywhere' to support the United States in its stand against 'communist aggression' in Vietnam. The Bolshevik leaders stirringly reissued the invitation of Karl Marx and his colleagues to the workers of the world to unite, on the alluring ground that they had nothing to lose but their chains and a world to win.

Ideology, in short, is a national interest rather in the way that international prestige is a national interest. Both are intangible things. Both operate below the level of pure rationality. Yet, perhaps for this reason, both are of considerable collective psychological importance. It matters very much to a state what its international standing is in the world, and, broadly speaking, both a state's sensitivity on this point and its international standing itself are proportionate to its position in the general ranking of the powers. Obviously the principality of Liechtenstein will not make –

and will be seen not to make – such a fuss about its international standing as will the French Republic. Status, we may note in passing, is partly a matter of what is generally conceded, partly a matter of (often prickly) self-attribution. A sort of international common sense prevails here. No one denies that Russia is a very important country, or that India is an important country, or that Indonesia is quite an important country. But self-attribution has its political effects too. In the second world war, after the defeat of France at the hands of Hitler's Germany, Anthony Eden, the British foreign secretary, had occasion to ask General de Gaulle, leader of the Free French based in London, why he made so many difficulties about being consulted over everything, and was so awkward about agreeing to certain policy decisions. The general replied, with ineffable *hauteur*, 'because France is a great power'. The world, including Anthony Eden, might have been forgiven for not supposing so, in the circumstances. But to De Gaulle the issue was vital. Posing, and genuinely seeing himself, as the representative – even the embodiment – of the *true* France, he believed that her destiny was bound up with the recognition of her major status.

Like prestige, a country's ruling ideology is an aspect of its international personality. As such it is an interest, to be defended and upheld by all appropriate means. In turn, as we have seen, it helps to define and to promote other national interests.

Lastly, we must notice the link between national ideology and *diplomatic style*.

More will be said of style. Here we notice that style and ideology reflect one another in the behaviour of a state. It will be simplest to take as an illustration an issue that is largely domestic but partly international in its implications, and still, at the time of writing, unhappily topical: the issue of Northern Ireland.

Without entering into the merits of the Ulster situation as it developed from the late 1960s, or the respective claims and interests of the inter-related parties to this passionate and violent dispute – the United Kingdom, the Irish Republic, the Protestant majority community, the Roman Catholic minority community, the Unionists, the Republicans in the North – we may usefully note how constraints upon the behaviour of the United Kingdom government represent an expression of its contemporary political style, and how this is conditioned by the liberal parliamentarist

79

value-system for which the modern United Kingdom professedly stands. The British government has, and asserts, its primary responsibility for the maintenance of law and order within its territory. It takes, and is seen to take, such steps as it can to uphold these. There lies the clue: *such steps as it can*. Theoretically, that government could have 'solved' the Ulster crisis in a matter of weeks. It disposed of the organized force to do so. It *could* have bombed the Creggan and Bogside areas of Londonderry flat, forcibly evacuated the entire Catholic population of West Belfast, and carried through (doubtless with considerable bloodshed) the ruthless deportation to the Republic of the entire Ulster Catholic minority. There was never the slightest prospect of any such action. By its known subscription to certain norms of conduct, by the public expectations held about that conduct on the part of both friendly and hostile states all over the world, and by its own assurances concerning policy made implicitly in response to those expectations, the British government was committed from the first, and was known to be committed, to the search for settlement, which would be acceptable to all parties. That at the time of writing no such settlement is in sight does not lessen the obligation to seek for it, an obligation *which is deemed to lie upon the British government even by those whose own practice in similar circumstances would be, and would be expected to be, very different*. Thus both 'wings' of the IRA, between 1969 and the early 1970s, perpetrated many acts which, if done by British soldiers in Ulster, would have aroused the bitterest denunciations and execrations – by, among others, the IRA. It is, again, difficult to conceive that the Soviet government, faced with a comparable challenge to its institutional arrangements and political authority anywhere in the territory of the Union, would have regarded its duty to the Soviet state purely in terms of a military policing function, using minimum force, and combined with a patient attempt at political conciliation and the search for an acceptable constitutional adjustment. *Nor would the rest of the world expect this to be the case*. The difference in international expectations derives from the differences in the political style of the countries concerned. To Soviet leaders the territorial and political integrity of the Soviet state, under the sole legitimate authority of the Communist Party of the Soviet Union, represents a very high value indeed. There is plenty of past evidence, in the Ukraine for instance immediately at the close of the second world war, and elsewhere,[8] to suggest that, faced with a challenge to the internal *status quo* which that party and its doctrines guarantee as alone permissible, the Soviet leadership would proceed to the *strongest measures* to uphold it. In short, the IRA could be thankful that it was not employing its terror tactics against men like its own members, or against the Russians. This is not, let us emphasize, a matter of Russians being 'nastier' or even simply more ruthless than Englishmen. It is essentially a matter of the degree to which, within the framework of the existing ideology, dissent is regarded as tolerable in a particular political community.

Thus we see from this example, chosen for its obviousness, how ideological assumptions, sometimes rarely articulated, and often lacking any loud or self-conscious proclamations of intent, do profoundly affect policy. They do so both in its formulation and its implementation. National style is a function of political traditions. These both mould and are moulded by the values of the society in which they are found. For better or worse, helping to ensure its national successes or contributing to its failures, ideology is inseparable from the collective political experience of any state.

We have touched on the influence of ideology upon national

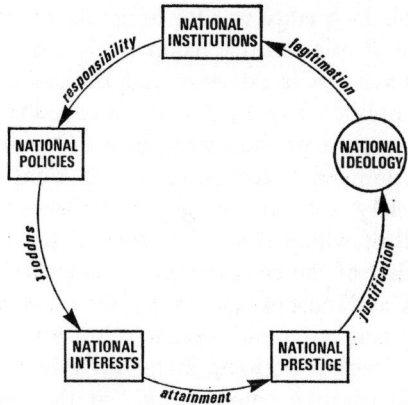

Fig. 5. The role of ideology in a national political system, in relation to foreign affairs

[8] The present Soviet Constitution guarantees the right of secession to each constituent republic of the Union. But one hesitates to contemplate the fate of any federal members actually attempting to exercise it.

81

style, and the way in which both affect policy in its conception and execution. For purposes of analysis it does become necessary to divide our notions and our data into categories. We do well to remember, however, that all these elements are interwoven, in the day to day and age to age living experience of a political community. Ultimately, power and doctrine, like the events and tendencies of history itself, form a seamless cloak. Fig. 5 shows how ideology justifies national institutions, how these generate policies in support of interests, how attained objectives enhance national prestige and how heightened prestige serves to justify the national ideology. Similarly, policy failures and hence reduced prestige are likely to bring a prevailing ideology into question.

Rich and poor countries

The second great diversity between the world's states which we are to notice is that of wealth, and of the variations of power – the capacity to have one's will in the world – which that diversity provides, as well as the very important unplanned, indeed unwished for, effects upon the poor and weak which the highly unequal distribution of economic provision among the members of international society brings about.

The fact of this inequality was for long taken for granted. Only from the middle of this century has it really loomed large in the minds of statesmen, their advisers and the politically attentive sections of their publics. For them it has come to loom as one of the most grave and urgent predicaments in world politics. The new concern has accompanied, and is associated with, the growth of international society, and the emergence of a large number of new states, nearly all of whom share a history of imperial subjection under one or other of the economically (and politically) advanced Western powers, and most of whom share too a condition of relative impoverishment and economic underdevelopment. Moreover, the 'have/have-not' division between states broadly coincides with a geographical distribution, north and south respectively. As between the northern and southern hemispheres there is a 'bipolarity of contrast' which poses its own grave problems for political leaders in both.

The pattern of power which is created by the division of the world into rich and poor countries is not simple in itself. Neither are the political and economic processes to which it gives rise, nor the effects which flow from them. Here we cannot do more than indicate in general terms some of the considerations that are to be borne in mind when we try to think about the overall problem of economic wealth throughout the world and its distribution. Politics, as we saw at the very beginning, is basically about who gets what, and how, and from whom, and by means of whom. International economic relations therefore represent a vital and pervasive aspect of international politics.

One basic problem is that poor countries tend to find their chief economic effort going into the production of 'primary' goods, that is certain kinds of foodstuffs and a wide range of raw materials. Correspondingly, primary producers among countries tend to be poor. One reason for this is that the economic infrastructure necessary to produce many primary goods tends to be relatively simple, and not to give rise to those secondary effects – such as diversification of labour – which in turn produce more wealth and more kinds of wealth. In this respect manufacturing countries with a developed industrial structure enjoy a great advantage *vis-à-vis* primary producers. Again, terms of trade tend to move easily against such producers. They may find themselves obliged to produce more and more at lower prices to buy the secondary products their populations increasingly demand. Moreover, in economically sophisticated societies, endowed with great purchasing power, the role of consumer choice, taste and fashion can play a large part in determining the share of the world market enjoyed at any one time by the suppliers of particular primary products. Technological innovation, too, can effect a wide measure of substitution by way of synthetic products for the traditional raw materials, thus restricting the scope of the primary producers' trade.

These and other factors have helped to motivate the urgent attempts of many poor countries in Asia, Africa and South America to industrialize; to achieve diversified, complex national economies to attain a higher level of economic self-sufficiency. (A low level of economic self-sufficiency, of the kind we call a 'subsistence economy', is no longer enough, although circumstances still impose it in places.) But this effort to modernize creates its own problems. It is difficult for poor countries to compete with the rich directly, in the same markets. Though production costs may be lower, this is likely to be true of quality as well. Deliberate disadvantage may also be imposed by advanced industrial countries in the form of protectionist measures designed to 'choke off' any new threat to their own industries.

Another problem concerns the question of political control. Few developing countries can achieve advanced economies without massive help from outside, whether in the form of direct aid or by investment on unsentimental commercial principles by foreign firms or sometimes governments. Sovereignty, not as a symbol but as a real capacity to direct one's own course, may be seriously compromised in the case of a poor country most of whose economic enterprise is under the ownership and the direction of foreign nationals. So far has this process gone in some countries that it has given rise to a concept of international relationship of which a good deal was heard in the 1960s – that of 'neo-colonialism'. The notion here is that the control of the economic life of State A by the nationals and even government agencies of State B may be so complete as to constitute, instead of an economic relationship between two sovereign powers, a relationship of dependence as between ruler and subject. The sense of this dependence, whether wholly justified or not, whether avoidable or not, has created deep resentments where it has been felt, and accounts for many of the nationalizations, appropriations and confiscations of industrial and commercial resources held by foreign interests which have occurred in various parts of the developing world during the last twenty years or so. Given the economic facts of international life, it is hard not to feel that there is a large degree of inevitability in both the offence and the reaction to it.

A further problem that has been widely studied concerns the possible internal effects of modernization. The process not only calls for sustained effort by political elites and economic managers in the countries concerned. It is also likely to have profound and at times devastating effects upon the traditional social structure of whole areas within developing countries, and hence upon the norms of behaviour associated with them. This has indeed happened on a wide scale almost throughout the present century. Where economic activity, for instance, tends to be essentially geared to the expression of social status, or to meeting purely current needs, the concept of an economic surplus for trade or investment being irrelevant to the requirements of the group, the breakdown of such traditional patterns of production within an extended family or tribal society may result in serious collective psychological shock. Some such societies, it appears, seem to have adjusted with remarkable speed and completeness. It is perhaps more true to say that their members have abandoned them. Social anthropologists have given devoted and scholarly consideration to the impact of rapid economic and technological change on such societies,[9] and their accounts leave us with a strong impression of much that is lost, whatever may be gained, in terms of cultural vitality and even actual mental health, by these pressures of innovation.

Another effect associated with modernization, and the growing transformation of society in the poorer countries, is what has been called 'the revolution of rising expectations'. Whatever disillusionment may have set in during recent years among some sections of predominantly young people in the Western world about the general desirability and moral excellence of a consumer-oriented society, peoples in poor countries do appear to feel deprived. Where, as has become commonly the case, such deprivation does not exclude them from access to cheap forms of mass communication, they have become aware of the relatively very high levels of amenity and consumption enjoyed in the economically developed countries on a large scale. The poor two-thirds of the world now know how the rich one-third live, and their response to the knowledge combines elements of admiration, envy and resentment, compounded by a sense, often expressed, that to some extent the privileged minority enjoy their luxuries *at the expense* of the world's poor. To what extent this sense corresponds with economic facts does not matter. In so far as it is felt to be true it carries far-reaching political consequences.

An important psychological factor at work in the process of bringing into independence nearly a hundred ex-colonial new states between 1946 and 1970 was the conscious assertion of a renewed human *dignity* on the part of the newly independent peoples. Black men, brown men and yellow men were to 'walk tall' amidst their newly sovereign nations, to walk as tall as their 'pinko-grey' fellows, East and West. (It is significant in this connection that Pandit Nehru in 1962 could remark that seen from east of Suez,

[9] Two typically valuable studies are: Margaret Mead, *New Lives for Old*, Mentor Books, New York, 1956, and *Cultural Patterns and Technical Change*, UNESCO, New York, 1955, edited by the same author.

85

the Soviet Union appeared as a 'Western' power.) The emotional satisfactions of the symbols of sovereignty cannot easily be exaggerated. But, in the shorter let alone the longer run, they cannot avail alone. Inescapably, the economic aspect of human dignity comes to demand the right to give richer meaning to the political dignity of acknowledged nationhood. For if sovereignty is ultimately to be more than a hollow status, it must become an instrumentality; a function by which political communities may direct their course. Such a function requires, indeed it presupposes, a sufficient economic capacity under the hand of rulers. Yet, paradoxically, the creation of such a sufficient capacity is made more difficult, as it is certainly made more piecemeal, by the very persistence in world politics of multiple and competing sovereignties.

Rising expectations have their vital effects within developing countries as well. In many – probably in most – poor countries there is an economic elite, largely if not entirely correlated with the political elite, which enjoys relatively enormous wealth, and consequent economic power. The moral and political tolerability of such numerically small groups continuing to recline among their conspicuous privileges is increasingly held up to hostile question in many of the countries concerned. Clandestine groups committed to violent revolution and the transformation of their societies, in the name of necessary modernization as well as 'justice', are active in several parts of the world, and threaten the stability and legitimacy of the existing order. We are bound to ask where they succeed in gaining power, as Fidel Castro did in Cuba, whether their success has really made less difficult and hazardous the kind of economic development which is felt to be urgent, and the benefits of which are intended to flow with ameliorative effects through the whole society. Successful revolutions may assuage a no longer bearable sense of collective grievance. But in the conditions that prevail in many parts of the developing world their effect in promoting sound economic development, the right kind of industrialization, the confidence of trading and investing interests abroad and long-term political stability at home, must seem problematical.

We must not forget either a very important consequence of the successful modernization of industrial enterprise and the attainment of a buoyant and innovating economy where these are achieved. This consequence is the progressive impoverishment and pollution of the planetary environment, as exploitative techniques become increasingly available in every part of the world. So rapid, and, many observers insist, so reckless has been this exploitation, and so far-reaching its effects, that it has been seriously questioned how much longer the 'life support systems' of 'Spaceship Earth', as Miss Barbara Ward has chosen to name our planet,[10] will function effectively. No prognostications will be made here. But some of the 'doom-writers', a salutary if uncomfortable group, and not necessarily the less well-informed among them, are expressing doubts whether human society, given the present rate of resource exhaustion and pollution creation, and their likely proportional increase if present policies remain substantially unchanged, can survive beyond the close of this century.

However that may be, it seems clear that a consequence of rapid economic development of the kind that has characterized advanced societies during the last hundred years could be a crisis of environmental viability, on a scale that would jeopardize the well-being, and perhaps the existence, of rich and poor nations alike.

Yet another worrying consideration is that the actual gap between rich and poor countries tends to widen. Partly this is a relative thing. Some poor nations do succeed with difficulty in improving their standard of living, but do so at a lower rate than do rich nations. In other cases the widening gap is of an absolute kind: the rich grow absolutely richer and the poor absolutely poorer. The problem yields neither to mere generalized goodwill, laced with pity, nor to exhortations arising out of the moral uneasiness of members of rich, developed societies who are endowed with a nagging conscience. Partly it is a question of given circumstances. Some countries have a greater growth potential than others, for reasons of geography, natural resources, even strategic importance to great powers. Partly it is a matter of the structure of international society itself. On the whole this tends to illustrate the scriptural maxim that to him that hath shall be given, to him that hath not shall be taken away even that which he hath. This, it must be said, does not seem particularly to be anyone's fault. Partly too it is a matter of the implicit choice of human beings to possess as much as they can, to subscribe to the values of a consumer society, to want – or to allow themselves to be persuaded that they

[10] Miss Ward published a book in 1966 bearing this title.

want – more and more things. Rich and poor alike in international society tend to equate possessions with happiness; the standard of living with the quality of life. Commercial pressures tend to reinforce this attitude. And not only does the conventional wisdom throughout the West at least, and in much of the Third World, assume its continuing timeliness and reasonableness, but economic growth, as an ideal and a technique, depends upon this assumption remaining a dominating one in the minds of peoples all over the world, whatever their current levels of investment and consumption.

At the same time it is fair to remember that this evidently world-wide preoccupation with the prospects of increasing material well-being has given rise in the West to strong pressures to attempt a substantial redistribution of wealth to the benefit of poor nations, and what in the long run matters more, a more equitable distribution of the means of *creating* wealth. This pressure derives partly from prudential considerations: world stability is assumed to be very much of a general interest and to be promoted by spreading prosperity. But moral imperatives are also very powerful in motivating much of the effort being expended on schemes of economic betterment in the developing countries. The various aid and relief agencies, the 'Third World First' movement, even the Voluntary Service Overseas scheme, all tend to profess a moral inspiration, and seek to encourage a sense of personal responsibility in all persons of good will in the rich third of the world towards the promotion of prosperity in the poor two-thirds. However, it is also necessary to notice that these schemes, however spiritually and emotionally valuable they may in fact be for those participating in them, have not as yet had any very marked effect in ameliorating the lot of the many hundreds of millions of human beings whose lives are passed in conditions of material deprivation, restricted opportunity and physical squalor which defy adequate description. This is not, we may remind ourselves, merely a matter of insufficient will for betterment. The actual structure of international relationships does not lend itself easily to the kind of rapid and radical reallocation of economic resources, on a global basis, which idealists sometimes impatiently demand. And although structural changes do take place over time, we shall examine in chapter 8 some reasons for doubting whether the kind of radical transformation of the structure that may be desirable in regard to making the world's poor richer could be carried out swiftly, easily or soon. Even within a single national territory the British experience, paralleled elsewhere, shows how difficult it is to keep the economic development of different areas in phase. On a global scale the problems that obtrude themselves nationally in this connection are multiplied and enlarged almost beyond calculation. 'One world' may beckon alluringly. But it is still, we may feel, a long way off.

One more consequence of the economic disparity between the states of the modern world may be noticed. It can have very wide-ranging effects. It concerns the economic implications of being a great power. A great power with worldwide commercial relationships and a national economy that touches the economies of others at many points cannot help but exercise a pervasive influence on very many other countries, particularly where their trading interests are closely bound up with those of the power concerned, or which are deeply penetrated by capital investment emanating from sources in the great power. Being economically very powerful means that those in relation to whom you are powerful are made hostages to your fortune. The Wall Street 'crash' of October 1929 set in train an economic depression in the United States that had grave repercussions all over the world. Most strikingly was this so in Europe. There the protracted political crisis of the Weimar Republic was sharpened by the general European depression, with ultimate consequences of worldwide significance. The United States had no interest in 'exporting depression'. The Americans simply could not prevent this happening, given the economic collapse at home. By the same token a number of economists have argued that the forms of American government investment in military and space 'hardware' during the middle 1960s stimulated a measure of inflation in the United States which helped trigger off inflation throughout the Western world. This effect, as it has been felt in Britain, worried cabinet ministers and old age pensioners alike.

In these instances three factors operate in complex relationship with each other. First, there is the large degree, already observed, of economic interdependence throughout the greater part of the world. Second, this interdependence functions through a system of multiple sovereignties, each with responsibility for the most important economic as well as political decisions. Third, the great

89

power base from which some decision-makers unavoidably operate places in their hands relatively enormous and inescapable influence, for good or ill, over the general well-being of others. Once more we may see how power is both defined and measured by the context in which it is exercised.

The big and the little

We come now to the third of the major diversities we have to discuss in this chapter. To the casual observer it is perhaps the most obvious type of distinction to be seen among states. Its effects, however, are complicated. Though it has significant links with the division of the world into richer and poorer states it by no means correlates entirely with that division. The society of states, we notice, is characterized by quite extraordinary differences in *size* between its members. Although the most powerful states in the world are among the largest, the two states with the greatest population totals, China and India, are by no means the strongest or richest. On the other hand, there are relatively small countries, such as Sweden and Switzerland, which give their citizens a high level of material prosperity, and which on various grounds count for a good deal in international politics as a whole. It is worth noting that, though territorially not one of the most considerable countries in the world, the United Kingdom, despite her 'demotion' from world-power rank, with all that that has meant for her citizens in terms of political and psychological adjustment, is still one of the twelve most populous nations in the world, and, on the basis of her Gross National Product, one of the seven richest. Federal Germany, one of the two successor states to the Third Reich which was totally overthrown in 1945, comes into the same category. Whatever opportunities or responsibilities in regard to either Britain or the Federal German Republic may be supposed to flow from these facts, they do suggest that ex-great powers are not easily divested of the benefits or the burdens of major status among the world's nations.

We have observed more than once in the course of this book that constraints of various kinds are laid upon all states, and mitigate, sometimes in very important ways, their freedom to act as they will. The existence of real constraints on the freedom of action of even the very greatest states is a significant feature of international politics, and sheds light upon the way in which the international system actually works. Whatever may be thought of his controversial political career, Sir Oswald Mosley often showed himself to be a perceptive commentator on world affairs. Writing shortly after the end of the second world war, he analysed the constraints that lay upon both the United States and the Soviet Union, in their mutual relations and in their capacity to do as they pleased in the rest of the world; the second set of constraints being inter-related with the first. So palpable did these limitations seem to be to Sir Oswald that he actually described the two powers as 'paralysed giants'. This was doubtless overemphatic. But the phrase contains enough truth to be worth recalling. It reminds us that the freedom of states, like that of individual men, is a relative thing, conditioned by factors of circumstance which states can and do modify by their actions, but which they cannot wholly control or escape from.

A popular game among students of American politics is known as 'ranking the presidents'. In this absorbing pastime various factors of personality, style, opportunity, luck, flair as between foreign and domestic policy-making, all come into the calculation. Similarly in the game of 'ranking the powers'. As with the presidents, there are many variables to take into account. These variables tend to alter in their effect over time. Their influence upon each other, and, severally and collectively, upon the standing of the state concerned within international society, may well tax judgement. Yet we all, consciously or not, play this particular game. We all have a sense of which are the most important or powerful or prestigious countries in the world. However, rough and ready rankings often fail to take account of considerations that may really affect a country's status to a significant degree. Let us take just one factor – population.

The national population is generally and quite rightly regarded as a resource; one of the most important resources which the state can utilize. Thus the state's citizens themselves represent, in their collectivity, one of the chief means by which their state can attempt to meet their needs and fulfil their desires. A nation's population is often described as one of the 'sinews' of foreign policy. Many times in recent history governments have gone to considerable lengths, by exhortations, rewards for large families, penalties, generally by way of extra taxation, for continued bachelorhood, etc. to encourage population growth in their countries. Yet we see that a large national population is by no means simply correlated with a high level of national prosperity, or with a proportionate degree of world power. While it is true to say that the greatest powers have relatively large populations, some powers, such as for example the Scandinavian countries, South Africa and the 'white' dominions of the Commonwealth, can play significant roles in the world, and provide relatively high living standards for most of their citizens, on the basis of comparatively small national populations. Conversely, a very large population can be a major constraint upon national power, and act, so to speak, as a net consumer rather than producer of prosperity. In such a case the government concerned may feel obliged to resort to urgent measures designed to discourage and restrict population growth. This, where it has been applied, remains notoriously one of the most delicate, sensitive and controversial areas of government policy. The most striking example of population size representing a major constraint upon the development of welfare, national power and international status in recent years has perhaps been India. But she is certainly not alone in her predicament. Increasingly, economically straitened political communities with relatively huge populations are seeking by means it is hoped will prove tolerable to the susceptibilities of their members to restrain mere growth in numbers. This effort is accompanied by an endeavour to improve the capacity of the existing population to provide for its own well-being. It is thus not the size of the national population which is chiefly relevant to the prosperity and prestige of a state, but the 'quality' of that population, in terms of the wide dissemination of acquired skills of all kinds, which makes possible both an enlargement of productive capacity and the development of a high level of indigenous civilization. So when we speak of population as a 'determinant' of national policy and the nation's standing in the world we realize that this is true both in a favourable and an unfavourable sense.

We see, then, that any ranking of the powers which will sustain critical analysis has to accommodate various factors which in any given case support each other, or pull against each other, and which are liable to change in their relative importance with the passing of time. We will now draw up a list of possible categories in which states may be placed, and suggest two states in each category as representative of the class. We will leave to the reader, if he pleases, to judge the soundness or otherwise of our choice by reference to the appendix at the end of the book.

Here is the classification:

  (i) Superpowers
  (ii) Great Powers
  (iii) Major Powers
  (iv) Medium Powers
  (v) Minor Powers
  (vi) Small Powers
  (vii) Nominal Powers

In the first of these seven categories we place the only present representatives: the United States and the Soviet Union. Among the great powers we place Federal Germany and Japan; among major powers France and Brazil; among medium powers Canada and India; among minor powers Ghana and Burma; among small powers Dahomey and Haiti; among nominal powers the Vatican City and Nauru. This sample choice implies that ranking is not determined by any one factor but by the way various factors are combined.

Where, to take one further example, would the People's Republic of China come in such a classification? With a Gross National Product of only upwards of forty billion dollars she is among the medium powers. But as a permanent member of the United Nations Security Council China certainly enjoys the status of a great power; a status enhanced by her possession of a limited thermo-nuclear capability. (At the time of writing an effective delivery system appears still to be in a formative stage.) But France too exhibits these features: is she not a great power? China, we remember, has by far the largest national population of any state in history. As many human beings live in China as probably existed on the entire globe in AD 750.[11] This immense population is still in the process of fairly rapid industrialization. On the whole, then, it seems sensible to classify China as a great power with a super-power potential likely to be realized within ten or fifteen years.

We cannot too sharply perceive that what matters very much more than absolute levels of wealth or military provision sustained by different countries is the way such varying levels determine the nature and quality of the relationship between the countries

[11] An estimate contained in Professor Carlo Cipolla's valuable *An Economic History of World Population*, Pelican Books, London, 1962.

concerned. A great power is not defined by absolute standards but by reference to other powers. In this respect all states have a defining role in relation to each other. It is not mainly by counting heads, guns, rockets or even dollars that a superpower is shown to be such, but by estimating the resources of states which are not super-powers, and are shown not to be so *by a comparison which arises out of the relationship between them and the superpower*. Thus 'ranking the powers' is only meaningful in the context of a society of states, the character of which will be largely determined in its collective behaviour by the disparities between its members.

Bearing this in mind we will bring this chapter to a close by con-sidering the international role of the smaller countries in the modern world. We do this as introducing another way of looking at the working of the international system, and also for the not un-remarkable reason that small states comprise more than half the total number in the world.

As so often when contemplating international politics we are brought up against the role of relativity. Variables abound. There are states plausibly regarded as small, with small populations but large territories, for example Mongolia, Chad and Mauritania; states with small populations and territories but comparatively large natural resources, for example iron-producing Luxembourg; states with small populations, territories and resources, for example Trinidad/Tobago and Rwanda; states with relatively large popula-tions but small territories, for example Belgium, Holland and Malta; and states with small populations and small territories but comparatively enormous resources, for example Kuwait. Such permutations can be interwoven with other diversities which challenge classification. What might be regarded as small states are found in all parts of the world. They vary greatly in their regional interests and their strategic significance. Some are developed, efficient and prosperous. Let Denmark stand for them. Some are so poor and ill-organized that their actual viability as states is fre-quently questioned. Perhaps Haiti and the kingdom of Laos may not too unkindly be cited as instances. Some exist in areas of acute strategic sensitivity, among them the two Vietnams, Israel, Jordan and Lebanon. Others, for instance Switzerland, the Irish Republic and now perhaps Cuba and Austria, enjoy the considerable advantages of their strategic unimportance. This reminds us that power is never merely a quantity. It is always also a factor of relationship. A small state of major strategic interest to a great one may virtually determine whole areas of that state's foreign policy. Dog-wagging tails are by no means unknown in international politics. Small states also vary at least as much in their internal stability, structure and ideological colour. They include advanced, stable Western democracies such as Norway; largely traditionalist despotisms such as Bhutan or the sheikhdoms of the Persian Gulf; newly emergent political systems of a modified Western type such as Lesotho; countries which have passed or are passing through periods of military dictatorship such as Dahomey and Greece, and communist People's Republics such as Albania.

In the light of all these and other variables it is not easy to lay down characteristics which identify the 'small state' as such. Let us, however, establish certain definite criteria, arbitrary though they may be. A small state, we may then say, is one with a population of less than five million but more than a hundred thousand, and a national territory of less than fifty thousand but more than five hundred square miles. In that case we find ourselves with a list of some thirty states. They range in location from Central America to south-east Asia, in economic and technological advancement from Iceland to Liberia, in geograhical type from the island of Jamaica to the inland mountain fastness of Sikkim, and in strategic importance from Israel in the Middle East to Burundi in a corner of Central Africa. On this showing even rigid limits of definition reveal considerable diversity. Moreover, this number excludes on the one hand many states somewhat bigger or more populous which could still very reasonably be classified as small states, and on the other a group, mostly found in Europe, whose members are tiny, alike in territorial extent, number of citizens, and, with one exception to be noted later, political importance. If we allow population alone to be the defining criterion, so including states of whatever territorial size with national communities of five million or less, the number of small states amounts, as at present, to no less than sixty-eight, nearly half the total number of states in the world.

If we leave aside the question of objective criteria, we may ask whether we can perceive a characteristic type of small-state political behaviour in international politics, which a significant number of states, clearly not major ones by any criterion, tend to practice in common. Here too great variety persists. Small states reveal differing diplomatic styles; as we have seen they vary in political complexion and international allegiances. Some attach themselves, thankfully or resignedly, to great alliance systems. Others cling to the concept, and the hope, of non-alignment. Certainly the United Nations Organization has been of the greatest importance to small states. It is the one international association they are all free to join without any commitment other than to the principles of the Charter, principles which, in upholding the integrity of all states, most pointedly operate to the benefit of states least able to protect themselves. As membership is a universally recognized symbol of sovereign independence the Organization is a very good friend to small states, some of whom, though unable to afford diplomatic representation almost anywhere else, contrive to send their five-man delegation to Lake Success. Within the General Assembly smallness is probably most consciously and consistently felt by states. Here groupings have sometimes manifested themselves in terms of a collective small-state resistance to what have been deemed to be unduly peremptory or overweening initiatives taken by one or other of the superpowers, acting either against each other, or, very occasionally, in concert.

In the population explosion of states that has occurred since the second world war, many of the seventy or so new states are small by one or more of the criteria suggested above. A considerable number of them are still in the throes of an intense nationalism, which has been known to be even reinforced by the awareness of their exiguous extent. Perhaps this suggests that there is something to be said for G. K. Chesterton's remark that the true patriot never boasts of the largeness of his country, but of its smallness.

But though the defensive self-assertion of some of these small states may be loud, their claims to contribute to world peace insistent (whether they purport to do so through the medium of the United Nations or directly in their relations with other powers), and their efforts to assuage the international grievances which are held to threaten world peace well-intentioned, it appears to be true that small states in general are best regarded as consumers rather than producers of international security. We might argue that their very vulnerability represents a useful function, since it enables great powers to use their own political and military assets to protect small partners, and perhaps to separate squabblers, so serving an acceptable great power purpose in the world. If small states did not exist, admittedly in almost embarrassing profusion, great powers might have to invent them!

For it appears that there is some need to justify the possession of vast power by reference to a moral theme of some kind. The Foreign Office official Sir Eyre Crowe, in a memorandum of 1907 that has become almost legendary, suggested that British maritime supremacy at that golden epoch might most suitably be linked with a commitment to defend the rights of small nations. It may be questioned how far Britain ever consciously adopted this justification. The Irish would demur. But the attitude was revealed during the first world war in many publications[12] and official statements about Belgium. It is in any case interesting to notice that moral considerations intermingle with more strictly ideological ones in the attempt to justify policy and its consequences. Political commentators may be tempted often to discount the role of moral scruple in international affairs: politicians hasten to insist on its relevance.

Dr David Vital, in his helpful analysis,[13] notices an element of self-righteousness in the behaviour of great powers. They tend to assume that the possession of power in itself confers a prescriptive right to exercise it, often with scant regard to the sensitivities of lesser states. We saw earlier in this chapter how defensively the Soviet Union felt obliged to react to criticisms of her subjugation of Czechoslovakia in 1968. In the Brezhnev Doctrine, laying down that fraternal socialist countries were morally justified in constraining an erring comrade by force if need be, for his own ultimate good as for the good of all, the self-righteous complacency of the powerful could scarcely go further.

However, this unendearing trait in great powers (and throughout this discussion we are of course including the two superpowers in this category) appears to be paralleled by a curious moralism often detectable in the attitudes of small states. Among some of them there is a tendency to believe that by reason of their very smallness they are somehow morally superior to great powers. Dr Leopold Kohr[14] developed a thesis that the great values of social life, security, conviviality, prosperity and serenity (by which last he appears to mean culture in general), are best upheld by state units

[12] *King Albert's Book*, published in 1915, is a good specimen.
[13] *The Inequality of States*, Oxford U.P., 1967.
[14] In *The Breakdown of Nations*, Routledge & Kegan Paul, London, 1957.

that are both numerous and small. We may think that there is some substance in Dr Kohr's contention, at least if we look at history rather selectively, and admire, for example, the court culture of many of the lesser German states in the eighteenth century. But it does not obviously follow that these values are best served by the multiplying of small sovereignties. Equally questionable might seem the implication, which the Kohr thesis clearly makes, that because large states tend to be *unavoidably* subject to over-government, social atomization, individual anonymity, collective passivity matched by violent minority dissidence and other evils, small states, assumed to remain relatively free from them, enjoy a *moral* superiority over large ones. It may be doubted how far small states are really better guarantors of the values Dr Kohr sets store by than large ones. But even admitting the case, we may feel that small states are simply luckier in this respect. The element of choice, which is inseparable from morality, would hardly seem to be present.

A further assumption frequently made by those who tend to believe in the moral superiority of small states is that they are inherently more peace-loving than great powers. The case is cited of Costa Rica, whose president on 1 December 1948 disbanded the entire Costa Rican army on the grounds that his country chose to tread the path of peace.[15] Gwynfor Evans, president of *Plaid Cymru*, the Welsh Nationalist Party, pledged that an independent Wales would husband resources and demonstrate virtue by dispensing with armed force. But *Plaid Cymru* demands membership for Wales of the United Nations. In principle, this would oblige Wales to maintain an armed capacity in order to contribute to the collective security which the Organization ostensibly provides.

Now, granted the continuance of an international system which is predicated upon the need of governments to defend their countries against the possibility of armed attack, states such as Costa Rica and an independent Wales become essentially security consumers at the expense of whatever relatively powerful neighbour or alliance group is prepared to protect them. Moreover, much historical evidence supports the view that where there are many competitors for security that valuable commodity becomes in progressively shorter supply. Wars may then be resorted to in an

[15] In fact the president was acting to forestall an imminent military *coup*.

increasingly desperate effort to produce it. As we saw in chapter 2 the Greek city-states, however much some of them may have met Dr Kohr's criteria of political excellence, were in practice unable to escape from a condition of chronic warfare so prevalent that war has been called the 'natural relationship' between them. The *Pax Romana*, we have seen, was imposed by a superstate, not attained by mutual agreement among a multitude of small states sworn to relinquish the sword.

There is little evidence that small states are more peaceable than great powers. It is rather that the former are less militarily effective than the latter, not more peace-loving. It has been strongly argued that the world is safest when international affairs are firmly in the hands of a very few great powers. So-called 'Concert politics' of the kind that was explicitly envisaged in the nineteenth century in Europe, is often held up as something of an ideal. While there may be good reasons for discounting this view it seems evident that small states are as eagerly engaged in pursuing their interests as are large ones. It is only that the area of influence they command is usually much less. If the exercise of state power is ever morally questionable we cannot help noticing that small states exercise it as readily as they can. There seems little evidence that the political initiatives of small states, however constrained, are characterized by a greater delicacy of scruple, or perceptibly more prudence, than those of greater neighbours. Small states seem very willing to invoke the support of the powerful where their interests may be served by it. So the great powers 'floundered into war'[16] in 1914 over issues deriving largely from the intransigent claims of small-state nationalism in the Balkans, and so the United States fought a major if limited war on behalf of the republic of Vietnam which could not assure its survival alone. Moreover, issues between small states may be at least as embittered as any dividing great powers, as was illustrated in the Middle East from the inception of the state of Israel in 1948. Nor, significantly, in that area were the great powers able to remain detached, but found themselves underwriting rival interests, with possibly the most far-reaching consequences for the future. All in all, we may well decide that small states appear to be imbued with as much collective self-assertiveness and generalized ill-will as large states may seem to be. Less moralistically, we

[16] A phrase borrowed from Sir Lewis Namier, *Vanished Supremacies*, Hamish Hamilton, London, 1958.

E

may recognize that they are equally locked in predicaments which determine policy. In any case, we may reach the conclusion that the belief in the superior virtues of small states is a romantic illusion.

Small states, in short, are great powers writ small. They behave as much like great powers as they can. Nor should we blame them for this. They belong to an international order which requires them to exercise what power they have, and to seek the favourable attention of larger states wherever they can. Nor can they escape from this international order without ceasing to exist as states. Any distinctiveness in small state behaviour arises not from any qualitative difference between small states and others but from the limitations their smallness places upon their capacity to implement significant decisions in foreign policy. Herein lies the chronic dilemma confronting small states. If they remain internationally quiescent their image on the world stage is likely to diminish into virtual invisibility. If they seek to expand their influence they may provoke constraining pressures from disturbed or interested neighbours, and so heighten their own vulnerability. As we saw earlier, a small state may exercise a seemingly disproportionate effect upon the foreign policy of a great power. Very often this arises because the geographical position or natural resources or ideological posture of the small state are of major strategic importance to the great power. The latter's anxious interest is thus stimulated in the first place by considerations *exterior* to the wishes or the preoccupations of the small state itself.

This perhaps suggests that the principal role of small states in international society is that of political *objects* rather than *subjects*. Although they may pursue lively international relations, especially with each other, so far as great powers are concerned they are on balance done to rather than doing.

We may now attempt to summarize what seem to be the significant aspects of the role of small states in the world.

(i) They perform a defining role in relation to great powers, whatever difficulties we may have in defining small states themselves. All power is relative, and it is evident that great powers are so in an international context in which they loom enormously larger than other states. It is the *fact* of a small state which gives meaning to the *idea* of a great power, and vice versa. On this basis a ranking of states can be attempted which is of explanatory use.

(ii) The international system has undergone a remarkable proliferation of small states during the middle decades of the twentieth century. This process has probably not yet come to an end. It serves the function of satisfying diverse nationalisms characterized by a common intensity. The continuing growth of nationalistic passion in our increasingly interdependent world is a striking feature of contemporary international politics which we will discuss in the next chapter. A consequence of the increase in the number of states is that the sphere in which the great powers are obliged to act becomes more complex, contains more imponderables and is probably more dangerous.

(iii) Small states occupy certain areas and provide occasions in which the interests of great powers, and most significantly the superpowers, may clash. The Middle East has always been likely since the early 1960s to prove a case in point. In this respect small states represent a preoccupation in international politics of grave importance for themselves and the rest of the world.

(iv) On the other hand small states may act as buffers, keeping superpower interests largely apart. Examples are perhaps Austria since the 1955 Peace Treaty, Switzerland and Sweden. This function may be assumed to contribute something to international security.

(v) Small states, acting for instance in United Nations groups, may exercise some constraint from time to time on the policies of the superpowers, at least when these policies are concerned not directly with vital inter-superpower relations but with areas where superpower interests are more readily negotiable.

(vi) Small states in a position of great strategic importance to the superpowers will always attract the urgent attention of the latter's policy-makers. Hence the foreign policy of such critically placed small states may have incalculably important consequences.

(vii) Small states in the developing world will generally wish to find themselves among the recipients of economic and perhaps diplomatic and even military aid, dispensed by great powers. As such they help to enhance the international prestige of the latter. Prestige is, for better or worse, a major interest of great powers. It might be said that the urgency of the interest is directly proportional to the importance of the state upholding it. Indeed, for the superpowers prestige is such a central and sensitive interest that, as in the Cuban missile crisis of 1962, each superpower may take quite elaborate diplomatic steps to safeguard the prestige of the other, in the essential effort to stabilize a dangerously dynamic situation.

(viii) We cannot leave entirely out of account that group of tiny states which were mentioned above. Perhaps we may say of such states as Liechtenstein and San Marino, for example, that they provide a picturesque, amusing, harmless, and for many observers curiously satisfying element in the international political system. Aptly have they been called the 'ceremonial states'. R. M. Lockley, the celebrated naturalist, remarked[17] that there is something in a small island 'that satisfies the heart of man'. We may feel the same about the handful of agreeably minute states. We may suspect that this, as much as anything, accounts for their survival.

(ix) All small states, particularly those adjacent to great powers, exist on sufference. Their survival is therefore significant. While it may be true that in some cases it is simply not worth any state's trouble to eliminate them, their continuing existence does bear witness to the constraining effect of international law – and morality – on state action. We are right to remember that in a world of power politics scruples remain a real, and even at times a decisive, factor.[18]

(x) We come now to that state which, as we hinted earlier, is exceptional, both in relation to its tiny size and its immense political importance. Indeed it performs a unique role in international politics. Vatican City provides an almost universally recognized temporal sovereignty for the Supreme Pontiff, thereby freeing papal institutions from dependence upon the territorial hospitality of a particular country – in this case, Italy. The Roman Church is thus helped to pursue that worldwide evangelical and pastoral mission, with which she believes herself to be charged,

---

[17] In *Islands round Britain*, Collins, London, 1945.

[18] A striking example may in fact be found in the case of San Marino. At any time during the past century Italy could have marched into the country and turned the 'Serene Republic' into a minor Italian municipality. No international crisis would have arisen. Italy would actually gain economically from the removal of what has been a haven for commercial tax evaders and illicit casino operators. On these grounds relations between the two states have sometimes been strained. San Marino's career as for years the only communist state outside the Iron Curtain was also a constant irritation. Yet, in honour of her pledge to observe San Marino's independence 'for ever', in return for the republic having given asylum to Garibaldi, Italy has scrupulously refrained from taking an action militarily and politically open to her.

essentially free of institutional bonds with any secular authority. This remains the fact, of course, although in certain countries Roman Catholicism is the state religion, and the Roman Church consequently the official religious organ of the state. The Irish Constitution affirmed, though it did not define, the 'special position' of the Roman Catholic Church in the Republic of Ireland. 'Catholicism', it has been said, 'is Spain upon her knees.' But Catholicism is clearly far more than this. Vatican City symbolizes the freedom of the Roman Church (and as that Church would insist her *necessary* freedom) to remain always something more. It has been argued that Vatican City is not really a member of international society because the papal government does not pursue specifically state interests by means of a foreign policy fashioned for the purpose. But this disclaimer ignores the quite definite international personality of Vatican City, as expressed in the exchange of diplomatic representatives with nearly all major countries and many minor ones throughout the world. Vatican City's foreign policy is admittedly specialized, being conditioned by unique interests of state. But as formulated on behalf of the conceived rights of the Roman Catholic Church this foreign policy certainly exists. Vatican City is undoubtedly a state. She possesses all the requirements of statehood. There are a territory and population. There is a legitimate government. The state enjoys a measure of diplomatic recognition wider than that accorded many other states. There is even a ceremonial armed force, together with a 'national' flag. It is perhaps fair to say that the force and the flag enable Vatican City, in addition to her diplomatic and political functions in relation to the interests of the Roman Catholic Church, to discharge the role mentioned under (viii) above with considerable *éclat*. When Pope Paul VI addressed the General Assembly of the United Nations he did so, and said he did so, as a head of state, whatever significance may have attached to his remarks by virtue of his theological office as Vicar of Christ.

Our conclusion then will be that small states play a not uninteresting and not unimportant part in international politics. The world is faced with the prospect of further technological advance. It is strongly urged in some quarters that the managerial needs and economic effects of such advance will compromise still further the real autonomy of the smaller nation-state. Reinforcing this pressure is said to be the problem of urgent material want arising in large part from the swarming increase in human population. There are also the potentially supra-national effects which are held to derive from a growing hostility between whole groups of nations confronting each other across great racial divides deepened by severe economic disparities. The argument goes that such considerations must bring more and more into question the continuing capacity of such states to meet the expectations of their peoples. There is doubtless a good deal of force in these views, which are increasingly being canvassed. Our last section in this chapter considers in particular one factor which many students of world politics regard as a critically important element in processes making for qualitative change in the modern international system. We refer to the role of *private* international institutions.

Non-state actors in international society

Now in this book we are concentrating, as its title implies, perhaps in a rather old-fashioned way on *states* as the principal actors on the international scene, and on their inter-relationships. And we suggest below why we think such a treatment to be justified, while recognizing the great value of treatments conveying a rather different emphasis. For it is of course perfectly true that non-state actors in international society play a large and evidently growing part in world affairs. The great international corporations and industrial consortia are coming to exercise a pervasive influence. While they generally remain essentially private bodies they tend to wield enormous economic power affecting often profoundly the collective life of whole areas of the world at large. For this reason individual governments and public international institutions seek increasingly to render them in some form publicly accountable. In some cases governments become active partners within the corporations concerned, contributing to the economic efforts involved, sharing in the making of policy and in the benefits secured. In other cases governments hedge round the activities of such private international bodies with regulations and restrictions intended to retain some measure of control in the hands of governments themselves over the public effects of large-scale private international enterprise.

Clearly the development of modern technology and the exploitation of world resources on a global basis make the emergence of such international corporations inevitable in those parts of the world at least where the pursuit of private economic endeavour for profit is acknowledged as a legitimate and even desirable activity. Even with communist countries, whose political philosophies and internal arrangements do not provide for the growth of huge private corporations, the great international firms have in many cases developed important and mutually beneficial commercial links. The fact remains that, quite apart from the role of the public international organizations, ranging from the United Nations to, for example, the local Customs Union between Switzerland and Liechtenstein, there now exists a large and growing number of international bodies, essentially private, with in many instances worldwide economic interests, and disposing sometimes of resources exceeding those at the disposal of many sovereign states.

From this fact the suggestion has followed that the workings of international society may more profitably be studied from the standpoint of the function of such bodies rather than from that of the role of states, and that the effect of the activity of the former may contribute very significantly to a transformation of the international system by means of the gradual supercession of the sovereign state itself.

No one would readily deny that this developing role of the great international corporation should be carefully assessed. A growing body of literature attests to the keen attention which many scholars of international politics and economics are now directing to the phenomenon. However, we may suggest that there remain good grounds for maintaining that the sovereign state is still the *principal* actor in the international arena. This may seem to be so even allowing for the marked inequality of influence which states command *vis-à-vis* each other and the international corporations themselves. We may concede that General Motors is a more momentous institution in the modern world than, say, the Republic of Andorra. But there are grounds for believing that major states remain more important than any private corporation.

It is certainly true that the policies of governments may be radically affected by decisions taken by boards of directors in these great international companies. For example, a decision by Chryslers to wind up all subsidiary and concessionary enterprises and agencies in the United Kingdom would almost immediately confront the British government with a serious economic dislocation in regard to industrial redundancy in certain critical areas. The day to day well-being of some thousands of British citizens would be drastically affected at once, or within a very short time, by decisions taken by mainly American citizens, acting according to their perception of the best interests of the American-based company whose own well-being represents one of their primary responsibilities. Private capitalism may thus, in its legitimate attempt to maximize its own advantage, produce tremendous public consequences both in and even beyond those countries whose political traditions sanction its operation. Indeed, the economic development or decay of whole regions of the globe – in extent far greater than the individual countries comprising them – may be directly affected by the wise or poor judgement or the good or ill luck of private international corporations primarily responsible to themselves.

Yet doubt may persist as to whether this really implies that such corporations must necessarily prove to be a decisive instrument in transforming the international system.

In the first place, where a direct clash occurs between the policies and interests of a private international body and those of a sovereign government the latter is likely to prevail, even though its intervention may well not be, at least in the short run, to the economic betterment of the state concerned. In reacting to the influence of foreign commercial interests inside their countries governments not infrequently exercise the capacity either to take over the interests involved outright, with or without compensation, or to assume a large measure of executive control over them. As but one of many instances in the developing world in particular, we may cite the case of Uganda at the end of 1972, whose then president, General Amin, moved against British commercial interests in his country in precisely this direct and forceful manner, despite the measured protests issued by the British government.

But more significantly (and herein lies our justification for the emphasis adopted in this book), *states remain the only institutions in world politics with the generally acknowledged right to coerce their members, and to claim an ultimate sanction in disposing of their lives and property*. Certainly in almost all countries, particularly all those with a pretension to civilization, this right is hedged about with all sorts of constitutional restraints, guarantees and norms of political behaviour. But it is there, and there uniquely. States, in short, alone monopolize *legitimate* force. That worldwide public international institution the United Nations can only use force at the behest and with the consent of its member states.

In fact everything that happens in international politics has reference sooner or later to the role of independent states. Bernard Shaw's Andrew Undershaft could boast that it was the great manufacturers, in his case of armaments, who 'paid the piper and called the tune', while politicians played with their 'caucuses and leading articles and historic parties and great leaders and burning questions and the rest of [their] toys'.[19] But it is still governments which in the end decide policies which will determine the use made of the arms the Undershafts produce; which in the realms of economic no less than military policy assert the ultimate authority to shape the role which public activity will assume within their states. The most powerful private interest must acknowledge and come to terms with, or assimilate itself to, or else be gravely challenged by, the national interest, which, however variously conceived, is in the last resort interpreted and upheld by statesmen.

Hence we venture to reaffirm the view that as interests assume that primacy in politics which we suggested in the first chapter, so state interests retain a corresponding primacy in international politics, and that this seems likely to ensure that for the time being states remain the chief, though by no means the sole, actors upon the international stage. We offer some examination of the possible role of *public* international institutions in transforming the international system, and hence the function of the sovereign state, in the concluding chapter.

Meanwhile, we may notice that not the least of the expectations peoples entertain towards their states appears to arise from a more or less universal desire for the demonstration of a national identity. Nationalism, urging its claims no matter how small the scale on which the assumed nationhood may operate, would also seem to ensure that states will remain a prominent feature – indeed the most salient feature – of the international system for as long as we care to foresee. And it is to the notion of the nation, and to some of the images and myths that surround it in the collective minds of peoples, that we now turn.

[19] In *Major Barbara*, Penguin edition, 1945.

Note on the psychology of foreign aid
Jesus remarked that it is more blessed to give than to receive. In some
transcendental sense this may well be true, but it is apparent from
experience that it is far easier. Many of us manage to give graciously;
many find it hard graciously to take. The expectation of gratitude
implicit in much giving represents a real if scarcely conscious psychological offence to many recipients. Largely, perhaps, this is because to
be in a position to confer benefits indicates a state of superiority. Herein
lies the heart of the predicament in which countries concerned with
making foreign aid available so often find themselves. If it is notoriously
hard to love the powerful, it may be hardest of all when they use their
power for our good. Similarly, it is difficult for the doers of good to
remain merely disinterested. Being human, they tend to look for the
reward of gratitude. Again, to take an example of the sensitive relationship between giver and receiver within the field of domestic politics, we
may see the champions of American Black Power trying their best to
destroy white racism as a political force while apparently reserving
their deeper hatred for white liberalism. Because, alas, the white liberal
is in the intolerably superior position of seeking to 'do justice' to black
citizens, to 'give them a square deal', to better their conditions. The
way of the would-be righter of wrongs is hard. The sincerity of white
liberals' desire to do good by the blacks is not in question. What the
latter seem to find intolerable is that society should be so arranged that
there is occasion for such white objectives at all. In the world at large,
the insoluble problem of international economic relations, as of inter-
racial relations generally, is how to meet urgent needs without appearing
patronizing. Nations as well as individuals tend to behave as if they did
indeed find it easier to forgive those who wrong them than those whom
they wrong, and by a comparable paradox, find it hardest to be cordial
towards those who do them good. Victims induce a sense of guilt;
benefactors a sense of shame. How heartily Nazis loathed the Jews
they massacred! How readily Europeans criticized Americans once
they were in full receipt of Marshall Aid! Thus white Americans, admitting it or not, see in black Americans a living reminder of an historic
injustice. Thus the material evidence in a country of another country's
foreign aid represents not only a means of economic development: it
is also a symbol of hated dependence. The easy pride of the rich and
powerful is readily matched by the fierce pride of the poor and weak.
May this perhaps explain why men resist the Christian gospel? For it
posits on the part of the Almighty a stupendous benefaction – salvation
itself – and enjoins on the part of His creatures an unceasing gratitude.
How is it to be borne? The Christian answer has traditionally been

that we cannot bear it, and that gratitude itself is a grace, infused into us by God to make possible the response He requires. But countries engaged in the generally unthankful business of giving foreign aid are in no position to confer grace. They can only confer benefits, and hope for the best, knowing that some of the aid, at least, is liable to be misused, and its providers to be abused. Unalloyed benevolence and pure thankfulness both and equally require on the part of those doing good and those being done good to true humility. And this remains, perhaps, the rarest of all human virtues, most seldom met with, it would seem, when individual human beings are congregated into nations, and their personal pride, which Gulliver, home from his travels, found so peculiarly detestable, is reinforced with a collective *amour propre*. Real and spontaneous gratitude may seem indeed a grace. Formal gratitude, proffered because it is expected, one uneasily suspects is the type most common between nations. It is little more than an aspect of diplomatic protocol. And gratitude of this common kind is a coin stamped on both sides. The device on the reverse delineates resentment. And resentment breeds dislike. No doubt, when a benefit has been received, the inner dislike felt is broadly proportional to the degree of gratitude outwardly expressed. All this is not to deny that foreign aid, in a number of forms adapted to varying need, remains essential, if international order is to be maintained. But what is necessary is often not what is agreeable.

4

The notion of the nation: some images and myths

We are Egyptians first, Arabs second and Muslims last – *Azam Pasha, first secretary-general of the Arab League.*

There is room for both the Sleeping Beauty and the Frankenstein's monster view of nationalism. It brings millions of people out of traditional corners into the global commerce of the modern world, and it induces a psychological climate conducive to bitter, irrational struggles over contested bits of territory. The good it does could all be done in other ways; but equally, it has contributed little more than a new vocabulary to the history of political evil – *K. R. Minogue.*

India a nation! What an apotheosis! Last comer to the drab nineteenth-century sisterhood! Waddling in at this hour of the world to take her seat! She, whose only peer was the Holy Roman Empire, she shall rank with Guatemala and Belgium perhaps! – *E. M. Forster.*

If you can engage people's pride, love, pity, ambition (or whatever is their prevailing passion), on your side, you need not fear what their reason can do against you – *Lord Chesterfield.*

The subjective nature of the nation

The nation is one of the most important psychological facts in human history. There may be continuing debate about what a nation really is; about its essence, and about the criteria which most convincingly define it. But there can be no doubt about the reality of the thing itself. Nations exist because they are believed to exist. All men assent, implicitly or explicitly, to the proposition that a certain class of human group, which is always on a relatively large scale, is properly thought of as comprising nations, whatever, in any particular case, may be the decisive criterion defining the nation. There are several more or less distinct constitutive elements which go into the making of a nation. They combine in various ways. Several may be of comparable importance together, or one or two may be clearly preponderant. But essentially a nation comes into existence when a sufficient number of human beings believe that they comprise a nation. Such existence is decisively assured when a sufficient number of people outside the national group are induced to accept that the nation exists. Thus we see that, like political legitimacy in the case of institutions and office, the reality of the nation is 'all in the mind'. What is also undeniable is that the powerful and often shrill demand for the continued assertion of an existing nationhood, or its reassertion where it is felt to be obscured by political forms that do not satisfactorily express it, represents a dominant theme in contemporary international politics.

What constitutes a nation?

Let us glance briefly at some of the constitutive elements that have proved important in giving rise to a felt nationhood, and *therefore* to the reality of nations.

Of them all, language has been one of the most pervasive. Linguistic nationalists[1] tend to insist that language is far more than merely 'a means of communication'. It is, they hold, a vital instrument in the shaping and colouring of the collective national personality. It enshrines the group culture. It is, in their view, the most important homogenizing force in society. While there remains a multiplicity of tongues, the human world will be divided into many nations. To the linguistic nationalist such countries as the United Kingdom and Belgium are multi-national states because more than one language is spoken by their citizens. Linguistic nationalism even goes to the length of trying to revivify 'local' languages now moribund or dead, in an attempt to assert a claimed nationhood, usually against a resented preponderant neighbouring nationhood. Thus the Cornish and Manx nationalist parties identify themselves strongly with the cause of the Manx and Cornish languages. The biblical myth of the Tower of Babel regards the 'confusion of tongues' as a Divine punishment and a human mis-

---

[1] Dr Brian Porter, with agreeable mischief, has called linguistic nationalism 'lingoism'.

fortune. To the linguistic nationalist it is a source of cultural enrichment and a validation of nationhood, both of which he regards as essentially 'good things'.

Geography has also been an historically important determination of nationhood. Frontiers not only frame the state territory but can go far to making real the national character of the political community within them. There is, for example, in diplomatic fact a Republic of Chad. Is there a Chad nation? The answer seems to be, Yes, if the citizens of the republic think that that is what they are. There are very many instances of arbitrarily delimited colonial territories coming to support not only independent states but newly self-conscious nations. A riverine strip of land in West Africa, belonging to Britain, was flanked by two French colonial territories. However improbably, this later became the kingdom of Gambia, its riverside population becoming an independent nation-state within the Commonwealth, and acknowledging Queen Elizabeth II as its head. Ruling elites in many of the newly independent countries of Africa have been urgently engaged in building nations within their ex-colonial borders from tribal communities who had no sense of national cohesion to begin with and indeed were often enough passionately hostile to each other. It remains to be seen how far over the long term the replacement of warring tribes by larger-scale competing nations will make for greater stability and prosperity in Africa and elsewhere.

The experience of ex-colonies is a reminder that state institutions themselves have been one of the means by which nations have come into being. Medieval England and France, for example, were states before they were nations. The relative and varying success of their kings in maintaining legitimacy and running their writ over the lands subject to their rule did much to create in their political communities a sense of nationhood which state institutions at once symbolized, fostered and protected. It seems probable that in ancient Egypt and old imperial China too the prestigious role of the dynasties did much to promote the collective self-hood of the 'People of Han' and the nation of the Egyptians.

Upon the complementary effect, whereby a felt nationhood gives rise to state institutions, we need not dwell here, for it has been one of the most evident and fateful processes at work in human history during the past two centuries. In the nineteenth century the kingdom of Italy and the German Empire were striking

examples of an urgent nationhood finding expression and a measure of psychological relief in the setting up of over-arching state
institutions. In the twentieth century rival and unassuaged nationhoods among the subject peoples of the Austro-Hungarian Empire
were enabled by the solvent of war to break out of the imperial
state structure of the Habsburgs, ancient and dignified but with its
legitimacy decayed, and to set up new state institutions designed to
satisfy clamant national demands. The facts that one of the successor states was itself multi-national (Czechoslovakia, as between
Bohemians, Moravians, Slovaks and Ruthenians), and all had
national minorities within the new borders in conditions of greater
or lesser disgruntlement, contributed duly to political difficulties in
the decades following the first world war. If nationhood is indeed a
blessing, it is never unalloyed.

We may notice one further fermenting agent in the production
of national consciousness, for it is one of the most remarkable.
This is religion. Historically, of course, both Protestantism and
Catholicism in Europe did much, during the formative period
of the European state system, to mould and colour what may be
called the 'collective life-style' of particular countries. Of equal
significance perhaps has been the role of religion in generating
a decisive nationhood in two modern nation-states, Israel and
Pakistan.

In neither case has the relationship between the collective religion and the sense of nationhood been a simple one, and we cannot
trace out all its effects and implications. But we may note a few
salient features. Though very different from one another, both
states were heirs of a great religious tradition; in the case of Islam
one that had informed and sanctified a major civilization; in the
case of Judaism one that upheld a distinctive exclusiveness that had
been proof against the eroding effects of two thousand years of
fairly consistent restriction and oppression. A complicating factor
in the case of Israel is the implication of a special collective 'apart-
ness', the fact, or the pretension, of being a 'chosen people'. This
aspect has given a peculiar quality to Jewish nationhood, and
a historically fateful determinedness to Zionist nationalism,
which sprang from the former but is certainly not identical to
it. The unremitting claim of Zionists that a Jewish state in
Palestine was and is a historical and moral necessity has been,
and seems certain to remain, one of the most important factors in

world politics during the twentieth century, and probably beyond it.

Nationhood defined by religious faith has been powerfully challenged. To Pandit Nehru and the secularizing advocates of a united independent India the concept of a separate nation of Pakistan based on the adherence of a minority of Indians to Islam was a political outrage. Underlying all the diversities of culture, language and physical type to be found in India, Nehru argued again and again, was a degree of ethnic and economic 'Indianness' which abundantly justified the conception of a variegated but single Indian nation. The resentment felt by the Congress Party of India at Mr Jinnah's 'new-fangled' notion of a separate Moslem Indian nation was understandable. Once concede Pakistan and the federal union of the rest of India would be compromised, perhaps fatally. But Moslem fears of being engulfed by the Hindu majority of the rest of India were decisive: Moslem inflexibility prevailed. Amid appalling bloodshed, disruption and turmoil the new confessional nation-state came into being. To date, the secular federated parliamentary republic of India has survived intact, despite enormous difficulties and through many dangers. Islam, on the other hand, has not proved enough of a nation-making bond to hold together a country uniquely divided by the geographical separation of its constituent parts. Political, economic and regional interests between them proved in the end irreconcilable, and the experiment of a unitary state representing a nationhood defined purely by religion ended, with more human suffering on a tremendous scale, in a 'rump' Pakistan in the west, and, in the east, a precarious but populous new state, representing as Bangladesh a Bengali nationhood which exists because Bengalis feel that it exists.

Nationality, nationhood and nationalism

We have been referring in this chapter to nationhood and nationalism. Before going further it would be well to distinguish terms. We are concerned here with three related but distinct ideas. They are *nationality*, *nationhood* and *nationalism*.

To take them in order, the first is essentially a legal concept. It concerns a man's status as a subject or citizen. It is what is concerned with his right to vote, if the political system gives him that right, with his duty to pay taxes or to serve in his country's armed forces. It is what appears on his passport. There is no such thing as Welsh nationality (as yet), any more than there is such a thing as English nationality. There *is* British nationality. Tudor ap Llewellyn is a Welshman and a British national. I am a British national and an Englishman. There are extra categories, such for example as 'citizen of the Commonwealth', and anomalous features, such as the 'right' of citizens of the Irish Republic domiciled in the United Kingdom (and born since 1949) to vote in British elections. But basically a man's nationality is a matter of his legal standing in relation to the state to which he belongs, to which therefore he owes allegiance – his state, not his nation.

Nationhood, as we have suggested above, is that sense of the existence of a nation, and of a man's feeling that he is a member of it. What the late Lord Morrison of Lambeth said of the English middle class may be applied equally to a nation – any nation. It 'consists of those who think they belong to it'. The sense of nationhood, which may wax and wane in a particular case, remains one of the most powerful forces operating in human society. Where its pressures culminate in the establishment of a state, it gives rise of course to a new nationality. But if nationhood touches nationality on one side it is no less linked with nationalism on the other.

For nationalism is the ideology which seeks to justify the emotions which give substance to nationhood by demanding for it an *institutional* presence in the world, and the international recognition of that presence. Nationalists generally hold that the state is the essential instrument through which the nation stakes its claim on the attention and consideration of international society. Hence, given the existence of the nation, it follows, according to nationalist theory, that the nation should be embodied in representative institutions of state. Very many nationalists are unwilling to accept anything less than full sovereignty. Some are prepared to settle for a form of autonomy for their nations of confederal or federal status. Essentially, however, nationalists stand for the politicizing of their nationhood. They tend to insist that whatever value may be placed upon the cultural splendour of their nation, or the contribution its traditions may make to the fullness of experience enjoyed by a multi-national state of which it forms a part, that nation cannot be entirely fulfilled, and attain a full collective satisfaction, unless it becomes in some form, and usually this is required to be sovereign statehood, a distinct political community. We should in fairness admit that the national pride and status-consciousness displayed by many sovereign states give countenance to the demands of unsatisfied nationhoods, and help to explain the reactive assertiveness of many nationalists.

On the other hand, if rationality played any considerable part in these matters, it is difficult to see why nationhoods should not in fact find adequate, honourable and satisfying expression in collective forms other than the nation-state, jealous of a sovereignty which modern conditions may make less and less real in terms of effective responsibility for decisions governing the well-being of the political community. Linguistic, cultural and regional autonomy clearly *need* not require the apparatus of statehood to be evident and effective. Yet though many in non-sovereign nations readily concur, there tends to exist a vociferous minority whose passion and devotion ensure that the nationalist issue remains alive, and contributes to the general perplexities confronting and surrounding government. By what has aptly been called 'the law of the persistent minority' these groups tend to get more and more of their way, at least in politically 'permissive' systems, because they are not opposed by a corresponding dedication but by relative inertia and indifference.

In accounting for extreme nationalism, as for political extremism of all kinds and for whatever cause, we must not overlook the interplay between stated objectives, the group pursuing them and the psychological tensions of the individual member. Generalized political grievances are only too likely to be linked with personal frustrations, personal inadequacies, and the complex psychopathology of real and imagined failure on the part of individuals. We have seen that in 'normal' politics motives are mixed, that articulated claims made in the course of the political process can both express and mask inner desires. So much the more may this be assumed to be the case with those who, as do some groups of nationalists, resort to terroristic violence. That violence often succeeds in eroding the will of opponents is no proof of the 'purity' or disinterestedness of the motives of its perpetrators. Some men appear to need hatred as a spring of satisfying action. Their psychological balance would be upset by the actual removal of the cause of offence. It is in fact dangerous for a man, whether dissatisfied nationalist or other type of extreme dissident, to wrap his *raison d'être* exclusively around a cause, for then its ultimate success or failure could be equally disastrous for him personally. If it wins he may be among those enjoying a new power and prominence. But he may also suffer a damaging sense of lost purpose, and become like those revolutionaries who, as Bernard Shaw once remarked, have to be shot when the revolution succeeds. If it loses, his total identification with it may involve his own destruction as a person. But, of course, it would be idle to expect commitment to causes, least of all perhaps to the cause of nationalism, to be determined by a large measure of rational calculation. Nationalists, when they think, tend to do so 'with the blood'.

It may well seem to us that the most unendearing aspect of nationalism, as of other and related forms of collective self-regard, is that which attributes to the nationalists' own nation an innate superiority to others. An element of such arrogance probably pervades all nationalistic sentiment.[2] The 'validity' of the believed superiority depends always upon arbitrary criteria, for instance when the relative technological and industrial advancement of my nation proves to me its *general* superiority, of an innate kind, over your nation, which happens to be relatively backward in these respects. The two sets of circumstances of course prove nothing of the sort. This aspect of nationalism is essentially doctrinal. Like all doctrines, it can neither be proved nor disproved. If, for reasons that may lie deep in my own psychological vulnerability, I choose to believe that the more generally distributed mechanical gadgetry in my country indicates her innate superiority over a country with less of it, that is what I choose to believe, and there is really nothing more to be said. The whole notion of *progress* implies change for the better. Change is inevitable: whether any particular change is progressive remains ultimately a matter of belief. If you choose to believe that the advent of the motorcar has rendered mankind 'better' or happier, and that if it was a native of your country who invented it, this shows a national superiority over other countries, no one can prove you are wrong. He can only disagree. However, a belief that developments in one's own country *are* both progressive

---

[2] In 'Notes on Nationalism', reprinted in *Decline of the English Murder and Other Essays*, Penguin, London, 1965, an essay first published in 1945, George Orwell discussed this and allied points in his briskest manner.

in themselves and indicate national superiority is one of the fruitful sources of nationalism.

Self-determination

A most powerful doctrine in world politics during this century derived directly from the subjective fact of nationhood through the ideology of nationalism. This is the doctrine of 'self-determination'[3] It was in obedience to this doctrine, dear to the heart of President Wilson, and subscribed to somewhat more cynically by his European colleagues as an aspect of power politics rather than as an ideal way of ordering the world, that the postwar settlements of 1919, however partially and imperfectly, were imposed.

A fundamental principle of democracy is that the will of the majority should prevail. That is to say, it should prevail in so far as it can be ascertained, and subject to its practicality, and in as much as it is interpreted aright by those charged with its implementation. The principle represents in practice a rough and ready method of making political arrangements which it is hoped will command general assent and hence prove conveniently stable. The problem lies in determining the constituency. The issue of self-determination has proved a notorious case in point. At what size of group, at what degree of homogeneity characterizing it, by what criteria defining it, does a group qualify for consideration as one capable and deserving of determining for itself the issue of self-determination? All national groups are more or less heterogeneous. All frontiers, existing or proposed, are more or less arbitrary. No possible settlement can therefore satisfy completely. In this connection, as in so many, Betrand de Jouvenel's dictum has force. There are no 'solutions' to political problems, only *settlements*, more or less unsatisfactory.

From the late 1960s the issue of Northern Ireland illustrated the difficulty of applying the doctrine. The Irish nation won a struggle with the United Kingdom for the right of national self-determination in 1922, when the Free State came into being. But the new Irish government never conceded the same right to the Protestant

[3] The late Professor Alfred Cobban's *The Nation State and National Self-Determination?* revised edition, Collins, London, 1969, is an indispensable short study of the subject. Also helpful is Professor F. S. Northedge's article, 'National Self-Determination: the Adventures of a Moral Principle', in *International Relations*, vol. 1 no. 3, April 1955.

community in the Six Counties (out of the traditional nine of historic Ulster), merely acquiescing in a political separation which that government could not prevent. Unionist self-determination was not regarded as legitimate in the South. If we take all Ireland as the constituency in question a majority of the people living there would have presumably voted for Irish union under the republican regime ruling in Dublin. If we take the Six Counties as a legitimate self-determining community, a majority would have voted for the continuing constitutional division of the island, and for the un-changed adhesion of the Six Counties to the United Kingdom. Whether or not the population of the Six Counties comprised a self-determining community is a matter of political dogma, to be affirmed by its supporters and denied by its opponents. The desire for self-determination is a psychological fact. The right of self-determination is a matter of political decision by those holding power. There is nothing self-evident about it, any more than there is about any other political rights. It exists if it is conceded by those with the power to withhold it. In practice the Irish republicans were driven to the assertion that Ireland was a 'natural unit', with an inherent right to political unity. The fact that before the English conquest Ireland had not been politically united, but instead was divided among warrior kings who were constantly fighting each other, was not held to be relevant. A doctrine of 'insular self-determination' developed; the belief that because Ireland was an island in the sea it 'ought' to be politically united. The fact that the nationalists advocating this doctrine tended also to support the political division of the island of Great Britain serves to remind us that consistency and logic retreat before the blasts of political passion, rather as truth (it has been pointed out) tends to be the first casualty of war. The Northern Unionists on their side were obliged to insist that they did, in effect, comprise a community sufficiently definable and sufficiently homogeneous as to merit the granting of a right of self-determination. What this meant at the time was that the shared doctrine of self-determination, as applied by each group to its own political, religious and psychological needs, operated in a mutually exclusive way.

All this is not to say, of course, that we cannot advance criteria for establishing the viability of a self-determining community – criteria based on known political and economic facts illuminated by the light of commonsense. In practice, however, commonsense has often to yield to the intractable clamour of prejudice, the more narrow and embittered forms of collective self-hood and sheer human wilfulness. In any case, self-determination as a political principle and objective arising from the psychological fact of nationhood and the ideology of nationalism remains an active issue in world politics, which, as F. S. Northedge remarks, can 'no more be ignored than the climate or geography of the world'.

The character of nations

Lurking in wait for us has been the problem of national character. Perhaps about no aspect of international politics are generalizations likely to be more misleading or less avoidable. Some commentators on international politics have come to feel that any statement about national character in general or the character of any nation in particular is subject to so much qualification that it is better left unsaid. Yet . . . we all feel that there is a palpable difference between Englishmen as a whole and Frenchmen as a whole, more indeed than there may be between a given Englishman and a given Frenchman. The historical experience of a people does much to colour its prevailing mood, its 'way of life', a phrase so vague yet so convenient; its mode of behaviour in international society. National character has been aptly likened to a smell, indefinable but perceptible. It seems probable that an actual collective genetic factor may be at work in influencing the character of national groups, particularly the more homogenous ones. This is most apparently the case with recognizable physical characteristics. Rash though the suggestion must seem, and however shaky its scientific basis, it is hard not to conclude from experience that, for instance, there is more than one type of Welshman and Irishman. The social and cultural implications of their Welshness and Irishness cut across the physical elements of differentiation between these definable sub-groups of Welshmen and Irishmen. We all know, on the other hand, how difficult it is to define 'the races of mankind'.[4] If racial characteristics elude satisfactory classification,

---

[4] The conventional classification of human races into 'Caucasian', 'Negroid', 'Mongoloid', etc. has been dismissed as unsatisfactory, together with sub-race categories derived from them. Some authorities reduce racial classification to the different blood groups. They are all agreed that existing mankind comprises a

how much the harder we may think it is to pin down convincingly the elements of national character. Yet they are felt to exist. Our notions about national character, whether our own or other people's, may be largely illusory. But illusions themselves are part of reality. They influence action, and thereby help to make the world what it actually is and not something different.

Just as the nation itself exists by virtue of a widely held belief that it does, so what is chiefly important about national character is what is believed about it. Doubtless, in whatever objective reality it may have, national character affects international politics. But we may never be in a position to know what the effects are. We can, however, be certain that people's beliefs about national character affect relations between nations, both those that are institutionalized as states and those that are not. Nowhere than in international politics is it more true that what matters is not how things are but how they are believed to be. Beliefs about things, after all, are part of what they 'really' are. No doubt but that the images people entertain in their minds about other nations will tend to be crudely generalistic, relatively ignorant and for the most part critically unexamined. But they persist. They can exercise powerful influences upon policy, even at the highest levels. Many of these mutual national images, it must be admitted, are mere stereotypes. But this makes them the more important. The very ease with which they can be absorbed by the mind tends to ensure that they will be widespread among the political community and hence the more liable to affect political decisions.

The role of national images

At the comparatively sophisticated and informed level of diplomatic interchange, as well as at that of mass prejudice and generalized myth, national images influence international relations *because they affect the expectations countries entertain towards each other*. The images may be friendly or hostile in character. They are themselves influenced by the perception of interests. And interests, we should not forget, are neither formulated nor upheld in a purely

single species. See, e.g., Sonia Cole, *Races of Man*, British Museum (Natural History), London, 1963. The single human species is called *Homo sapiens* – 'wise man'! – and sometimes, to distinguish us from our defunct Neanderthal relation, *Homo sapiens sapiens*.

rational way, for interests engender feelings. Habitual and largely unquestioned attitudes, inertia, the bent of tradition – these also help to define a nation's self-image of its place in the world, of its claims upon the consideration of other nations, and its actual collective image of those other nations.

To take just one historical example, given the existence of the Indian Empire of Britain in the nineteenth century, the defensibility of its north-western frontier was a major – and largely rational – concern of British policy-makers. The greatest threat to the integrity of that frontier was perceived to be the Russian Empire, expanding eastward and southward in a manner comparable in many ways to the contemporary opening up of the Great West in the United States by American pioneers. In consequence there grew up in Britain a collective image of Russia as uniquely dangerous, sinister and aggressive, about whose attitude and policies it could only be safely predicted that they would be hostile. For England, the Crimean war was in great measure an outcome of these suspicions, which reinforced the will of the British government to try to prevent by military means any further weakening of the Ottoman Empire at Russian hands. In 1852, on the eve of that war, Sir Edward Creasey, the Professor of History in the University of London, published a justly popular work, *The Fifteen Decisive Battles of the World*, which echoed public anxieties by writing in this vein about the significance of the Battle of Pultowa between Peter the Great and Charles XII of Sweden in 1709:

What Russia has done since that time we know and we feel. And some of the wisest and best men of our own age and nation, who have watched with deepest care the annals and the destinies of humanity, have believed that the Sclavonic element in the population of Europe has as yet only partially developed its powers: that, while other races of mankind (our own, the Germanic, included) have exhausted their creative energies, and completed their allotted achievements, the Sclavonic race has yet a great career to run: and that the narrative of Sclavonic ascendancy is the remaining page that will conclude the history of the world . . . [Russia's] rapid transition . . . from being the prey of every conqueror to being the conqueror of all with whom she comes into contact, to being the oppressor instead of the oppressed, is almost without a parallel in the history of nations . . . the successors of Peter have, one and all, carried on an uniformly aggressive and uniformly successful system of policy against Turkey, and against every other state, Asiatic as well as European, which has had the misfortune of having Russia for a neighbour.

What mattered was not whether such writing represented an accurate assessment of Russian achievements, or a correct interpretation of Russian intentions, but that it expressed a popularly held mental image of Russia which was to influence relations between both Russia and England for another fifty or more years. It is a passage that breathes the very spirit of a cold war.

However discreetly, indeed exclusively, statesmen may appear to pursue high policy, they cannot afford to ignore, and need to some extent to identify with, the popular images of other countries held by the citizens of their own. Nor need we expect that the run-of-the-mill parliamentary deputy or MP will be free of such trammels. On the contrary, the more genuinely representative he is, the more his susceptibilities will reflect those of his constituents. Meanwhile, the images persist, and at least add a certain colour to international relations. We have long dwelt in a political universe peopled with such curious creatures as chilly, hypocritical but (in their own eyes) essentially fair-playing Englishmen, dour Scots, quarrelsome Irishmen, sensual 'Latins', pleasure-dominated Frenchmen, stolid but bullying Germans, devious Welshmen, mournful and emotional Russians, gloomily moody 'Slavs', oily Greeks, brash Americans, inscrutable 'Orientals', cowardly Italians, tight-fisted Jews, venal Indians, thick-skulled 'Africans', jealous Spaniards, permissive Swedes and other varieties, all more or less unlovable. These crude simplifications, at times approaching the grotesque, are all widely disseminated, and if not exactly maintained with passion, linger among the untidied litter of collective national minds to have their imprecise effects. That they are all more or less wrong matters far less than that they are believed. Perhaps younger people are breaking free of them, with the experience of uniquely widespread and informal travel abroad, although G. K. Chesterton declared that he found nothing narrowed the mind like travelling.

Again we must notice the importance of national images as giving rise to national expectations. If we tend to behave according to our prevailing image of ourselves, we may well react to our perception of the image others hold of us, behaving in the way we gather they would consider likely or typical. To the French is widely attributed a rather prickly national pride. However hard it may be to demonstrate empirically, French sensitivity in this respect may be somewhat sharpened by the French awareness that other nations expect Frenchmen to reveal it in their dealings with them. There is of course a great deal of giving dogs bad names and hanging them about this aspect of national image-making. Thus the arrogant Englishman who said of Welsh nationalists that they did not have an inferiority complex but were simply inferior, probably provoked just the defensive reactions which would tend to confirm his prejudices.

There are, lastly, natural limits upon our capacity to know and understand each other, either in groups or as individuals. Reality of whatever kind can only be apprehended through the screen of our perceptive apparatus. There is no way of knowing how much 'objective reality' is distorted by this. The subjective nature of our perceptions is part of the objective reality of our being. As with men, so with nations. British people cannot 'know' the Chinese people in any ultimate sense whatever. They can know only their own perceptions of the Chinese. What they like, or admire, or hate, or fear are the impressions that the objectively existing Chinese impose on their sense perceptions. Indeed, the process is less direct still. Most of us obtain our impressions of the Chinese at second or third hand. If I form an opinion of Chinese political behaviour from a popular journalist's review of a book on the subject by a political scientist my mind has in fact developed impressions of impressions of impressions. This essentially subjective aspect of all knowledge makes the images men form of each other, whether as individuals or groups, at once limited, limiting and inescapable. Our reaction to the image formed in our minds of the benevolence or otherwise of another country is influenced, positively or negatively, by the image we hold of ourselves, of our country's qualities, motives and actions. In 'normal' conditions, where feelings of destructive self-hatred are largely absent or dormant, self-images will no doubt be generally favourable, and the benevolence of other groups towards us will be assessed mainly in accordance with how far the image we have of them is congenial to that which we have of ourselves. Thus for Britons, who entertain the notion that they are 'democratic', to understand that Norway is a 'democracy' will tend to evoke in them certain definite if not particularly intense feelings of friendliness and approval towards Norwegians as a national group. These reactions, while not much dwelt upon by British people at any particular time, by filtering through the political system have some influence, however diffuse and unarticulated, upon British policy towards Norway, not least by making it easy to maintain smooth relations at the diplomatic level. And we see in fact that Anglo-Norwegian relations are usually not merely correct but cordial. This is an instance of the effect of ideological congruence on international relations. Ideologies are, in addition to their roles noticed in the last chapter, bound up with the activity of image-making. It is certainly true that the prevailing cordiality of relations between Britain and Norway depends to a large degree upon a coincidence of some interests, as for example in the field of European security, and to the absence of any serious clash of interests. Still, the favourable prejudice created by reciprocal and approved democratic images plays its part in maintaining cordiality.

We see then that nations exist, though their constitutive elements vary in importance, in nature and in the way they combine or exclude each other in a given case. Nations exist as groups of human beings 'out there', in international society, but they do so by virtue of existing in the minds of those who comprise them. They remain the single most important legitimation of statehood. They engage the emotions and loyalty of their constituent peoples to a degree which continues to enable state governments, acting in the name of the national cause, to dispose of the lives, liberties and property of their subjects, in short to make as far as necessary absolute claims upon them. Although there are nations which are not, and may never be, embodied as states, and states which embody more than one nation, there is in the contemporary world a positive relationship between the intensity of a felt nationhood and the demand for statehood to give it expression. The politicizing of nations, in some of which the sense of nationhood is still very recent or only 'emergent', to the level of sovereign statehood, has been one of the most dynamic and dramatic features of international life in this century.

If the state may properly be regarded as in a sense the supreme instrumentality by which the nation makes its presence felt in the world, and pursues its purposes, the state itself disposes of various necessary means in acting on behalf of the nation. These means represent together the *power* of the state. It is to the role of state power in international society that we turn in the next chapter.

Note on the role of national images

That political image-making which is so potent a factor in the way peoples think about themselves and each other has for some two centuries and more been a special function of political satirists, especially in the cartoon. In the pages of *Punch* and similarly prestigious periodicals elsewhere the art attained the height of a dignified and almost semi-official commentary upon public affairs. There was bluff John Bull. Top-booted like Mr Pickwick and wearing a Union Jack waistcoat, he expressed a certain bafflement about the world, and postured in an undefined relationship with Britannia. She, armed with helmet, shield and trident, moved majestically through many a weekly political cartoon, and survived on the British coinage until decimalization in 1971. There was Germania, pictured generally as a rather overblown Rhine Maiden. Westward across that notable river dwelt Marianne, wearing her cap of liberty, and looking for the most part coquettish and charming. There was Uncle Sam, ruggedly masculine in cotton planter's broad brim, starry vest, striped pants and New England goatee. In south-eastern Europe lurked a dark-visaged, portly and rather helpless looking personage in a fez, over whose future there always hovered a Question. These and other giants and giantesses cavorted about the international system, exchanging diplomatic courtesies, snubs and occasional blows. They were, as H. G. Wells called them in *The Outline of History*, the tribal gods of the nineteenth century. Parallel with them, and equally reflecting the political cartoonist's often brilliant simplifications, was the international menagerie. This included the British Lion, whose tail it was such an impudence to twist, the Russian Bear, whose embrace was thought by so many to be the hug of death, the French Cockerel, game but vulnerable, and a number of Eagles. There was the German Eagle, brooding and unpredictable; the Russian Eagle, twin beaks averted inscrutably. There was the American Eagle, supposedly soaring in democratic freedom. There was the Austro-Hungarian Eagle, nervously facing two ways, its flappings increasingly ineffectual. These and other symbolic creatures snapped and snarled their way through the jungle of international politics. Fashions change, not least in political mythology. Both giants and beasts are rarely seen nowadays. Instead, the equally venerable tradition of depicting actual statesmen as representative of their countries dominates the political cartoon. Hence we see the United States in the shape of her president fighting in Vietnam, or a British prime minister grappling symbolically alone with the intractable problems of the national economy. However, one unprepossessing latter-day animal, of almost apocalyptic aspect, may be mentioned. This was the fascist Hyaena, sired by communist polemic out of anti-Western hostility, and supposedly skulking through the murk of East-West relations seeking to devour progressive people's democracies. It did not succeed. It probably hardly existed. But – political symbols and myths remain important because politics is important. The image-making cartoonist's shorthand continues to be a vital component in political communication.

5

The instrumentality of power

We will now discuss in a little more detail the struggle for existence
– *Charles Darwin*.

But Power has natural charms for those who desire its use. . . .
Whoever does not wish to render history incomprehensible by
departmentalizing it – political, economic, social – would perhaps
take the view that it is in essence a battle of dominant wills, fighting
in every way they can for the material which is common to everything they construct: the human labour force – *Bertrand de
Jouvenel*.

Political power grows out of the barrel of a gun – *Mao Tse-tung*.

Danger – states co-existing overhead! – *C. A. W. Manning*.

Power is the capacity of an individual or an organization to have
his or its way. It is rightly regarded therefore as an attribute, or
quality. But what matters is the fact that power is only functional
in terms of a *relationship* between the power-holder and some
other person, institution or thing upon which the power can be
exercised. Political power is a special aspect of the concept of
social power: it prevails in those special relations between individuals or groups which we suggested in chapter 1 may properly
be regarded as political. Until a relationship exists power remains
implicit or potential only. An obvious example not involving the
complexities of relations between persons would be a weight-
lifter. He only demonstrates his power not by asserting how strong
he is but by bringing himself into relation with a set of weights
which he wills, and perhaps manages, to lift. Power, then, although
quantitative, is an aspect of relationship. All power, to be real,
requires a context in which its realization can take place. Power

indeed represents the accomplishment of the purposes of a will, but is recognized in its effects.

In this chapter we will examine briefly five aspects of international power, drawing out some of the implications arising from our general theme as developed in the first three chapters. The aspects are: the relationship of power to security; the measuring of power; power as a net cost; the balance of power; and the varieties of power.

Security as a desired good

In their unremitting search for security, states seek to acquire, retain and enlarge national power, the principal means by which security may be attained. As we have seen, security represents the primary traditional function of the state, which exists to protect its citizens and their well-being. The problem of security is central to the predicament in which the members of international society find themselves. In order to do what they should for their citizens, states must do what they can to ensure their own survival. This responsibility imposes upon them an inescapable need to pursue security. We may recall here the analogy which treats security as a scarce commodity, one that is universally desired and for which there is competition, more or less fierce, between the members of international society. There are various methods by which states seek to 'buy' their sufficient share of the scarce commodity. Often several are combined. An important state is likely to try to buy security through investing relatively large amounts of the national resources of money and manpower into armaments and the creation and maintenance of effective armed forces. In a sense states 'choose' to do this. But equally states rarely feel free to do other than try to ensure that they are as strongly armed as practicable. What is 'practicable' in this connection clearly depends in the ultimate upon the willingness of the political community to accept the balance struck by their rulers between national defence and the things that have to be sacrificed to attain it; the guns and the butter. But nations do expect to be defended, by one means or another. Some idealists have argued that *if* states would agree to render themselves equally defenceless, and to devote the resources released from military investment to social purposes, causes of international conflict would tend to disappear, so making military defence unnecessary. All one can say is that this view has not convinced either the world's statesmen in general or their publics. There is a good deal of trust in international politics; there has to be for it to continue. But the nature of international society effectively inhibits the development of that absolute trust between states which would make universal and total disarmament rational and feasible. It is conceivable that international society may change in ways that increase international trust, which in turn would encourage further international change. But it seems to be the case, partly because statesmen and their peoples generally behave *as if it were the case,* that such change will be slow, uncertain and piecemeal. Implicitly, statesmen agree with each other that there is too much at stake for any of them to embark on hasty, dramatic and unilateral initiatives that *might* invoke a reciprocal goodwill, but might as readily – or more readily – tempt the ill-disposed to take an unscrupulous advantage. Statesmen cannot be sure, and they have a duty not to be rash. Each will recognize too that other statesmen can be no more certain of his intentions than he is of theirs. This is not because either he or they are bad men, or even merely unpredictable men. It is because they are in a competitive situation. In this situation, as statesmen, they have what all of them will invariably regard as an obligation upon them to seek first, not the Kingdom of Heaven, but the safety and prosperity of their own kingdoms. There are counsels of perfection, and there are political necessities. They may not be mutually exclusive, but are rarely merely coincident. It is such considerations which justify us in describing the members of international society and their policymakers as being locked in a predicament. They did not choose it: their chosen actions are taken in response to it.

Meanwhile, it is obvious that armaments produce wealth in the form of an increased Gross National Product derived from the wages of arms workers, servicemen, etc. and the profits of the arms manufacturers. But there remains a net cost: the investment in other forms of production foregone for the sake of the defence spending. The problem for any government is how to ensure that adequate amounts of security are purchased by this particular outlay. As in all fields of policy-making, this is ultimately a matter of political judgement.

The exercise of sound judgement is one of the most precious and most necessary skills of political leaders and their advisers alike.

In the matter of military power alone many factors have to be taken into account in the reaching and implementing of decisions. Some are essentially political, as for instance in the perception of external threat and the assessment of hostile intentions. The old formula is useful here:

$$\text{Perceived Threat} = \frac{\text{Understood Capacity}}{\text{Assumed Intentions}}$$

whereas, of course,

$$\text{Actual Threat} = \frac{\text{Real Capacity}}{\text{True Intentions.}}$$

The statesman cannot certainly know the latter, and has to plan on the basis of the former, and to rely on good information, loyal and intelligent advice and his own 'informed intuition' in trying to bring the former as close as possible to the latter. There are technical factors, such as the obsolescence rate of existing weapons, which itself is related to the innovating will and capability of potential enemies. If no one else is making surface-to-surface nuclear missiles one's own slow old aeroplanes may remain a credible defence, and even provide a credible retaliatory threat. The statesman has to judge the willingness of his own nation to bear the economic and – even harder to assess – the psychological burdens of a systematically modernizing military capacity, and to measure this against what his sources of information suggest is the corresponding willingness of such countries as he may have reason to believe are or may be likely to become hostile to his own. The warheads of Britain's celebrated nuclear deterrent armoury all point east when they are in operational position, not west or south.

Among the security options from which the statesman must choose are membership of an alliance system, or the attempted practice of 'non-alignment'. Here too the choice is not made in a vacuum, but is influenced by all kinds of pressure, arising from the perceived political sympathies and antipathies of important sectors of opinion in the statesman's own nation, the standing that nation enjoys in the eyes of other nations as a potential ally, the degree of possible danger to it deriving from the disapproval or resentment of countries against which the alliance is defensively directed, and not least the pressure that arises from the statesman's own temperament and prejudices. There was, for instance, a good deal of personal distaste and moral disapproval on Pandit Nehru's part of the postures adopted by both sides during the developing East-West cold war, as well as a responsible consultation of Indian national interests, wrapped up in the Indian prime minister's decision after 1947 to pursue a policy of non-alignment. And, as the Indian experience shows, policies proclaimed on a basis of high principle may have to be radically modified in the light of political and military realities.

We saw something in chapter 3 of the role of non-alignment in providing a motive for great powers to seek to augment their influence and prestige by various forms of aid, economic, diplomatic and often military, offered to non-aligned countries, many of which have been among the poorer and weaker states of the world. The facts of power politics are on the whole highly compelling. It was a fact that a number of these countries, however free from East-West cold war entanglements they wished to remain, found themselves obliged to resort to one side or the other for the help they needed to pursue their own purposes in international politics. In some cases they were constrained to accept aid they were in no position to decline. Great powers, in their relations with some would-be non-aligned smaller states, have been known to behave a little like the literary patron in Dr Johnson's famous rejoinder to Lord Chesterfield, and to 'encumber [them] with help'. In the case of Egypt, noticed earlier, it is perhaps not too fanciful a judgement to suspect that both the late President Nasser and his successor, in receiving massive Soviet military aid in their confrontation with Israel, gave more hostages to political fortune than either their ideological prejudices or their conception of the long-term interests of Egypt would by themselves have led them to wish. It would clearly be naïve to expect foreign aid to be genuinely disinterested; the nature of international society ensures that it will not be. In very large part both the giving and the receiving of such help derives from the urgent and unrelenting need to seek for security in a world of power politics.

Linked with the analogy which regards security as a scarce commodity is the notion of states as being either net producers or net consumers of security. The same state may, of course, be each in turn at different epochs. Broadly speaking, we may expect to find a positive correlation between the size and importance of a state and its capacity to act, for most of the time, as a net producer of security. From the proclamation of the Truman Doctrine in 1947, which offered assistance to any state resisting communist subjugation or subversion, at least to the early 1970s, the United States may properly be regarded as the major producer of security in the Western world, acting in this regard as much as the 'arsenal of democracy' as she had done during the second world war. In the NATO and Warsaw Pact alliance systems, the members of each contribute, according to their capacities, to a general pool of mutual security which is deemed, in each case, to guarantee the members of either multilateral alliance against threats from the other. It was the role of non-communist European countries in the immediate postwar years as net consumers of security which motivated the American policy of containment. Greece and Turkey were particularly regarded as vulnerable to Soviet pressure, and the United Kingdom, wearied, impoverished and bent on social change at home, was neither able nor willing to act as the producer of Greek and Turkish security, relinquishing the responsibility with some relief, whatever the cost in diminished international prestige may have been, for the great trans-Atlantic wartime ally to take it up.

We see, then, that security is a fundamental justification of state power. As the state exists in part to protect its citizens from each other by means of internal order,[1] so it must seek to protect them from threats to their safety from without. Except for the greatest powers this function is less and less dischargeable on the basis of unilateral national forces. Alliances tend to be entered into with a good deal of caution, even reluctance, for they represent a substantial constraint upon effective sovereignty more or less in direct proportion to their real effectiveness. But the needs of security have overridden such misgivings. Even France, which withdrew from the military obligations of NATO, on the grounds that her sovereignty was being unacceptably compromised by the defence structure that had been developed, remained within the protection of the alliance, since any conceivable Soviet initiative against France, lying in the heart of the NATO system, would have posed an immediate threat to the other partners. The development

---

[1] It was the absence of such internal order, provided by a stable government, which Thomas Hobbes in a famous phrase declared made the lives of men 'solitary, poore, nasty, brutish and short'.

of multilateral alliance systems among those countries which possessed, and by possessing were most directly threatened by,
nuclear weapons, is an aspect of that process of transformation of
the sovereign state from a territorial entity which could be defended at its borders to one which was irresistibly penetrable. This
process began with the development of effective manned air-
power, and reached its decisive phase when such air-power was
supplemented and then largely superseded, at least as between the
superpowers, by the existence of unmanned nuclear weapons, in
operational readiness and poised for their deadly flight. The
'shell-back state', on this conception, became the 'soft-centre
state'.[2] For the greater part of the nuclear epoch the only effective
defence was regarded as a real retaliatory response capability in
kind. At the time of writing it remains to be seen whether the
development of efficient anti-ballistic missile systems (ABMS) will
prove so successful as to restore a genuine frontier defensibility of
the states possessing them. A major inhibiting factor in their rapid
evolution has been their appalling expense, which has occasioned
hesitations on the part of the superpowers themselves. Another
possibility, of which some hopeful signs emerged in the 1960s,
has been that of actual strategic arms limitation by international
agreement. This agreeable prospect was presaged by the 1963
Test Ban Treaty; the so-called 'Nuclear Clean Air Bill'. This was,
as far as it went, a real achievement, not least in its psychological
effects. Its principal limitation was that only those nuclear powers
signed it whose programmes of tests in the earth's atmosphere were
already complete. However, the fact of the agreement may have
had some constraining effect elsewhere. By the early 1970s the
two superpowers were conferring with some earnestness and to
some purpose on proposals to limit nuclear proliferation, and to
reduce or halt their own bilateral arms race, on the ground that
enough was enough, and that there should be sought and might be
found a more rational way of achieving mutual security than by
expensively building up bigger and bigger potential responses to
greater and greater threats.[3] On the other hand, the primacy of

[2] See J. Herz, *International Politics in the Nuclear Age*, Columbia U.P., New
York, 1959.
[3] The Strategic Arms Limitation Agreement of 1971 between the United
States and the Soviet Union, together with undertakings to cooperate in space
ventures and other matters, signed in Moscow by President Nixon and Mr
Brezhnev, General Secretary of the CPSU, was generally held to represent an

interests prevails. This can always be urged, in theory, against what might be regarded as a common interest in world peace. We cannot expect, and should not expect, either the Soviet Union or the United States to take steps which might actually jeopardize their respective national interests. Among these must remain their own security. High among their policy priorities also comes the security of their partners and clients.

On the other hand, there has clearly been a marked change in the complexion and style of relations between the two superpowers since the days when, as Anatol Rapoport pointed out,[4] the United States saw herself principally as the defender of a legitimate world order against a communist adversary both implacable and ubiquitous, so that a social revolution anywhere could be seen as a challenge to American interests. From the late 1960s onwards those interests came to be regarded by American policy-makers in a less rigorously ideological light, leading to the suggestion in some quarters that world politics was in process of developing a renewed phase of a Concert of the Powers, in which the superpowers particularly would conduct their affairs and attend to their interests in the context of a relatively stable international order acceptable to both, and with much less emphasis on self-righteous assertions of doctrinal motives and justifications. We shall see.

We come now to one other aspect of security in relation to power. By the closing stages of the first world war *collective security* had come to seem to many intelligent and well-meaning men, among them President Woodrow Wilson, to be a preferable, indeed necessary, alternative to the discredited *balance of power*. The war was understood by many of them to have been an outcome of 'balance of power politics'. In a sense, of course, this was clearly true. The balance of power was an acknowledged feature of international politics before 1914, and the war had in fact taken place. But these idealists came to persuade themselves that the

important further stage in the process of *détente*. Russian authorities declared that the agreement helped to meet the most urgent current need to eliminate the risk of thermo-nuclear war. Mr Nixon, in a broadcast in Moscow, admitted on his part that as great powers, the two countries would 'be competitors, but need not be enemies'. This significant admission reflects the realities of power politics, while giving some hope for enhanced restraint in its exercise. In June 1973 Mr Brezhnev, visiting the United States, actually declared the cold war to be over.

[4] In his excellent introduction to an abridgment of Clausewitz's *Vom Kreige* (*On War*), published by Pelican Books, London, 1968.

balance of power could somehow be dispensed with; that it was a *chosen* method of conducting international relations, rather than an inescapable feature of an international order comprising competitive sovereignties, which clear-headed practitioners had simply recognized as being in operation. The principle of collective security was institutionalized in the League of Nations, a device for maintaining international peace which owed much of its inspiration to the vision of President Wilson himself.

Collective security as a way of ordering the society of states was based on four premises. First, there was the assumption that international *aggression* would be equally clearly defined in theory and identified in practice by all the states in the collective security system. Second, it was assumed that aggression by any state would be equally repugnant to and regarded as equally contrary to the legitimate interests of all these other states. Third, and following directly from the second, it was assumed that all members of the collective security system would prove equally willing to fulfil their pledges to take all necessary action, including if need be the waging of war, to check and punish an aggressor state. Fourth, there was an implicitly assumed broad equivalence of power among the members of the system, whereby each could contribute effectively to any necessary economic or military sanctions against an aggressor.

In practice none of these premises proved to be well-founded. To take the last first, the disparity of power between members of the League was so great that some remained net consumers rather than producers of security, and then found the commodity in fatally short supply when the crisis came. (Both China and Abyssinia were members of the League of Nations.) Japan and Italy, both members of the League, declined to interpret their actions against China and Abyssinia respectively as aggression. Other League members discovered that their own economic and political interests did not permit them to pursue vigorous sanctions against the states whose actions were declared by a majority of the members to be aggressive. It is easy now to say that the League failed because its conception did not sufficiently take account of the realities of international politics. But it did achieve a few successes, and helped to motivate a second attempt, at the end of the second world war, to institutionalize a means of maintaining international peace and security. We discuss the role of the United Nations in chapter 8. Here we may just notice that the United Nations Organization differed significantly from the League. Its comprehensive worldwide membership made it a much more authoritative body. Its structure reflected realistically the effects of the wide disparity of power among its members. It aroused more sober hopes, and on the whole has probably caused less acute disappointments. But it did consciously embody the notion of collective security. Indeed the phrase has retained enough of its normative colour to be applied freely to almost any defensive alliance system, which is deemed to acquire a measure of extra international respectability by being called a system of collective security: the term has been deliberately applied both to NATO and the Warsaw Pact.

Ultimately, the difficulty about the doctrine of collective security in its pure form is that if it were practicable it would hardly be necessary. The whole notion presupposes a degree of mutual benevolence among states sufficient to enable them to agree to act together *disinterestedly* to deter or punish an aggressor, and deprive him of the fruits of his aggression. But if states were as benevolent and disinterested as that it seems very unlikely that any one of them would commit aggression in the first place. It is arguable that states have a duty not to put the interest of another state before their own. Generosity between states, on this view, is always, and necessarily, an outcome of the calculation of advantage to the state acting generously. It is not the duty of a statesman to deploy national resources in acts of merely disinterested charity, for he manages them as in effect a trustee, acting on behalf of a political community. Even the lend-lease arrangements made by the United States in favour of Britain in wartime, which Winston Churchill called 'the most unsordid act in history', and the implementation of the Marshall Plan after that war, however much the beneficiaries gained by them, are properly to be seen as in the ultimate interest of the United States, which had no desire to be confronted with a possible Nazi victory or a possible communization of Europe. So far as the pure doctrine of collective security is concerned, the very factor of self-regard at the expense of others which unavoidably characterizes much of the behaviour of states, ensures that it must remain if in principle desirable in practice unattainable. At the level of practical international politics, the notion retains value as conferring a certain air of moral propriety – even excellence – on institutional arrangements which can be seen to make some contribution, in their deterrent effects, to international order.

Measuring power

In considering the measurement of international power we need to remind ourselves once more that power is an aspect of relationship. There is no meaning in power as an absolute quantity. What matters is to *measure power at the margin*. Let us, by way of example, imagine a total aggregate of the instruments of military power at the disposal of the United States: her aircraft, warships, guns, rockets, nuclear warheads, armoured vehicles, etc. and add to them her total number of operational service personnel. This vast assembly of military units amounts, let us assume, to a factor of 20. A similar aggregation of the items of military capacity in the Soviet Union amounts, let us say, to a factor of 17. Clearly the *real* military power of the United States *vis-à-vis* the Soviet Union is a factor not of 20 but of 3. And this almost absurdly simple calculation does not allow for the intangible elements of political will, service morale, strategic judgement and tactical skill. All kinds of considerations affect the real – and realizable – power of a state in the given complexion of international politics at any particular juncture. It would be misleading to assume that the big battalions are necessarily or merely arithmetically so much the more powerful than smaller ones. It could be argued that unusable power may as well not exist. Indeed, such power may well represent a net subtraction from the well-being of the state that possesses it, since it implies the foregoing of other goods, which have been sacrificed in the effort to acquire it. For a state to sustain a high opportunity cost for the sake of possessing an extensive military establishment which in the existing circumstances cannot be usefully deployed on behalf of rational purposes to the advantage of the state represents a real policy failure. We have been speaking of military capacity because it provides a simple example of the relativity of power. But the same principle applies in regard to other forms of power. We saw in chapter 3 some of the effects of the great disparity of power in the international system. The implication was evident there that even economic power, for instance, cannot simply be quantified and left at that. The economic power of a large neighbouring state may be so resented by a weak state, and have such political consequences inside the weak state, that it may seriously interfere with the pursuit of the large state's policy towards the weak one, proving an actual policy hindrance instead of support.

In attempting to measure a state's power, then, we have to try to allow for the effects of all kinds of variables which influence the freedom a state enjoys in its exercise, and thus determine the real power of the state in distinction to its ostensible power. A close analogy may be made with the changing real value of money over time as against its denominational value. We should always remember that a particular situation may confer a peculiar strength on the weak and impose a peculiar impotence upon the strong. For actual power is never an abstract thing, but is always determined by the context in which its possessors find themselves.

The costs of power

We have already seen that power, however much its use may bring about desired results, also incurs a net cost. International theory tends to assume, as a basis for analysis, that states seek to maximize their power, rather as elementary economic theory assumes for the same purpose that firms seek to maximize their profits. But the amount and kind of power a state needs and therefore seeks depend upon the particular aspect of national well-being for which the power is required. In some circumstances states will be driven to devote comparatively enormous resources to military demands. Britain 'standing alone' in 1940 against Germany and Italy began the process of maximizing the amount of wealth and productive effort she could devote to the war effort, until in the later stages of the conflict some 45 per cent of British GNP was directly linked to it. In other circumstances a state will find itself with the desire and the opportunity to invest heavily in social provision of various kinds, which Britain largely did when that war was over. Power, we must repeat, is not only an instrument for attaining given purposes. It is also a resource, for the increase of which other resources have to be expended. Power always involves a cost. In this respect power itself can be looked at as a commodity, the production of which calls for an outlay of national energy, and the foregoing of other things citizens may wish to possess. States in effect 'buy' by this means the power they desire. By the same token, states vary not only in their actual power, both in the number of power components they hold and in their liberty to deploy them, but also in their *need* for power. A small state on good terms with a powerful neighbour, and firmly protected by it from any threat of external interference, will not need to devote national effort to acquiring the military capacity it potentially could. When Costa Rica in 1948 unilaterally disbanded her army she could do so in safety because as a member of the Organization of American States, and enjoying the traditional protective effect of the Monroe Doctrine proclaimed by the United States, she was amply secure without one. Thus we see that states need different amounts and kinds of power at different times.

International politics being never static, statesmen have to try to keep in balance the degree of power their states need to fulfil their purposes and the costs such power will entail. Great states obviously enjoy more power than small ones: this is what makes them great states. But because they are great states they need to maintain a corresponding degree of power. It is a matter of observation that prestige attaches to great power status. Historically great powers have been reluctant to descend to a lower rank in the hierarchy of international society.[5] Moreover, the stability of international order tends to require that states do not oscillate rapidly in their power ranking. The sudden overthrow of a great power has a highly disturbing and transforming effect on international politics, as much as does the rapid rise of a new great power. While, for instance, the elimination of the great power status of the Third Reich in 1945 by conquest was generally welcomed throughout Europe and the world, it had profound effects, among the most far-reaching being the concentration of major power in the hands of superpowers, one completely and one partly extra-European. A pattern of power based on the preeminence of the principal states of Europe in world affairs, already in marked transition before 1939, was decisively changed. In political terms, this was one of the greatest costs borne by Europe for the attempt of a leading European Power – Nazi Germany – to create a European New Order under its leadership.

[5] Both France and Britain, in their different ways, illustrated from 1945 onwards the difficulties ex-great powers have in adjusting to a lesser standing in the world. Both, according to their differing styles, made a relatively successful adjustment. The role of Charles de Gaulle in infusing a new national confidence into the French people, who had found defeat in war bitter, postwar decolonization hard, and domestic political stability elusive, can hardly be overstated.

All states need some power. Some states need a great deal of power, if they have a high prestige stake in international society. Power can be gambled away, as Hitler gambled it. It can be wisely husbanded by political leaders, or recklessly used up. But its acquisition and retention always represents a major charge upon the resources, both psychological and material, of any national community.

The balance of power

We have already touched upon the balance of power as it was generally regarded by the idealists who sought to create after the first world war a viable system of collective security in its place. We must now look a little more closely at the notion and the fact.

Historically, as we noticed earlier in this book, the balance of power has been a prevalent feature throughout the whole period during which the collective life of mankind has been characterized by a multiplicity of autonomous political units. In ancient Greece it was a fact, about which even the speculative Greeks do not seem to have consciously reflected. By the beginning of the eighteenth century it had been fully conceptualized, and erected into a norm of international politics. The European state system was then almost wholly dynastic, and sovereigns generally acknowledged the principle of the balance of power as a common interest. Even when a state was eliminated, as was Poland at the great partitions, it was sacrificed in order that the balance of power could be maintained among its destroyers, in this case Austria, Prussia and Russia. However, it may be necessary to stress once more that although rulers may deliberately seek to maintain a balance of power, and shape their policies with its requirements consciously in view, they do not originally choose it: they find themselves in a situation which implies it. This must be so wherever there are rival or competitive sovereignties. Bearing this in mind we will probably incline to the opinion that the whole moralistic attack on the balance of power was misconceived. States could not choose to pursue balance of power policies, because that was the position they were in. All they could do, meanwhile, was to try to transcend their position, and develop an alternative mechanism for carrying on international politics. The mechanism tried was collective security.

In a partial form it still has political and institutional relevance in the working of the international system. But it clearly has not superseded the balance of power. In fact, the United Nations has provided an arena in which balance of power politics is carried on.

There are, however, different forms of the balance of power. A number of simple models can be outlined by way of illustration. One great state may be approximately balanced by an alliance of several lesser states, which together produce a rough equivalence of power (Fig. 6).

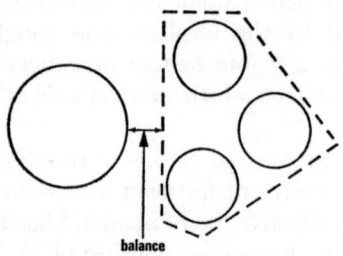

Fig. 6. A one and many-type balance

Allied groups, the members of each group being roughly comparable to each other, may be in balance (Fig. 7).

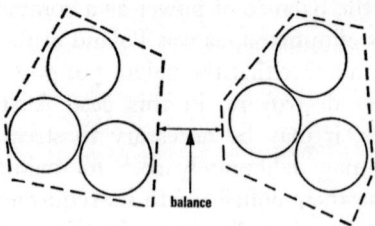

Fig. 7. A balance between opposed groups of comparable powers

A 'chandelier' type of balance may exist (Fig. 8). Here states of comparable power confront each other, their weapons 'turned impartially in all directions'. The great power 'concerts' of the eighteenth and nineteenth centuries were very broadly of this type. Alliances which are formed in the maintenance of this kind of balance tend to be comparatively short-lived, and not to be coloured by strong ideological congruences among the allies or ideological cleavages with the states against which alliances are formed.

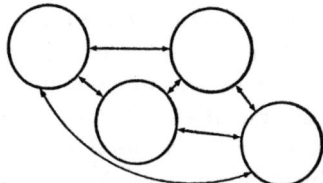

Fig. 8. A chandelier-type balance

A balancing state may sometimes manifest itself – a power putting its weight now on one side, now on another, to prevent either from achieving a decisive hegemony (Fig. 9). Widely regarded as the classic role of Britain during the period of European dominance in the world, the balancer may conceivably emerge in the future as one of the three powers, America, China and Russia.

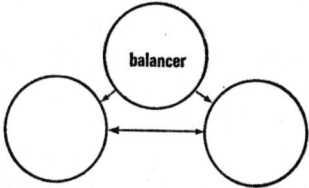

Fig. 9. The role of the balancer

We have seen already that the acute phase of the cold war, now past, reflected another form of power balance, of which the Peloponnesian war was an historic early example: the bipolar balance (Fig. 10).[6]

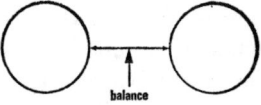

Fig. 10. A bipolar balance between great powers

[6] A mathematician friend pointed out to me the tautology involved in 'bipolar'. How many *poles* can there be? But 'a polar balance of power' might give rise to misunderstanding, and the practice of statesmen and commentators over more than twenty years perhaps sanctions the usage. So I let it stand.

The post-1945 balance of power was not anticipated – at least in their institutional arrangements – by the devisers of the United Nations Charter. It seems fair to say that general peace, as distinct from general war, allowing so to speak for the fighting of local and limited wars, has been maintained since the second world war by an effective power balance between two great defence systems, East and West, and not by the functioning of anything closely approaching a global system of collective security. The nearest thing to a collective security operation since 1945 has been the Korean war, in which North Korean 'aggressors' were opposed by forces contributed by members of the United Nations acting under the United Nations Charter. Essentially, however, this conflict was a limited war between the communist and free worlds, in which the latter fought to prevent an extension of communist power into South Korea, across a line where the two 'worlds' touched.

A general system of collective security, we have suggested, is likely to remain unworkable. Partly this is because the conception involves the fundamental contradiction of regarding all the member states as simultaneously potential aggressors and enemies of aggression, thus making the system either impracticable or unnecessary. Partly it is because collective security implies ultimately some form of world authority, capable of enforcing its will on any or all member states. It is a proposition of this book that such a world order remains a very remote possibility. In these circumstances the members of international society continue to be involved in a security dilemma. The twin horns of it are the prospect of states surrendering their freedom when challenged, and of being prepared to face the risks and loss involved in trying to defend it. What relieves the sharpness of the dilemma is the existence of an effective balance of power. There may be argument about whether a bipolar balance of power in the world is more or less stable than other forms. What matters is that a balance should exist, and function, whether or not it is consciously tended. In modern conditions the world balance is in fact examined very deliberately, and ways of making it surer are actively canvassed. The balance at its nuclear level may be called a 'mere balance of terror' by those who desire something different to keep the world relatively safe, whether for 'democracy' or other forms of political order. But mankind have long lost their nuclear innocence, and the world is what it is. If the critics wish their disapproval to carry weight it is incumbent upon them to produce a workable alternative. Collective security, on the old idealistic basis, evidently will not do. Meanwhile a balance of power is essential to the perpetuation of such peace and stability as exist, and the present one remains, after all, 'the best balance of power we have'.

Varieties of state power

It is worth turning our attention to some of the varieties of power if only because it will remind us that military power, probably the most easily recognized and understood form of power, by no means stands alone, and in the day to day life of political communities in their relations with each other is not generally the most important, only, when it is invoked, the most dramatic.

If we take *political power* itself, and understand by it the overall capacity of a state to organize its other forms of power in order to have its will in the world, we shall see that effective political power is closely bound up with the notion of legitimacy; the imputed right of policy-makers to direct the activity of their states towards the attainment of accepted national goals.[7] Political power, so conceived, may be considerable or insignificant, depending on the resources and standing of the state in international society, and on how firmly based is the policy-makers' mandate. Power is never unlimited in practice, as dictators and absolutist rulers could attest. In particular situations, as we have seen, even the greatest states may be effectually prevented from accomplishing desired purposes. Dearly would the American leadership during the two decades after 1949 have liked to encompass the elimination or transformation of the communist regime in China, for example. There simply was no way open to American power-holders, even when their domestic support for the objective was most evident and vocal, to do this by any means which would not have entailed unacceptable – and largely incalculable – political risks. On the other hand even comparatively minor powers, given skilful leadership, together with luck in the conjuncture of international affairs, may be able to make a considerable impact on international politics in ways that

[7] See note on legitimacy at the end of this chapter.

serve their interests. The defiance of the United States by revolutionary Cuba was successful. The Swiss, the Swedes, the Icelanders, the Yugoslavs, to name but four nations, have all fulfilled their limited international roles during the last quarter century with a good deal of effectual flair.

Economic power, like other forms of power, is really an aspect of political power, in that it represents the availability of economic resources for use on behalf of policy. We saw in chapter 3 some of the consequences following from the great disparity of economic power among the members of international society, including the fact that in the economically interdependent modern world none of the major features of economic activity – boom, recession, inflation, innovation, automation, etc. – can develop in any important country without affecting very many other countries. We will have noticed too the capacity of industrialized states to stage spectacular recoveries even after total defeat in war, assisted it may be by their victors, who in turn suffer from the effects of economic crises. The American humorist Art Buchwald was so struck by this phenomenon that he suggested that the easiest way for the Americans and the British to resolve their economic problems, particularly in relation to the balance of payments and the strength of their currencies, was to arrange to be defeated in war by the Russians, who would then presumably set them on the way to recovery and prosperity, while ensuring for themselves obstinate problems concerning productivity and the international role of the rouble!

All countries seek prosperity. However, the nature of international economic relations is such that it is often hard for this to be attained by one country except at the expense of another. The application, wherever possible, of the device of *comparative advantage* would seem at first sight to offer a rational way through this difficulty. By this means each country concentrates on a range of commodities it is best fitted to produce, exchanging them on the most favourable terms for the goods they need which happen to be most efficiently produced by other countries. To some extent this actually happens, but does not bring greatly or rapidly increased prosperity to primary producers, who find it hard to sell their products in the markets of producers of manufactured goods at a margin of profit which enables them to satisfy the home demand for the manufactured goods. So, as we saw in chapter 3, most of these primary producers seek strenuously to industrialize, thereby spreading still further the ill effects, as well as the good effects, of that kind of economic development, at the same time coming into direct competition with the manufacturing countries who are meanwhile striving to induce each other's populations to buy imported manufactures in preference to home products, driving home producers to demand import restrictions of various kinds; a demand governments would often like to accede to in order to improve the national balance of payments. 'We must have', say manufacturers in effect, 'a high domestic demand in order to lay down the broad productive base on which increased exports can be raised.' But stimulating home demand by restricting imports tends to provoke retaliatory restrictions elsewhere, and so inhibits the very increase of exports which governments urge manufacturers to bring about.

Ultimately difficulties of this kind derive from the nature of international society itself. States are obliged to seek their own advantage in order to flourish. National economies must engage in international competition. Even the growth of regional economic communities seems likely chiefly to lift the problems of multi-national economic relations to an inter-regional level in which they may prove equally intractable. Much international economic activity *is* cooperative. But to wish that economic power should operate throughout the world on a basis purely of cooperation is to invoke in the international sphere the famous old Bolshevik formula, 'From each according to his capacity; to each according to his need'. This has the merit of epigrammatic elegance. As a world policy, however, it represents an internationalist utopianism far removed from the facts of power. While communist regimes have been comprehensive economic regulators all along, it is also true that both national economies and their interactions have been increasingly regulated by governments and their agencies throughout the non-communist world.

Of this willingness to try to structure international economic relations for the general benefit of mankind the limited but not imperceptible achievements of GATT, the General Agreement on Tariffs and Trade, may stand as the symbol. On the other hand, the three UNCTADs so far held – the United Nations Conferences on Trade and Development – have proved comparatively negative and disappointing, particularly the last, held in 1972.[8] Urgent needs were indeed sturdily canvassed. Ways of meeting them eluded agreement. Many went empty away.

The direct use of economic power as a constraining or punitive instrument may be briefly mentioned. In wartime states use every military means at their command to crush their enemies' will and capacity to resist by inflicting damage on their economy. It is noteworthy how much economic destruction many countries have sustained before the determination to fight gives way to a willingness to surrender. The use of economic power alone to constrain or punish states has in general proved even less successful where it has been tried. The threat of economic sanctions to deter aggression and their imposition to punish the aggressor were envisaged by the proponents of collective security under first the League of Nations and later the United Nations. The record is not impressive. Fascist Italy completed the conquest of Abyssinia despite the partial and half-hearted sanctions imposed by League members in 1935. In Rhodesia the regime which illegally declared independence unilaterally in 1965 was not overthrown or seriously weakened by sanctions which were at first very generally applied by members of the United Nations. The trouble with the attempted use of economic power in this way is that there is no feasible method of ensuring that countries formally obliged under the Charter to impose sanctions will in practice bear the loss and inconvenience which the sanctions entail for them. It is of the nature of international obligations that their enforceability is in general limited. That does not make them any less obligatory. But it does have important and decisive political consequences. The limited experience which international society has had of the use of economic power in the form of sanctions does not encourage us to expect that they will prove particularly efficacious in the future.

In a world-famous sentence Clausewitz declared that war was 'the carrying on of policy by other means', other, that is, than politics and diplomacy. In later chapters we shall examine certain implications of this saying which arise in the era of nuclear weaponry.

---

[8] Even the declared aims of the UNCTADs apparently do not command universal support. It was waspishly suggested at the conclusion of the third UNCTAD that the conference was a device whereby 'the poor could apply their thumbs to the jugulars of the rich'.

Here it reminds us that *military power*, no less than economic power, is intimately bound up with political decision-making. Military power represents the capacity of a state to pursue its objectives by the exercise, or the threat, of armed and organized violence in international society. It also, as we shall see, symbolizes the *will* of the state to act in this manner.

The role of the military establishment of a state, which embodies that state's military power, can be briefly summarized under six heads.

First, it is the traditional (and by no means superseded) instrument by which the state defends its territory and citizens from armed attack. It may do this unilaterally, or, as within NATO and the Warsaw Pact for instance, in coordination with forces of other states with which it is linked in an alliance system.

Second, armed forces help as necessary in the maintenance of internal order. The operations of the army in Ulster are a British example. Generally speaking, this function of the military role is the one most reluctantly invoked by governments and least welcome to service personnel. But its importance is often crucial.

Third, there is that aspect of 'aid to the civil power' which takes the form of rendering assistance in dealing with natural disasters or industrial accidents, etc. The resources and training of the military in such circumstances often prove extremely valuable. Where industrial unrest seriously threatens essential communications or distributive services the military may be called in to maintain them. But this is a delicate task, and where governments are sensitive to public pressure it is called for as rarely as possible. In some countries, for instance communist China, armed forces themselves perform a major industrial task, acting as worker-soldiers, and building roads, peasants' cooperatives, citizen's housing and so forth. This role is normally not acceptable or appropriate in countries where organized and legal trade unionism acts to protect the rights of civilian workers.

Fourth, a limited role is discharged by the national forces of certain states in the field of international peace-keeping under the aegis of the United Nations. Operations of this kind have taken place since 1946 in Palestine, Cyprus, Congo (Kinshasa), West Irian, Kashmir and the border between North and South Korea. Limitations on the acceptability of particular national units for peace-keeping purposes arise mainly from the political posture of the country concerned. In general the forces of non-aligned states have most easily been able to perform useful service in this connection, and Irish, Swedish, Ethiopian and Indian troops, for example, have carried out a policing function under the United Nations Secretariat with considerable success and aplomb.

Fifth, armed forces indicate the national will. Whatever prudential or even moral considerations govern their actual deployment in any given case, there is an implicit assumption that when a state invests costly resources in a military establishment it intends to make appropriate use of it. For most countries, most of the time, the military establishment acts as a deterrent capability, but its operational effectiveness significantly reflects the national will. We may draw an analogy here with the mutual threat display of many species of animals. Such threats, in so far as they deter attack, economize force, and possess biological advantage. Armed forces in their visible manifestations serve a double function, in fact, quite apart from actual military operations. They pose a threat to a potential foe; they offer a reassurance to the home community. Some countries, by reason of history, tradition, political style and perhaps psychological vulnerability, rely on the demonstration of national will much more openly than others. The Soviet authorities make use of their military resources in this way with a conspicuousness that a fastidious observer might even regard as blatant. Every anniversary of the October Revolution Red Square thunders with the almost interminable rumble of an immense procession of military hardware, diversified with formations of well-drilled human beings. The West, perhaps more confident, perhaps more fundamentally stable, seems not to need to rely so openly or so often on the effects of such sombre theatricalities. Certainly Trafalgar Square in London provides the scene for almost every conceivable public demonstration except that of British military preparedness! Whether this is evidence of an alleged British tendency to play things down is hard to say. His late and biblical majesty, King Ahab, a monarch not without wit, reproved his enemy for boasting while still putting his armour on, instead of waiting to boast when, victorious, he was taking it off. What to Ahab seems to have been pretentious folly, to the British might seem just bad form. However, whenever civilians are entertained at some military Open Day or other, and treated to the display of effective weaponry in action, the purpose served is not merely a bit of extra training, useful though that may be, but the achievement of reassurance, for both military personnel and spectators alike. The former can feel they know their job and do it with efficiency and zest. The latter can feel the safer. Both groups gain psychologically from the letting off of these purposeful fireworks. To reassurance is closely linked the question of morale. Will does not operate in a vacuum but in a context. Challenges to the national will to defend interests and meet obligations are always liable to arise. Some flexing of the psychological muscles, so to speak, serves to keep the will fit and hard. This too is a motive for the occasional public demonstration of the military's capacity to act as it is designed to do. There is also the hope in the minds of statesmen that it may induce a certain thoughtfulness on the part of potential enemies.

Sixth, armed forces symbolize the identity, cohesion and sovereignty of the political community to which they belong. Costa Rica cannot easily be shown to have enhanced her national standing by her unilateral disarmament. National forces express visibly the right of the nation to stake claims upon the attention and respect of international society. Of course they are not alone in this. To a great extent the niceties of diplomatic protocol do the same, and diplomats insist, quite rationally, on how valuable such niceties are in helping the international system to function more or less smoothly. Servicemen tend to be strong traditionalists. Traditions are kept green mainly by the use of symbols, visual, auditory and behavioural. We need only notice how resistant soldiers have been in Britain, however unshakable their general loyalty, to changes in the nomenclature and structure of ancient military units, hallowed by many associations and a long continuity of communal experience. And it is evident too how keenly the authorities set about creating viable new symbols in place of those dicarded for administrative or economic reasons. No one would be better pleased than the British minister of defence, for instance, to know that soldiers serving in the comparatively new Royal Regiment of Wales felt about it as proudly as they did about the older units merged to create it. Even the sovereign pontiff, as we noticed earlier, enjoys titular command of an armed force. In this case it is almost wholly symbolic. 'How many divisions does the pope have?' asked Stalin once, jeeringly. He thereby missed the point. Admittedly he had another point, and a vital one. Power is our capacity to cause others to behave as we wish. In international society a traditional and fundamental aspect of power has been the possession of effective armed force. On this ground Stalin's armies counted and the Papal Guard did not. On the other hand, moral influence is also an important factor of power, and in this respect the papal presence in the world will widely be regarded as significant. Even the Christian Church has had ascribed to it the splendid biblical phrase, 'terrible as an army with banners'.[9] The pope's freedom of action is symbolized by his temporal sovereignty, which in turn is symbolized by his ceremonial troops. Political autonomy, where it prevails, tends to be passionately valued, and the military establishment remains a prestigious expression of it. So the People's Republic of China has her national forces, nearly three million strong, not counting a civilian militia claimed by her government to number some two hundred million,[10] and the 'Serene Republic' of San Marino has her standing army of some seventy-eight, which on mobilization goes well into three figures.[11] So Luxembourg in 1914 and again in 1940 opposed the German thrust gallantly if unavailingly with her national forces of some two hundred and fifty men. (Her current contribution to the strength of NATO is more than double that figure.) So the British have laid up regimental colours and other trophies with grateful pride in garrison churches up and down the land. We saw in chapter 4 that many things go towards the definition of a nation. Not least among them is the symbol of the nation's armed might. This need not be 'militarism'. The British, for instance, have perhaps been one of the least militaristic peoples ever to have enjoyed the status of a great power, yet few nations have more affectionately cherished the symbols which express the national defensibility. The charming and intelligent Margaret Schlegel, in

[9] By the late C. S. Lewis, in *The Screwtape Letters*, Geoffrey Bles, London, 1942.

[10] See *The Military Balance*, published and up-dated annually by The Institute for Strategic Studies; a most useful source.

[11] In August 1944 the German Army in Italy, retreating from the British Eighth Army, violated San Marino's neutrality, despite a number of notice boards along the frontier announcing in three languages, 'Neutral – keep out'. San Marino protested, mobilized and declared war on the Third Reich. Field-Marshal Kesselring's forces continued to advance into Sammarinese territory, and the following day a German platoon captured San Marino's army.

E. M. Forster's *Howards End*, probably represented British attitudes fairly, half-German as she was, in hating war but 'rather liking soldiers'.

We have discussed the sixfold role of military power, common to the forces of all states, with some difference of emphasis between each aspect in particular cases. We will now touch on the problem of civil-military relations in general, for these represent one of the most sensitive areas in which legitimate authority seeks to utilize resources for the attainment of national objectives. Civil-military relations appear relevant to a discussion of state power in international society because as an instrument of such power the military appears to be both essential and, potentially and often actually, uniquely dangerous.

All armed forces pose a political problem. In two ways: both as claimants upon resources and more importantly in relation to their control. We may imagine a continuum between total and unchallenged civilian control at one end and complete military domination of the community at the other. Few states approach either pure type. All civilian regimes recognize military influence. And where military regimes hold sway they are influenced in various ways by civilian pressures. In fact, it is usual for them to be intermittent in their power role, and to alternate, sometimes admittedly at rare intervals, with civilian governmental authority.

Towards the 'stable civilian order' end of our spectrum we may place two states very different in their general political and diplomatic styles: the United Kingdom and the Soviet Union. There is in the one case the very strong British tradition of service loyalty to constituted authority, even when, as during the first world war, the senior men in uniform tended to have little respect for their political overlords, whom they dismissed as 'frocks', from the frock-coat which was still very much part of the conventional dress of politicians. So powerful is this tradition that the Curragh Incident of 1913, in which some army officers threatened to disobey government orders in respect to policy in Ireland, may be regarded as entirely exceptional. In the Soviet case, civilian control is firmly exercised through the dominating role of the Communist Party at all levels of administration and government. No military challenge to such domination would be tolerated. Moreover, the possibility is made more remote by the fact that the top military leader themselves are invariably party members. The American experience is different again. There has very rarely been a military challenge to the Administration, and when one seemed to be developing, in the case of General MacArthur's dispute with President Truman over policy in Korea, the president's firmness ensured the general's eclipse. At the same time, an American political tradition has tended to propel the nation's top military figures towards the White House from time to time, not with very happy results. None of the three generals who became presidents – Grant, Garfield and Eisenhower – commanded in their political role the sureness of touch which made them eminent as soldiers.[12] Military influence over American policy, emanating from the Pentagon, has undoubtedly been sometimes very strong. Indeed the American experience gave rise to what was called by its begetter, Harold J Lasswell, the 'garrison state hypotheses'. In bare outline this hypothesis held that modern military requirements and demands loomed so large among the economic considerations of national policy, that military chiefs, in combination with the managers and executives of the defence industry, would come to dominate whole areas of both domestic and foreign policy, effectively determining the posture of the state in relation to its own citizens and to international society. The garrison state was never fully accepted by political theorists, but it was a salutary reminder of the obligation lying on the shoulders of the civilian political authorities to try to ensure that policy was not dominated unduly by the claims of national defence, legitimate, timely and essential though they were, nor by service personnel charged to implement it, nor by the arms industry.

In the Soviet Union the Communist Party monopolizes legitimate power. The party directly controls both the government and the armed forces, partly through the government, partly through political officers, attached to units, whose tasks include surveillance and political education. High-ranking office-holders, civilian and military, are invariably party members. But the party remains primarily a civilian organization. In the Soviet Union, therefore, and in people's republics constituted along similar lines, civil-military relations are stabilized under civilian authority.

[12] General George Washington was a special case.

In Britain (and some other Western European countries) political parties are not formally constitutional components of the state structure. They are unofficial but recognized political associations competing for power. Their access to power is governed by conventions and rules linked to electoral results. In Britain herself the arrangements are almost wholly conventional, but have the authority and force of actual law. The government firmly controls the armed forces which act only under its political direction.

In many Latin-American countries (and in other parts of the world: Latin-America stands here as the type) there is usually a plurality of political parties competing for power. They use the armed forces if they can as an instrument for gaining power or for denying it to others. The armed forces themselves frequently play a direct political role, both in association with parties and on their own account.[13] In general, if not invariably, military regimes seek to civilianize their power sooner or later. They do so either by entering into coalitions with civilian groups which suit them politically, or by handing over formal governmental authority to an approved party, with which military personnel will seek to remain influential. Occasionally, as in the case of Egypt's Gamal Abdul Nasser, ruling soldiers become in the course of time themselves effectively civilianized. In any case, the inescapable compromises and manoeuvrings of politics often prove uncongenial to military men. Moreover, outright military regimes are widely felt, and widely feel themselves, to be irregular, even makeshift. They represent emergency conditions. Often they seem to be analogous to the 'tyrannies' through which so many ancient Greek city-states passed. Pressure from the political community to modify them sooner or later in the direction of 'normal' constitutional forms is usually strong.

An attempt is made in Figs. 11–14 to indicate the salient features, in simple form, of the 'communist', the 'British', the 'American' and the 'Latin-American' patterns of civil-military relations and the norms of political power prevailing.

[13] In some parts of the world the *coup d'état* has been so common as to represent almost an institutionalized method of giving various groups within the political elite a turn of office and power. Bolivia sustained 193 *coups d'état* in 147 years. Only rarely have Latin-American armies been used in an offensive role externally. Their principal importance has been as political instruments for bringing about governmental and – increasingly of late – economic and social change inside their respective countries.

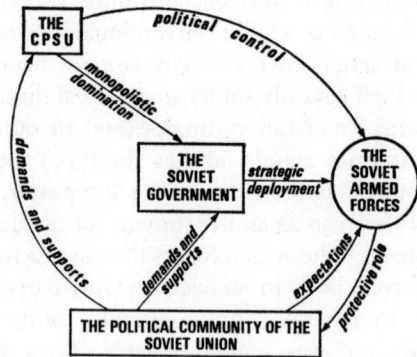

Fig. 11. The communist (Soviet) pattern of civil-military relations

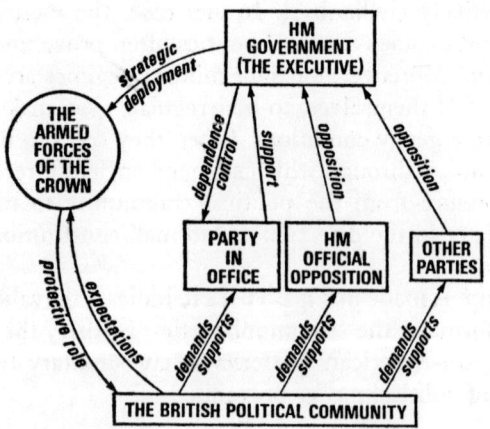

Fig. 12. The British pattern of civil-military relations

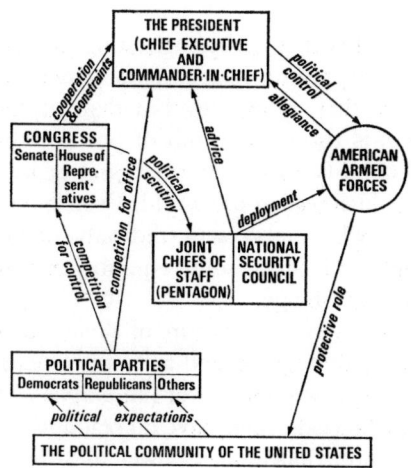

Fig. 13. The American pattern of civil-military relations

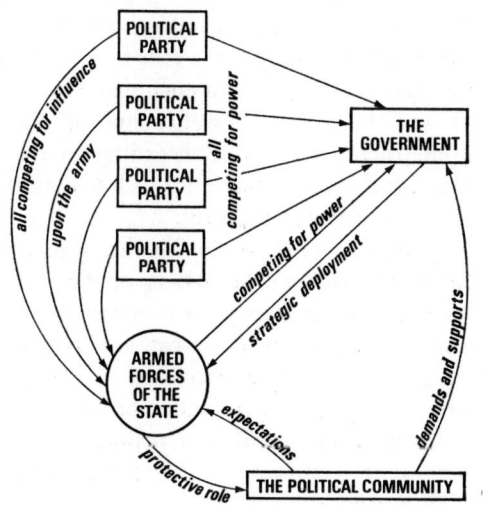

Fig. 14. The Latin-American pattern of civil-military relations

157

Conclusion

We may conclude this chapter by suggesting that power and countervailing power represent instruments which states use consciously to pursue their objectives, but that implicitly one of the central objectives is the equilibrium of power, which will ensure that degree of stability in the international order which enables states to do their business in the world. Even highly dynamic and revisionist states, which may seek radically to alter an existing balance of power, still desire some equilibrium; one that will be peculiarly to their advantage.

Although states have some measure of choice as to the amount of power they will try to acquire, and as to the chief forms in which they will seek to express their power (an emphasis that is likely to vary with circumstances), states have no real option about whether to seek power or not. States need power in order to exist, and to serve the purposes of their peoples. Power and responsibility are closely correlated in international society. A logical circle develops here. Great states, by definition, are very powerful. Because they are great states their responsibility for the maintenance of a tolerable and viable international order is proportionately great. To discharge this responsibility they need great power. But all states need some power, for they need to be able to manipulate the international environment sufficiently to ensure as far as possible their own survival and thereby the well-being of the populations dependent upon them. All states, according to their scope and status in international society, therefore seek to conserve and as far as may be to enhance their own power.

It is precisely because all states do this that at any given epoch a working equilibrium exists in the society of states. But no equilibrium is ever static, though it may prove relatively stable over long periods. An existing balance of power can very seldom be taken for granted. It is always tending to move towards an imbalance. It must therefore be adjusted, with more or less deliberation and success, in the direction of either a restoration of the original equilibrium or – more commonly – the creation of a new one. In Kenneth W. Thompson's words:

The business of statesmanship and diplomacy under these conditions is to limit the struggles and restrict their scope. The means available are a mixture of military power and diplomacy employed in *the unceasing pursuit of new balances of power and rough equilibriums among contending parties.*[14]

A critical reader may suggest that in this discussion we have ranged rather loosely between the concept of power as the ability to bring about effects and the components of power from which this ability derives. We must hope we have not blurred this valid distinction in an endeavour to show that – to borrow a theological formulation – the *substance* of power and its *accidents* are in an important sense aspects of one another. The ability to do something only exists in so far as the means are available. No discussion of international power which did not refer to its components would go beyond mere abstraction. Exclusive concentration upon the components of power would fail to provide any conceptual framework within which to accommodate them. In any case power, notionally and in its applicability, in both its wholesome and pathological aspects, lies at the very heart of politics, of which international politics is but a special case.

However, power in international politics – as indeed in most of domestic politics – is very rarely mere 'naked power'. It is hedged about, adorned is perhaps a more appropriate word, with a cluster of constraints, scruples, norms and rules of conduct. They form part of that context in which power is always exercised and which alone gives it significance. In the next chapter, therefore, we examine one of the most difficult aspects of our subject, which none the less also lies at the core of it, and the status of which political philosophers and not least theologians have worried over for many generations: the role of morality and law in international politics.

Note on legitimacy

This is an important aspect of power, though not essential to it, since power can be and often is exercised without any legitimacy. Generally speaking, the holders of power are anxious to ensure that their power becomes and remains legitimate. What this means is that power is recognized as *properly belonging* to its holder. He is deemed to have the

[14] From *Political Realism and the Crisis of World Politics*, Princeton U.P., New Jersey, 1960. My italics.

right to exercise it. Notice that he is *deemed*. There are no self-evidently inherent rights to power and authority. Instead there are sets of arrangements, conventions, customs, many of which are dignified and usually strengthened by being given the status and sanction of law. Together these arrangements have the effect of apportioning power to persons. But the legitimacy and authority of power, like the reality of the *nation*, lie essentially 'in the mind'. Power is legitimate so long as it is felt to be so. Legitimacy is an attribution of right to the exercise of power. The tyrants of the Greek city-states were not necessarily or even often oppressive and arbitrary rulers. The *tyrannos* might and sometimes did govern well. The point was that his power lacked legitimacy. He wielded it irregularly. Admittedly, the extra strain arising from the lack of legitimacy affected relations between *tyrannos* and his political community. In his endeavour to maintain his power (very frequently on behalf of the lower classes in the state against the opposition of aristocracies) the rule became tyrannical in our sense, a sense in which Aristotle in the fourth century BC was already using the word.

Legitimacy is as important in international as in domestic politics. Without it a working international order would be virtually impossible. The interests of all members of international society would then suffer. Internationally an important aspect of legitimacy is clearly diplomatic recognition. A government does not become internationally legitimate because it effectually exercises power within the borders of its territory but because it is generally recognized as doing so. From this there is needed only the single legitimating step of agreeing that it has a right to do so: the step from *de facto* to *de jure*. Regimes rise and fall. Legitimacy is accorded and withdrawn. The fundamental point is that persons ultimately give legitimacy to institutions and those who run them by believing that legitimacy attaches to them. Once the belief is eroded, legitimacy wanes. The ruler, or the government, or the international order itself 'loses the mandate'. The fading of legitimacy is a serious thing, because its effect is inevitably de-stabilizing. A given *status quo* may be felt to be good or bad, just or unjust, but its rejection is always attended by psychological strains and tensions, and the risk of a breakdown of order which may be a good deal less tolerable even than the discredited *status quo*.

We notice in this connection that every post-revolutionary regime seeks to legitimize its institutions as rapidly as possible by propaganda and the coercion of dissidents. It is recognized as essential to create a new, accepted *status quo* as soon as may be. So-called charismatic leadership has a strong self-legitimating quality in it, when it derives from the glamour and attributed glory and virtue of the leader. But he too will seek, sooner rather than later, to establish his personal ascendancy on a basis of institutional legitimacy. On the other hand, some institutions, for example the papacy, are endowed with such authority and prestige in the minds of those who accord them legitimacy that they confer a degree of charisma on those individuals who represent them. There can thus be the charisma of the man and of the office. In both cases the charismatic quality works for the strengthening of the sense of legitimacy, which in turn enhances the quality of charisma.

In any case legitimacy is jealously cherished by those invested with it, because so much is at stake. Gibbon remarked that Augustus was sensible that mankind were governed by names. And as Peter Sharp has put it, 'It is a small step from laughing at the king to asking the court jester to make laws'. One of the profoundest political parables in European literature is Hans Andersen's story of the emperor's new clothes. He was splendidly attired so long as he was deemed to be, in the context of the norms which obliged his subjects to assume that he would always be suitably dressed. The self-deception arising from this norm of behaviour was strengthened by the sanction of being thought stupid or unfit for their posts if they could not see the new clothes. But the eye of a child was innocent of these constraints. 'He has no clothes on!' 'But,' cried all the bystanders at last, 'after all, he has no clothes on!' And thenceforward the emperor walked in his procession, naked indeed.

6

Morality and law in international politics

Morality is the custom of one's country and the current feeling of one's peers. Cannibalism is moral in a cannibal country – *Samuel Butler*.

Small nations have a moral obligation to rouse the conscience of the world – *Pakistan official*.

Morality can only be relative, not universal . . . the search for an ethical norm outside politics is doomed to frustration. The identification of the supreme reality with the supreme good, which Christianity achieves by a bold stroke of dogmatism, is achieved by the realist through the assumption that there is no good other than the acceptance and understanding of reality – *E. H. Carr*.

Are not Religion and Politics the Same Thing? Brotherhood is Religion! – *William Blake*.

No man, I fear, can effect great benefits for his country without some sacrifice of the minor virtues – *Rev. Sydney Smith*.

To do the right thing is usually the right thing to do – *Viscount Grey of Fallodon, British foreign secretary*.

The nature of morality

Morals are rules of behaviour. They exist in a social context. Robinson Crusoe alone on his island could not behave morally or immorally, save in so far as his relations with the animals around were concerned. Any wanton cruelty on his part towards them might properly be subject to moral judgement. But morals clearly entered the situation when Crusoe encountered Man Friday. There was then a society, and norms of conduct between its members became implicit. The proposition we are making here is that morality is socially determined, and depends on an assumed capacity for choice. This is not to enter the question of whether our actions are in fact determined. It is enough that we behave in general *as if* a real element of choice governs our actions. The choices we make are in turn at least partly governed by our conception of what is admissible on moral grounds. Men behave differently from each other in part because their notions of what is moral differ. But reference to some norm is implicit in all action, even in that very large area of activity in which no interior debate about morality takes place. The implicit assumption we make there is that our actions are so to speak morally negative; they do not conflict with norms although neither are they prescribed. My decision to smoke a cigar rather than a cigarette may be prompted by mere preference, or by considerations of medical prudence, but is of no moral significance. If I choose to smoke in a non-smoking carriage I am in breach of regulations and flouting a norm of behaviour, and my conduct properly becomes subject to moral censure, and, if persisted in, possible penalty. Although ideas about the status of morality differ this does not affect our understanding of its function as a device for regulating social behaviour. Thus we may believe that moral rules are implanted by God (though then perhaps we need to explain their diversity), or derive from social habit or represent a prudential response to past experience. It does not matter to the analysis of the role of morality in human affairs.

No area of social behaviour lies outside the scope of moral judgement. Morals apply to relations: sexual, political, commercial, and so forth. They are rules intended to govern the behaviour of *individuals* in relation to each other. Thus there is morality as between men, morality as between citizens on one side and their governments on the other, morality between firms, acting as individuals, and morality as between states. These last can behave morally or immorally towards each other because they are notional group-persons, collective superbeings, whose relations are subject to understood norms. Even a relationship of hostility is morally constrained. Warfare between states has traditionally been subject to regulation, so that there have been deemed to be not only moral and immoral causes of war, but moral and immoral methods of waging it. The application of moral considerations to the conduct of states assumes them to be persons. Such imputation of personality to states is no less logically necessary to the whole concept of international law. The personality of states is basic to the theory of diplomatics. Without it morality and law among nations have no reality. Indeed the idea of an international society itself becomes meaningless. There are collections of things: there are only societies of beings.

By virtue of their imputed personality, then, states have moral and legal relations with each other. There is a third criterion for judging the actions of states, closely linked with the criteria of morals and law; that of prudence. All three reinforce each other. Prudential considerations may clearly be influenced by moral scruples, and the sense of obligation to observe international law is an aspect of the morality of states. Similarly, in the calculation of its own interest and advantage a state will have regard to its international reputation, and its dealings with other states will normally reflect an expectation of reciprocity. And as with ourselves, the behaviour of states towards each other may be judged in a positive or negative way. We may say that the state ought to act thus, or is obliged to act thus. Here there is a positive prescription. Or we may say that in taking certain action the state is not in breach of any rules to which it is subject.

Earlier in this book we noticed that there are two basic conceptions of the state. The first regards it as a means, the second as an end. Neither view affects the imputation of personality to the state, nor the standing of the obligations, moral and legal, that any state assumes by its very existence in the world of states. However, it is true that many who regard the state as an end, to which men serve as means, adopt a somewhat mystical view of the personality of the state, whereas most who regard it as a means to the achievement of the purposes of its members, uphold its personality in the notional sense, agreeing that the state is *to be thought of* as a person. In the matter of the obligations of the state towards its own citizens, as distinct from its obligations towards other states, our judgement of its actions is critically affected by the view we take of the nature of the state. Those who regard the state 'biologically' tend to think of it as the *end* of the individual rather as the whole body may be regarded as the end of the single cell. Up to a point this seems to have been essentially the concept underlying the ancient city-state. Its claims upon its citizens, however successfully defied in particular cases, were absolute. On the other hand the *polis* (from which we derive our word *politics*) was regarded both by Plato, in many respects the classic theorist of the absolute state, and Aristotle, as the necessary means to the attainment of true human excellence. The mechanistic view of the state, by contrast, implies that it is no more than a kind of convenient, even necessary, machine. It is interesting to note that this view of the state, in which states exist to serve the needs of their subjects, was in essence that of the political authoritarian Thomas Hobbes. He maintained that men establish governments to save them from themselves, and from each other. It is worth remembering that it is a form of this Hobbesian 'realism' that actually inspires much of the idealistic theorizing which insists that only world government, of one kind or another, will give the society of states and the community of men true security. The functional view of the state also includes the special case embodied in Marxist doctrine, in which the state is regarded as the institutional expression of the class structure of society. The conception of the Marxist state is fundamentally anti-Hegelian, or, as Karl Marx himself put it, Hegelianism stood on its head. Yet though Marxism thus rejects Hegel's view of the state as a superbeing to whose purposes men serve as means, communist countries since 1917 have been characterized by regimes as rigid and coercive as those set up by ideologies inspired by the alternative conception of the nature and status of the state.

Nevertheless, despite the experience of peoples in communist states, there remains a vital distinction between the two views of the state, so far as the relations of state with citizens are concerned. For if the state is an *end*, to the fulfilment of which its individual members and their interests are subordinate, the state has no moral duty to uphold those interests. If it does so it can only be because doing so serves the interest of the state itself.

Now, in practice most states do not uphold this absolute view of the self-justifying nature of state action. Instead they claim that they serve, and exist to serve, the needs and wishes of their citizens. That is to say, *people commonly think of states in this way*. For claims made by the state, though real claims, emanate of course from the minds of people. Most of us appear to believe that states demand obedience in order to ensure, so far as they can, their own survival, so that they can continue to serve the ends of their members. However, even this functional view of the state both requires and enables it to make more comprehensive demands on its members than any other society or institution to which persons belong will normally do. These demands, in fact, as we have seen earlier, are generally held to be broadly proportional to the benefits the state confers, in terms of general safety, welfare, the rule of law, collective prestige and opportunities of reasonable advancement and self-fulfilment.

For better or worse it is evident that modern conditions empower states to exercise a much greater degree of direction over the lives of their subjects than in earlier ages. Especially is this true in those parts of the world where state structures are characterized by a high level of bureaucratic competence, and the availability of modern techniques of social management. It was the combination of such techniques with technologized industry which gave both world wars their 'total' character. At the same time these developments helped to ensure that the belligerents would prove capable of enduring total war for periods of several years, and of recovering from some at least of its salient effects relatively quickly.

The instrumental view of the state, we suggest, is the one commanding the most widespread acceptance in the modern world. That it coincides with greatly increased state power over the lives of citizens has important implications. It arises because of increased expectations peoples entertain about the 'Good Life' in general. These expectations oblige governments to take more power to themselves in an endeavour to meet them, principally by greater regulative interference in economic affairs, by efforts to control physical environments, and by providing minimum standards of communal welfare. But the more citizens ask of the state machinery, the more scope states demand over the direction of their lives in order to be able to do what they ask. In modern conditions of international intimacy, responsive policy of this kind in the domestic field impinges more and more sharply on the interests of other states, so that the growth of human expectations affects the whole area of foreign relations.

It is evident too that many acts performed by states in what has been called their 'private domain' have important international effects in regard to widely held norms of political morality. Thus internal policy may colour a state's reputation as a civilized community. The treatment by the Third Reich of her Jewish citizens, and the great Soviet purges of the 1930s, are familiar examples.

The current *apartheid* policy of the Republic of South Africa, providing for the so-called 'separate' social and political development of black and white peoples in that country, attracts much worldwide moral disapproval.

The mention of *apartheid* reminds us how close the connection can be between political morality and ideology. Ideologies not only justify policies but often claim to be justified by morality. That twentieth-century type of *Homo sapiens sapiens* known as Soviet Man has often had claimed for him a higher form of political and social morality than that prevalent in bourgeois society. When the cold war freeze was at its harshest many members of the free world warmed themselves in the glow of a valued sense of ethical superiority, often fired by a belief, firmly urged if sometimes theologically imprecise, of the unique moral excellence and peculiar truth of some favoured form of Christianity. If ideologies generate much of the steam that drives political machines, their own dynamism is frequently enhanced by the special moral worthiness that is claimed for them. Countries that are ideological partners will sometimes remind each other not only of their shared political values but of the supposed high morality those values represent. Thus we may notice that much of the inspiration behind the European Movement since the second world war derives from an articulated sense of the 'shared heritage of Western civilization', and of the moral congruity between the closely related forms of 'Western democracy', which is regarded as deriving its norms of respect for the individual, of the attribution of inalienable rights to him, from a specific if in many ways residual Christian ethic. By the same token many Christian critics of communism have considered it, not entirely without sympathy, as a form of perfectionist Christian heresy, despite its official 'godlessness'.

The moral overtones of ideology find expression in a sense of obligation which goes along with the calculation of advantage. Fascist Italy thought both to serve her interests and discharge her comradely obligations by entering the war on Germany's side in June 1940, although many considerations might have suggested the wisdom of remaining neutral. It was for moral reasons, stimulated by the experience of the second world war, that Falangist Spain endured a period of relative diplomatic isolation after its conclusion. The European Economic Community is morally, as well as strategically, a 'security community' – an association of states between the members of which war has become a contingency so remote as for all practical purposes to be safely ignored, whatever disagreements between them may arise.

Morality among men and states

In 1932 appeared a remarkable book by the distinguished German-American Lutheran divine, Reinhold Niebuhr, called *Moral Man and Immoral Society*. A deeply considered study of the moral predicament in which statesmen and peoples are placed by the conditions of international society, the book remains timely for its theme is perennial. Dr Niebuhr brought out with earnest clarity a distinction which he saw between the ethical sensitivities which characterize the dealings of most individual men, most of the time, with each other, and that subordination of morality to power which he saw as characteristic of relations between states. Yet the argument, as summarized by the book's title, does pose an antithesis which we may feel cannot be accepted as it stands. For society, whether domestic or international, is inherently neither amoral nor immoral.

In particular, states are not amoral, as some have sought to argue, for in being faced, through their representative agents, with a range of possible choices of action, one of the criteria by which they decide their chosen course is the moral one, that is to say, the presumed rightness of that course against the presumed wrongness of an alternative course. Statesmen are human, and human conduct, when pursued in the context of a political role as at other times, is influenced by scruples, often, admittedly, not very exacting ones. Nor are states essentially immoral. The actions they choose to take do not invariably reflect the subordination of moral considerations to others. To take an example, successive British governments tried to find acceptable settlements to the problems of Rhodesia and Northern Ireland in the late 1960s and afterwards. In this difficult task they were never able (and doubtless had no wish) to disregard the question of Britian's *moral* obligation to ensure, if possible, the fashioning of constitutional arrangements which would guarantee to the black majority in Rhodesia and the Unionist majority in Ulster conditions of life that could fairly be regarded as meeting their acknowledged political expectations, often loudly proclaimed as rights. Britain had to attempt this while responding to clamant demands by the Rhodesian white minority and the republican minority in Ulster. Policy had to avoid the appearance of a betrayal of either majority community. In fact the word *betrayal* loomed large in discussion on both issues. One can, however, only betray a person, group or cause towards whom or which one has contracted obligations. All obligations have a moral aspect, because to meet them is what we *ought* to do; that is what is meant by obligation. In the case both of Rhodesia and Ulster advice was not wanting to the effect that other considerations, of prudence and expediency, should be decisive. Yet in both cases Britain acknowledged a duty to try to keep a balance between expediency and morality while she grappled with the problems. If politics is the art of the possible, what *is* possible depends in part on its moral acceptability.

This is not to deny the important truth that where only one course of action is open, such action cannot, by definition, be immoral, for, as we saw earlier, morality implies a capacity to choose. Frequently, in fact, statesmen plead the absence of an alternative (in terms of 'practical politics') as justification for what they actually do.

That states have less moral sensitivity than many individuals may readily be conceded. Indeed, there is much to be said for the view that this is necessarily the case. States, that is to say, may have to be more ready than individual men normally are to take decisions in the light merely of expediency and self-interest. Even so, it seems safe to say that no statesman would relish, or could long sustain politically, a serious charge of moral indifferentism in his public role. Even Hitler, one of the most thrusting and dynamic statesmen of modern times, who made of power not merely an instrument but a cult, was none the less careful to adorn his spectacular initiatives in foreign policy with as telling moral justifications as he could devise. And in this he was greatly helped by the fashionable doctrine of 'national' self-determination, which, with all its anomalous features, secured for German revisionism a good deal of sympathy in many liberal and idealistic quarters.

The distinctiveness of state morality

However, while we may be satisfied that international relations have their moral aspect, the distinction between the morality of

states and the morality of men is a vital one. To some of its important implications we must now turn. The English philosopher
Bernard Bosanquet, in his important work, *The Philosophical
Theory of the State*, developed the argument that states are moral
beings whose morality is necessarily different from that of individuals and should therefore be judged accordingly. This doctrine
provides a useful point of departure, provided we bear in mind that
it does not matter, in this connection, whether we believe the
state to be an actual organic being, or a being by imputation, which
is what this book assumes.

Firstly, then, Bosanquet held that states cannot commit certain
types of wrong that are open to men. We might take as an instance
the purely selfish exploitation of another person's body in pursuit
of unrestrained sensuality. This is strictly inconceivable to the
state. We may express an emotional reaction to events of which we
disapprove by such phrases as 'the Nazi rape of Poland', or 'the
communist seduction of Cuba', and such metaphorical language
may symbolize political facts. But it contributes little to an explanation of the nature of the political processes involved. While a
statesman may be a libertine in his private life he cannot be in his
public role. In what sense, then, if any, can a state be said to
behave selfishly? Presumably by seeking political or economic
advantages without regard to the understood rights or the well-
being of other states, who may lack the power to prevent this.
Obviously men can act in such a way in relation to other men. But
the nature and structure of international society ensures that self-
regarding activity will dominate the behaviour of its members, and
will be readily justified by the plea of political necessity.

Some political theorists suggest that 'crimes' of the state are
really the private doings of men, acting *ultra vires* on its behalf.
This brings us to the question of the distinction between a state
and its government. The acts of a state are acts of its government,
as these in turn are acts of the individuals who compose it. How
far may we assimilate men to the government they comprise, and
that government to the state it both rules and represents? In
diplomatic theory, completely. But analysis cannot simply be
satisfied with that. In relation to acts that have generally been
condemned on moral grounds, the commission of which may even
have been codified as a legal offence, for example genocide, the
problem remains of attributing to a state guilt which has been

incurred by its government, and more strictly, by the persons forming that government, or their agents.

The Nazi government's treatment of European Jewry, for instance, was almost universally condemned. Among other things it did not even accord Jews the minimum consideration due to persons as sources of claims.[1] The concentration camp officials, we may suppose, were clearly guilty of moral outrage. The government which issued their outrageous orders was also guilty. By a logical extension the state in whose name that government acted was guilty too. The nation, which acquiesced in these acts of state, may be supposed to share in the guilt. Yet it is difficult not to think that the guilt differs both in measure and even in kind as between these several entities. We might perhaps suggest that guilt was *direct* on the part of the officials and their superiors, whereas the German people at large shared in what might be called *constructive guilt*, in that their support of their government encouraged its policy, rather as a marriage partner whose behaviour drives the spouse away may be charged with 'constructive desertion'. As for the personified institution, the Third Reich, we might charge it with *notional guilt*. These distinctions may not have much practical effect, but do represent an attempt to define responsibility for what happened to real people in the 'real world'.

For it would seem unsatisfactory to concede that the German nation as a whole bore no collective responsibility for what was inflicted upon German and other Jews during the twelve years of the Nazi regime. For one thing, it is very hard to believe, except on a highly idiosyncratic view of political realities, that the destruction of European Jewry was 'necessary' for the survival of the German state, which had therefore no choice in the matter. We may feel, by contrast, that a plea of necessity has some plausibility in regard to some at least of the measures taken, which were admittedly harsh, by the German authorities operating in the conditions that prevailed along the Russian front after 1941. But even then their desperate situation arose from the earlier choice – the decision to attack the Soviet Union.

In any case the moral question has to be faced of the warrant for the acts concerned to have been as drastic as they were. As

[1] For a clear discussion of the status of persons, see S. I. Benn and R. S. Peters, *Social Principles and the Democratic State*, Allen & Unwin, London, 1959, chapters 1, 2, and 3.

Professor Manning pointed out,[2] the duty of a general in wartime is to win his campaign. But if he can do it without slaughtering large numbers of women and children, which in that case would be merely wanton, he has a moral obligation not to slaughter them. This is an application of the principle of 'the proper parsimony of means' to attain a given end. The destruction of Dresden by allied bombers in February 1945 has been much debated in this connection. The justification was that though the attack may not have contributed in proportion to its frightfulness to the collapse of the German will to continue the war, there were grounds at the time, deriving from received strategic doctrine, for believing that it would. Certainly, in conditions of total war moral constraints on strategic policy become extremely hard to apply. When, however, an act of state cannot plausibly be justified by reference to moral, legal or prudential criteria, where does responsibility lie? In one sense, as we suggest above, with the whole community, in another with each individual member of it, in a third with the actual perpetrators. The entire German people was *not* arraigned at Nuremberg in the war crimes trial of 1946, only those who made and carried out the policies which allied jurisprudence defined as criminal. But the accused were regarded as representative. They had determined, with massive popular support, the posture of the Third Reich in international politics. And this imputed collective responsibility was not an empty thing. The German national community as a whole honourably repudiated the acts of the Nazi regime done in its name, and marked this repudiation by such acts of reparation and compensation as were open to it. Where responsibility is indirect in this way even the individual may do something on his own account to discharge it. For example, an Englishman may happen to believe that his country behaved badly in some respects towards the Irish during the years of crisis before the institution of the Free State in 1922. That is to say, he may feel that some of his country's 'necessary' acts in those years were unnecessarily severe. Assume that he was born in 1930. He clearly has no direct responsibility whatever for them. Yet he may feel the pressure of a kind of shared historical responsibility, so to speak, for acts done in his country's name. While he may normally be expected to give his own national state the benefit of any historical explanations that may be going, he may also feel a moral

[2] C. A. W. Manning, *The Nature of International Society, op. cit.*, p. 20.

duty, in trying to understand why what happened did happen, to judge Britain's actions as honestly and impartially as he can, and at least not complacently to assume that because his country did them they were *ipso facto* right.

It appears to be a fact of experience that people do tend to apply relative moral standards to acts of state, according as to whether their own countries did them or suffered them. And of course this occurs in the sphere of personal relationships as well. Few people, to revive a once current phrase, 'cry stinking fish'.

Associated with the above tendency is a habit of bestowing moral censure upon other countries that are embarking on policies one's own has quietly or reluctantly abandoned. This may rather smack of the Duc de la Rochefoucauld's familiar maxim that 'old people give good advice to compensate them for no longer being able to give bad examples'. Elizabeth I, we may suspect, would not have been in the least scandalized by the attitude of certain con-temporary Afro-Asian heads of government towards the indepen-dence of the judiciary. Mussolini's attempt to create an imperial Italy attracted a good deal of earnest finger-wagging in liberal circles in Britain, despite the history of British enterprise in gathering, during an earlier epoch, the far-flung pickings of empire. But by the 1930s Britain was a *status quo* power, and wished only that others were too, and so incurred not unfairly the charge of expressing a convenient rather than convincing 'selectivity of indignation'.[3]

All this is not to suggest that in international affairs moral judgements have no proper application. Rather is it to remind ourselves, as Sir Herbert Butterfield sagely does,[4] that it would be timely if peoples and states would judge each other as fellow-sinners, and avoid assuming the mantles of self-appointed record-ing angels.

Another distinction between the moral behaviour of states and men is said to be that when a state 'does wrong' its whole level of life is under judgement, and not merely the single wrongful act, whereas, although some individuals may suffer from a degree of moral eccentricity, which gives a bent to all their actions, most

[3] Mussolini is said to have snorted on one occasion during the Abyssinian crisis, 'Whenever the English accuse me of aggression, I look at the map'. A *non sequitur*, perhaps, but one can understand the *duce's* irritation.
[4] In *Christianity and European History*, Oxford U.P., 1952.

moral lapses on the part of men are simply that – lapses – acts contrary to the prevailing direction of scruple or conscience. A state's wrong-doing, the argument runs, reflects a general tendency in that state's political style. Acts are understood in terms of what it is natural for that state to do. We may think there is much validity in this view by virtue of the high degree of persistence that is shown by basic national interests, and the consequent continuity of policy which a state's activities reveal, even during and often following periods of revolutionary change. Although we need always to be wary of glib generalizations about national character as determining the moral quality of states' behaviour, to suggest that states do tend to develop a characteristic moral style, as they clearly do a diplomatic style, seems to accord with observation. The diplomacy, as it were, acts as the vehicle of the morality.

The condition of sovereignty itself, it has been argued (by Bosanquet and others), is another feature distinguishing the morality of states from that of individuals. Sovereignty implies the supreme authority of the state to formulate its own policies and to execute them, constrained only by the countervailing power of other states, and not by any 'moral tradition'. This proposition seems more dubious. It is certainly true that sovereignty is a vital determinant of how states do conduct themselves, and of how they judge their own behaviour. But to dismiss moral traditions altogether from international society appears to be unwarranted. Such a moral tradition may be neither so powerful nor even so continuous among states as within domestic societies, but states are influenced by moral restraints, and these form part of their style of relationship with other states. Moreover, a prudential consideration with very many states at all times is their moral standing in international society. Statesmen are invariably ready to advance moral justifications upon challenge, as well as reasons of expediency, for actions taken by their countries. Even 'choosing the lesser evil', or 'seeking the greater good' as explanations of policy have a moral basis. If there has to be a choice between evils, there is an implicit obligation not to opt to do the greater. An existing good may be modified or abandoned for the sake of what is conceived to be a better. For example, the complex of motives leading the United States to try to extricate herself from the Vietnam war may fairly be summarized as expressing the belief that to end the war had become a lesser evil, even if it left matters not as the United States would wish them to be, than to go on fighting. Clearly the United States Administration may have had the most pressing political reasons for withdrawal, which had to be balanced against strong political reasons for remaining. But the decision – whichever way it went – would not lack an element of moral justification. Again, a redefinition and perhaps ultimate abandonment by the United States of its obligations towards the Kuomintang regime on Taiwan, for the sake of preserving more normal relations between America and China, may fairly be regarded as representing, in the eyes of American policy-makers, a greater good than the maintenance of the old rigid commitments. The loyalty of the United States to her friends is doubtless morally approved, not least by Americans themselves. But it may properly be modified or reinterpreted if thereby hostile suspicion between the United States and a major adversary is lessened and world stability, from which all may gain perhaps, is enhanced.

It is also true that the interests of states are not morally exclusive. There are no grounds for holding that sovereignty, or any other characteristic of the state, lifts it above moral considerations. The theory of 'my country right or wrong', advanced in this sense, cannot be rationally justified at all. It is one thing to say that citizens owe a special loyalty to their state in return for the means to a satisfactory life, which the state exists to guarantee and in modern conditions largely to supply, but quite another to say that the citizen has an obligation to support his country, whatever it may do, merely because it is his country. It has been pointed out,[5] moreover, that there is a difference between recognizing that in general everyone tries to do his best for his country, even if only by not actually harming her, and laying down as a moral principle that he should do so. For in that case a contradiction follows. A Frenchman would be in the position of approving actions of the British government if they served British interests while having to disapprove of them if they injured French interests. In other words, for him to prescribe the principle that we all ought to do our best for our country may mean that he is actually failing to do his best for France by approving actions injurious to her.

The most powerful objection to the doctrine that the moral quality of a state's action is determined by its sovereign nature lies

[5] By Benn and Peters, *Social Principles and the Democratic State, op. cit.*, p. 288.

in an appeal to the contingent situation. This appeal is commonly made by statesmen themselves. On the 'absolute' view of sovereignty, war and confiscation carried out by states can never be equated with murder and theft. But the rightful application of the latter categories to state action depends on the circumstances. As Professor H. B. Acton has pointed out,[6] soldiers killing each other in an unjust war might well be regarded as murderers; in a just war, not. The difficulty of course lies in the fact that the justice or otherwise of the conflict is precisely the moral question which states engaged in it are likely to settle in their own favour. And the question itself might well defy the judgement of either historians or moral theorists. The normative force of their conclusion would be in inverse proportion to its tentative nature.

L. T. Hobhouse took the view that the private standard of morality is simply superior to the public one, and therefore should prevail over it. Niebuhr appears to have come close to this position in some respects, though he stressed the tragic aspect of statesmen's predicaments. For this qualitative distinction between one kind of morality and another does present difficulties.

Count Cavour reputedly remarked, 'If we did for ourselves what we do for our country, what rogues we should be'. But the prime minister of Piedmont none the less seems to have believed passionately in the rightness of what, as a statesman, and as the architect of Italian unity under the House of Savoy, he was doing for his country. These acts included the support of a deliberate military challenge to a *status quo* which was unquestionably legal, and to Austrians seemed neither unreasonable nor unfair, and a deal with Napoleon III so characteristic of *realpolitik* as to appear cynical. But he did what he did *as a statesman*. We are brought immediately to the consideration of what Professor Manning, in his slightly whimsical manner, called 'the role of the Role'. A moment's thought will remind us that men commonly play several roles at the same time. The moral expectations we entertain towards anyone depend on the role he fills in relation to us. He may be at once a husband, father, churchman and foreign minister. In this last capacity his moral obligation is to discharge as ably as he can his political duty, which is to defend, and perhaps to extend, the interests of his country. If the perceived interest of

[6] In a masterly critique of Bosanquet given at a seminar in the London School of Economics.

his country requires him to do something which affronts his conscience he must either suppress his scruples or resign. What in his situation would represent a moral failure would be, while remaining in office and therefore responsible, to avoid doing what his country's perceived interest required. It may be hoped that such a predicament, in which a statesman's judgement, moral values, integrity and career are all locked together in acute crisis, will not often arise in practice. But the possibility is always present. The buck must stop somewhere, and President Truman, shrewd if homely, had a card on his desk to remind him that the buck stopped there. The story is told, which, alas, may be apocryphal, of Sir Charles Napier, soldier and perhaps wit, who would appear to have well understood the nature of political necessity if, as is related, he announced the successful occupation of Sind, then in turmoil, by telegraphing home the one word *Peccavi*, remarking to his aides, 'and a fine, humane piece of rascality it will prove'.[7] The essence of the statesman's situation is sharply percieved by Arthur N. Gilbert:

> The emphasis on policy as it grows out of . . . the optimistic liberal perspective is inadequate for an understanding of the total and complex international situation. The tragic perspective, which conceives of entities as being locked into positions as well as creating policies, is probably closer to reality.[8]

Another aspect of state behaviour which is held to affect its moral quality concerns the question of coercion. The exercise of coercion, the argument goes, is a necessary part of the functioning of the state, both internally, and, potentially at least, in external relations. On this view states may legitimately coerce their own subjects, and in certain circumstances the subjects of other states. This in effect is an aspect of sovereignty. It implies the existence of sanctions not normally available to private individuals. In so far as such coercion may be necessary, moral criteria apply to its mode, extent and severity.

[7] We may here recall the pleasant story of the old Scots Presbyterian minister, who had occasion in his sermon to refer to the condign punishments meted out by Jehovah to certain unfortunates in Old Testament history, and commented, 'The Almighty is obliged to do some things in His official capacity He would scorn to do so as a private individual'. Quite so.

[8] In 'International Relations and the Spirit of Tragedy,' *Yale Review*, Autumn 1970.

The essential distinction is that while the exercise of coercive violence may, in some circumstances, be necessary for the individual, as in claiming the 'right of self-defence', in the case of states such a right of coercion is to be regarded as a *defining* aspect of their activity. States are those entities which have a right to coerce. This doctrine has important implications for the concept of the legitimacy and moral propriety of war. The point to establish is that states have an understood right to coerce, and find themselves obliged, in a world where they remain primarily responsible for their own survival, to attempt to coerce each other.

It is further argued that a difference of condition in the morality between states from that between men arises from the relatively small number of members comprising international society. As there are only some 145 states in the contemporary world morally idiosyncratic behaviour among states is likely to be more momentous socially than among individual men. For example, the elimination of one man by murder in a large population normally represents a proportionately much smaller disturbance of the social system than the elimination of a state by conquest would be likely to do in the international system. An exception might be the assassination of a political leader who, though powerful, had no longer the support of a stable and legitimized political structure beneath him, and whose removal plunged his political community into anarchy. States, as we have noticed several times in the course of this book, tend to be highly persistent institutions, usually surviving even military defeat. The complete disappearance of a state, in a total population of states that is still comparatively small, and whose members, even the weaker among them, therefore enjoy a high degree of conspicuousness, represents a serious dislocation, relatively speaking, of the international order. This fact itself appears to act as a prudential constraint on states tempted to embark on a course of political immorality. The worldwide opprobrium directed towards the Soviet Union after her absorption of the Balkan states of Lithuania, Latvia and Esthonia in 1940 was not insignificant, even though protests and disapproval did nothing to restore these small countries to membership of international society. Naturally, the force of this moral constraint depends upon the system of moral values prevailing in the society of states at any given epoch, and on the degree of deference which states pay them. In the eighteenth century, for instance, the aristocratic tradition of rulership created a moral climate conducive to the survival of large numbers of tiny sovereign entities, particularly in the lands of Germany. (It was a popular nursery notion that there were as many states in Germany as there were days in the year. The nearest parallel was the 550 or so princely states of India, under the paramountcy of the British Crown after 1876.) It was partly moral scruples, as well as a recognition of mutual interest and the absence of implacable ideological conflict, which helped to ensure the comparatively limited violence and duration of warfare in the period. The balance of power, a consciously held political value at this time, reinforced moral considerations. Thus Russia declined to complete the destruction of Prussia, although at one stage of the seven years' war this became a feasible objective. The partition of Poland in three stages was felt, at least by some of the perpetrators, to be contrary to the moral proprieties that should influence inter-state relations, and after the upheavals of the Napoleonic wars the tsar, Alexander II, tried if not too successfully to create Polish institutions under his rule that would satisfy the national susceptibilities of the Poles in Russian Poland.

Something analogous to the 'princes' trade union' of the eighteenth century may be seen, it is perhaps not too fanciful to suggest, in the tacit agreement of modern heads of state and chiefs of government not to seek to defend national interests by contriving each other's physical elimination, even where relations between their countries are hostile and mutually threatening.

Again, the implicit acceptance that such things are 'not done' is linked with practical and prudential considerations. Where hostility or conflict prevail there is almost certain sooner or later to be a need for negotiations over the issues concerned. There must then be someone to negotiate with, preferably someone in power, who will be in a position to implement any agreement reached. Inducing government instability in your enemy by having his rulers assassinated might yield immediate advantage but could create serious obstacles in the way of a long-term settlement.

In the conditions of total war, when the insistence grows that nothing less will do than total victory, the assassination of enemy leaders may be canvassed and actually plotted.[9] But this technique

[9] In regard to the practice of international espionage, *Time Magazine* in an issue of 1972 carried an article on the role of the American Central Intelligence

for gaining military ends seems to be seldom practised, and is certainly rarely successful. In general the avoidance of assassination as an instrument of policy, and its relegation in effect to terrorists acting without authorization and very often directly against their own governments, represents a norm of international conduct. Hence it is of real moral significance.

Modern mass nationalism has many roots in the revolutionary Europe of 1789 to 1815. Articulated, as we have seen earlier, by a number of political philosophers, particularly in Germany and Italy during the nineteenth century, the ideology of the nation-state received a great impetus from the piecemeal but widespread recruitment of more and more social classes to the 'constitutional nation' which shared in the political processes of state. Democracy, despite what many political radicals assumed, did not cut across national barriers. It strengthened them. This development also affected attitudes towards international morality. Under the influence of what was a broadening of the political community within the state the moral value of state action came to be more readily and less critically equated with its political success. It is suggested that this consideration too distinguishes morality between states from that between individuals.

This is not so much a matter of 'my country, right or wrong', a principle which declares unswerving loyalty while admitting a possible moral distinction in the acts my country may perform. Rather is it a matter of 'my country, always right so long as it is successful'. A questionable doctrine, we may well think. The philosopher Henry Sidgwick reproved it, complaining that it was in line with a 'neo-paganism' in which the state had become a new diety; a religious cult-object. Gods do of course lose credibility from time to time. Should the 'divine' state fail signally in its purpose, then indeed, in E. M. Forster's phrase, may 'a strong light beat into heaven'.

But gods also have considerable powers of self-renewal. The state persists because the needs it serves continue. Revolutions create new structures and norms which then attach to themselves the old devotion. Holy Mother Russia gives place to the Socialist

Agency, in which the strategic removal of individuals was admitted to have been accomplished on occasions. Such acts were described as coming under an accepted category of 'dirty tricks'. The article pointed out, however, that the CIA was making far less use of 'dirty tricks' because experience showed their limited usefulness.

Fatherland (psychologists might find the gender change significant), which in return for more abundant promises requires an even sterner and more demanding worship. In the so-called totalitarian regimes of the twentieth century the state as the cult-object of a secular religion has been no mere analogy. Thus Mussolini, in his way a theorist as well as would-be practitioner of totalitarianism, declared that 'the state is the synthesis of all the material and non-material values of the race',[10] and again, 'all within the state, nothing outside the state: nothing against the state',[11] a resounding if imprecise slogan. We may well be thankful that resistance to this 'total' view of the state has been as determined, and perhaps on the whole more successful, than the attempts to impose it. Nietzsche, in his emphatic way, declared that 'God is dead',[12] a statement not susceptible of demonstration. But in any case many people may be expected always to find the state an unconvincing and unsatisfying substitute. As for morality, it may be strengthened, though not necessarily so, by religious belief. We would probably feel bound to consider, however, that the religion, or quasi-religion, of 'statism', as proclaimed by some dictators and denounced by some philosophers, cannot be seen to have enhanced the scrupulosity of morals in international politics, rather, perhaps, the reverse.

On the other hand, as we have had occasion to reflect upon earlier in this book, states are not in a position simply to act according to what some believers at least would claim to be the peculiarly Christian virtue of meekness, what might be called, not too flippantly, 'other-cheekliness'. Granted the nature of international society, we have recognized that there is a powerful case to argue that states *ought not* to act in such a way; that to do so is to fail in their duty to their subjects. Yet many 'tender-minded' thinkers, Sidgwick among them, have urged that states should nevertheless cultivate the humane virtues of tolerance and peaceableness. The obstinate difficulty is that these qualities, however admirable we find them, may sometimes be observed not to pro-

---

[10] Quoted in Sir Charles Grant Robertson, *Religion and the Totalitarian State*, The Epworth Press, London, 1937; a 'Social Service Lecture' still well worth reading.

[11] *Ibid.*

[12] A *graffiti* on the wall of Euston Underground Station read: '"God is dead." – Nietzsche.' Underneath was scrawled in another hand, '"So is Nietzsche." – God.'

mote national security. Moreover, if men expect states to practise these virtues, they imply in fact an equivalence in the moral value of acts done by entities as different as states and men, although we have considered good grounds for admitting that this equivalence does not apply.

If this is the case we are driven to the conclusion that states can only practise a specifically state morality. If, as is powerfully suggested by the remark attributed to Count Cavour quoted above, (p. 176), statesmen find themselves confronted by agonizing conflicts between their private moral perceptions and their evident public obligations, this is their predicament, inescapably bound up with their role. And as President Truman is said to have put it in his pawky way, 'If it is too hot for you, stay out of the kitchen'. No one is obliged to be a statesman. But statesmen are obliged to do their political duty.

The role of international law

We must now turn to examine briefly the relationship between morality and *law*, as they apply to international society.

Other things being equal we all accept that abiding by the law is itself a moral duty. When other things are not equal, when, that is to say, what the law lays down is felt to be intolerably at odds with prevailing moral assumptions, an appeal may be had to some so-called 'higher laws', or to a primacy of moral perception which 'obliges' the perceiver to break or simply disregard the law as it stands. Now law, whether domestic or international, always acts as a conserving force. It sanctions the *status quo*. Society, again whether domestic or international, is essentially dynamic. Its tendency to change over time constantly presses it against existing legal barriers. Breaches of international law, when they occur, are often justified less by appeal to the compulsion of naked self-interest than to the supposed moral rightness of the action taken as against 'mere legal niceties'.[13] It is evident that in many cases a

[13] The Indian invasion of Portuguese Goa in 1962 is an instructive instance. The action authorized by Pandit Nehru's government was a gross violation of international law, both in regard to treaty arrangements dating back to the sixteenth century, and to the Charter of the United Nations, which binds member states not to resolve disputes by force. But as an initiative on behalf of Indian self-determination against a residual European colonialism (whatever the wishes of the Goanese may have been) the Indian action claimed in effect a moral pri-

moral claim masks, or rationalizes, the intrinsic self-interest. In any event, the situation in which states choose to flout international law, however strong their motivation (and it is likely to be compelling: international law is seldom lightly brushed aside) poses a real danger to the smooth working of the international order. The very existence of this order, if law was generally disregarded within it, would be gravely jeopardized.

What it is essential to grasp is that law by definition is *binding*. It is frequently pointed out that while domestic (very often called municipal) law has in it an inherent element of command, international law represents only an auto-limitation on the defining condition of sovereignty which characterizes states. But does this distinction really constitute a difference? If it does, then international *law* should really be called something else. The distinction between 'true' law and unenforceable law is sometimes held to have been made by the great nineteenth-century jurist John Austin on the ground that only properly instituted governors have a right to be obeyed, possessing alone the right to issue rules, whereas no such governor exists in international society. In which case the question – is law binding because it is law or law because it is binding? – resolves itself into the claim that the quality of bindingness derives from sanctions available to a law-giver.

Now in one sense it is obviously true that law cannot bind of itself. That is to say, it does not constitute a category of rules which have an *intrinsic* capacity to bind those subject to them. But if law is binding by definition, which is the proposition put forward above, then law is that which is deemed to bind, whether in any actual contingency individuals or states observe it or not. Law, on this view, does not bind because it is supported by sanctions, applied by available enforcement machinery. On the contrary, they apply because law is binding. Nor is the *status* of law altered by the degree to which it may be disregarded. Austin himself may well have been concerned to show not that law proceeds only from a person or an institution having the right and the means to command, but that the sociology of the question indicates that, empirically, municipal law is found overwhelmingly to possess this character.

macy over existing law. In the prevailing ideological climate colonialism had become morally discredited and anti-colonialism morally respectable. Mere law came nowhere.

In subjecting themselves, in fact, to something they agree to call law, states implicitly admit that they are bound by it. In so doing, and in their observance in practice of recognized legal arrangements between themselves, in the generally accepted usages of 'civilized states' – admittedly a somewhat question-begging term – and in the acknowledged obligation to fulfil treaty commitments (*pacta sunt servanda*), states demonstrate their indisputable legal personality.

Further, *law is normative*. It is something which those subject to it *ought* to obey. Thus we see that a legal criterion for judging the actions of states is, by a logical association, assimilated to the moral one.

Moreover, the effectiveness of law, whether among states or men, is promoted by those elements of voluntarism and habitude which are to be found in all obedience. Indeed, one of the most notable aspects of international law is that the largely unenforceable remains largely observed. And of course behind this custom of observance lie motives of expediency and convenience, as well as, there seems no doubt, perfectly genuine moral delicacy. It may evidently be in the national interest of states to be reliable allies, for instance, until and unless very weighty reasons persuade them to modify or withdraw from their undertakings within an alliance; yet they do prove on the whole reliable allies. It may be nationally expedient for statesmen to seek to appear honourable in their dealings with each other, but it is highly probable that they will derive real personal satisfaction from a consciousness of behaving in ways consonant with honour. Neither morality nor law, of course, operate *in vacuo* but in a context which shapes them and which they in turn help to mould. The constraints upon statesmen in seeking to act morally and to uphold law are often perplexing. But they never make either morality or law merely irrelevant. We may ponder again the implications of Lord Grey's dictum quoted at the head of this chapter. At first sight it may appear no more than a somewhat portentous platitude. Reflection is likely to suggest that it summarizes a whole philosophy of international politics.

In chapter 4 we touched on the ideological aspect of the doctrine of national self-determination. Here it provides a useful instance of the links between international morality and law. Under the Charter of the United Nations member states which had been granted trusteeship over dependent territories had a legal duty, by the provisions of the Charter, to promote self-government in these

territories, leading ultimately in very many cases to full independence. Duties imply complementary rights. The states concerned
had the right to discharge their duties in ways that would promote or
at least not injure their own national interests. Other member
states of the Organization had in turn the right to require trustee
states to carry out their duty towards their dependent peoples
properly and wholeheartedly. The dependent peoples themselves,
however, had no *legal* right to independence. At best they comprised nations, and it is states which are subjects of international
law. Hence nations as distinct from states can only have what we
might regard as a moral right to independence. On the other hand,
we may well feel that this moral right enjoyed by dependent peoples
gave rise to an implicit claim (often explicitly made) to press
upon trustee states their legal duty to bring about their independence as expeditiously as was reasonable, that is to say in circumstances judged to be in the interests of both parties. The only issue
was one of timeliness. The principle, once the legal arrangements
laid down by the Charter were in force, could never be at stake. In
fact, the process of bringing trustee territories to independence
(for the good or ill of their peoples) is at the time of writing virtually
complete. The 'moral right' deriving from expectations, and the
legal duty deriving from undertakings, have advanced hand in
hand, so to speak, towards a common fufilment.

International law, then, exists; it is binding, which is simply to
say that it is true law, and its quality is not compromised by a
possibly well-founded suspicion that it is as well observed as we see
it to be less because states are scrupulous than because the obligations it imposes upon them tend to be minimal. Nor is it compromised by the absence of a political sovereign over what N. March
Hunnings perhaps rather wistfully terms 'the Family of Nations'.[14]
Finally, the relationship of international law with international
morality is intimate, continuous and in a real sense reciprocal.

The doctrine of double effect

An important problem connected with morality among states is
that of *intention*.

A choice of action clearly implies an intention to achieve a given

[14] In *International Law in a Nutshell*, Sweet & Maxwell, London, 1959. Someone once asked, 'Why cannot the nations behave as one family?', receiving the
answer, 'The trouble is, they do'.

objective. How far is the statesman to be judged by the known or stated intention behind his decisions or by their observed effects? If a policy intended to secure a good end has disastrous results we may question the judgement of the policy-maker, his failure perhaps to take critical factors sufficiently into account; his executive ability; his capacity to choose the best people to carry out his wishes. We may, in short, charge him with a failure to fulfil his responsibilities. But may we properly either impugn his motives or attach moral blame to his actions?

Saint Thomas Aquinas resolved the difficulty to his own satisfaction by endorsing the doctrine of double effect. Briefly, this laid it down that moral judgement was to be directed towards intentions, so far as these could be known, not results. Let us suppose, for example, that a ruler embarks upon a 'just war', that is to say a war in self-defence or on behalf of a righteous cause, and fights it by means which are morally consonant, that is using minimum necessary force, sparing the innocent, etc. Then let him as a result suffer a defeat which involves the occupation of his country, the destruction of his cities, the misery of his people and their death in large numbers. Now quite apart from any moral difficulty deriving from such a good cause coming to such a bad end, the effect of that ruler's action is not, according to the doctrine, subject to proper moral judgement, because he intended something very different.

Similarly, the intention of destroying Hamburg and Dresden by saturation bombing, and of dropping atomic bombs on Hiroshima and Nagasaki, was to achieve a morally acceptable end, namely the speedier conclusion of the second world war. Let us presume that it was genuinely believed that such acts were necessary to bring about this result. If so, the fact that the contingent effect was the killing of hundreds of thousands of unarmed civilians, of all ages and both sexes, has, on this argument, no moral relevance, since the intended effect was simply to hasten the end of a destructive war. To urge that saturation bombing did little if anything to break German resistance, or that the Japanese would soon have surrendered anyway, is merely to express opinions which there is no way of knowing are certainly correct about the actual military situation at the time; opinions which happen to differ from those held then by the persons responsible for prosecuting the war.

186

Yet the doctrine of double effect does raise the question whether there is any class of acts, the incidental effects of which are known to be likely to prove so dire that no intention, however good, and no necessity, however absolute, could provide a moral justification for doing them. The question is raised, but cannot be conclusively answered. For ultimately it is a matter not of fact but of value. The outright pacifist, for instance, answers it affirmatively by announcing his conviction that in no circumstances is armed violence justified: that its use is always immoral because intrinsically more evil than any conceivable situation which could be changed by using it. But this simplistic doctrine, however sincerely advanced, and however much courage adherence to it may demand in given circumstances, is not open to the statesman. He remains obliged to make judgements, unavoidably pragmatic and piecemeal, about the comparative worthiness of one course of action relative to another, and to relate each to intentions and goals. The statesman must, in fact, always recognize that while ends necessarily justify means, means inevitably modify ends. If 'the sacred cause of Irish unity', for instance, were to be achieved as a result of widespread terror, murder and destruction the result would be different in all sorts of ways, political and psychological, than if Irish unity ultimately came by means of peaceful political evolution. However, the fact that means affect ends does not imply that any particular means can simply be dispensed with. If its necessity is perceived as part of reality then necessary it is. To the attainment of the end of national security, for example, military means remain an assumed necessity. Responsible statesmen are therefore obliged to accommodate them within the overall defence policy of the state. This is why it is almost impossible to envisage a pacifist prime minister. What absolute principles of military defenceless-ness the pacifist is free to choose for himself the statesman is not at liberty to impose on his political community, most members of which will at any given time demand to be defended.[15]

While in practice the doctrine of double effect is – implicitly for the most part – widely followed, it remains rare for any end to be regarded as so excellent as to justify any means, however base. Sooner or later secondary effects do influence opinion. The moral quality of good intentions is sooner or later vaguely felt to be compromised by the relative evil of the means used to fulfil them.

[15] The pacifist option is examined at length in the next chapter.

Thus there is considerable likelihood that those holding the conviction that their cause is intrinsically so excellent that it justifies any means whatever to attain it, and who act accordingly, will lose the support of those on whose behalf they purport to act. They will do so partly at least because of the degree of moral revulsion inspired by the effects they produce. Revolutionary guerrillas, for instance, claim in an image much used by their spokesmen, to be 'fishes swimming in the stream of the people's support'. When the often indiscriminate misery they inflict evaporates the sanction they require they can find themselves gasping in the mud. It does not really do, in the long run, to maintain the stance of unilateral arrogance assumed by an IRA leader in 1972, who, on being asked what measures his organization took to prove genuine popular support for its programme of bombings and shootings, replied simply, 'We do not need a mandate to fight this just war'.

A residual rationality also enters the matter. For the employment of means to an end which were such as to make its attainment impossible would be both immoral and irrational. Immoral, because the attainable end provided the moral justification for the use of means to attain it. Irrational, because the means used prevented the very result which they were intended to bring about. Thus it would be doctrinaire but not irrational to resolve to lay a large part of the world waste in order to extirpate communism or capitalism. The morality of such an act would from the perpetrator's point of view depend on the degree of intrinsic evil believed to inhere in either communism or capitalism. It would, however, be simply irrational to destroy the whole world in order to deliver it from the evil of communism or capitalism; as irrational as it would be to cut off one's head to cure the toothache. It could of course be argued by an advanced eccentric that communism or capitalism are so evil that a world in which either flourishes would be better destroyed. But that is precisely not the view of those who wish the world to be saved from such supposed evils, and who seek means to save it.

The question arises whether the world has now reached the point at which a doctrine of double effect has no longer any relevance. If the two superpowers became involved in a thermonuclear war the intention of neither would be the destruction of the world. Yet this could be the effect. Does this not clearly imply that the use of thermo-nuclear weapons as a means of attaining given objectives, since the 'double effect' could be the destruction of everything, is inherently unjustifiable either morally or rationally? In effect, statesmen with such means at hand have answered 'Yes' to this question, for they have denied any intention of striking the first thermo-nuclear blow, and have affirmed the purely deterrent nature of their respective capacities. Indeed, it seems fair to say that their moral scruples have gone further than this, doubtless helped along by considerations of expediency. For it remains a fact that, granted that both the communist and capitalist worlds after 1945 regarded one another with self-righteous disapproval, nonetheless the Soviet Union, which had the means for a year or so after that date to overrun Europe, almost certainly without inviting an American atomic response, refrained from doing so. By the same token, the United States, from 1945 until the early 1950s, enjoyed an atomic monopoly and hence the capability to unleash a preventive and almost certainly decisive strike against the Soviet Union, a course she was actually urged in some quarters to adopt, and refrained, at least partly it would appear on the ground that the attainable end – the destruction of Soviet power – would not morally justify the means which its attainment required. The sharply perceived threat of communism was countered in other ways; ways which did not eschew armed force but used it in a containing and deterrent role. In short, it does not seem wholly absurd to suggest that, given the assumption that on one side the spread of communism was regarded as a great evil, and on the other as a great good, both American and Russian policy in those years before prudential mutual deterrence was clearly established shows itself to have been both morally and rationally irreproachable, although at the time policy-makers and their publics on each side were psychologically disabled from perceiving this.

The moral status of states

Before leaving the subject of morality and law among states we must briefly examine the notion of the state as a *prescriptive idea*. This idea is particularly associated with a number of German philosophers of considerable influence in the nineteenth century, and in a seminal way with Hegel.[16]

[16] Georg Wilhelm Friedrich Hegel, 1770–1831.

Put very simply, the idea suggests that the state *ought* to exist. There is in the nature of states a given goodness and in their being a given rightness. Hegel in fact actually ascribes to the state an intrinsic sanctity derived from God Himself. He writes: 'The state is the Divine Idea as it exists on earth'.[17] It follows from this that the more fully a state is 'realized' the less wrong it can do. States in effect do wrong things because they are imperfectly realized. States are thus to be conceived as 'becoming' rather than 'being'. (We may contrast this notion with the view that the state is a being at all only by imputation, although *by imputation* it remains 'really and truly' a being.) The ideal state, on the prescriptive conception of it, could by definition do no wrong at all. However, while this proposition may be necessarily true, it has no relevance to the situation of actual states.

We may well be disposed to think that some of the greatest miseries inflicted upon mankind have arisen from the action of states in seeking to realize their statehood in an absolute sense, and demanding to that end the total subjection to them both of their own subjects and of other states. The whole conception of the *herrenvolk* carried idealist implications of this kind, since there would be something morally amiss in a world order in which the 'natural masters' did not in fact rule.

It follows further from this prescriptive idea of the state that men *ought* to live in them. The state comes to be regarded as the natural form of human association, of which stateless societies represent either an aberration or merely a primeval stage. The state, moreover, is thus not merely more powerful than other forms of human association that may exist within or outside it, but is endowed with absolute rights over them. We may trace the roots of this total view of the state to Greek political theory: Aristotle, we remember, held that man was a 'political animal', that is, he attained his special excellence (*arete*) only in the *polis*.

Now, historically the state is only one of a number of forms of association. Admittedly states have come into existence all over the world. Despite the diversities we considered earlier in this book states share those common features, such as sovereign status, diplomatic recognition, a population, a territory, a government, which together enable us to classify them as states. But it is by no

[17] In *The Philosophy of History* (trans. J. Sibree, 1857), Willey Book Company, New York, 1944.

means clear why this institution, worldwide in distribution as it is, should be any more 'natural' than other forms of human association. Many would argue that it is less natural than some, and would urge the primacy of the family in this connection. To retort that the state is 'the family writ large' is merely to adopt a 'folkish' doctrine that does not tell us really anything more about the nature of the state.

Whether or not we find the prescriptive idea of the state convincing we cannot but notice that a further question is often asked. What is the *prescriptive form* of the state? Those who are eager to detect a significant enlargement of human personality in those national societies that permit a wide measure of personal liberty and of participation in political processes, at the level both of formulating and executing policy, have seen the prescriptive form of the state in 'democracy'.[18] But though we may prefer that type of state, it is not easy to see that it is *any more of a state* than other types. As A. J. P. Taylor has remarked, 'States will be states'. The existence of democratic constraints on governments, the right of interests to organize themselves autonomously, the access of individuals generally to wide educational and professional opportunities – these are all ultimately preferences with a doctrinal basis to them. To demand either that all states ought to fulfil them, or that only states which do are 'true' states, or on the other hand to declare that only autocratic states fulfil the true requirements of statehood, is to develop a 'mission theory' of the state which has nothing to do with what states actually are.

It is noteworthy that as against the prescriptive idea of the state Marxist literature has urged the prescriptive claim of an ultimately stateless society. Hegel standing on his head with a vengeance! We have mentioned earlier the Marxist view of the state as the institutional expression and guarantor of the class structure of society; as the instrument by which a ruling class, whether a traditional aristocracy, a bourgeoisie or the proletariat, coerces the ruled. This feature is undoubtedly true of states historically, and Marxist political analysis shone a hard light upon the structures of present and past political communities in pointing it out. But it is difficult to see why states should necessarily institutionalize class divisions, or that a classless society, assuming such to be possible

[18] For example, R. M. Maciver and Charles H. Page, *Society*, Macmillan, London, 1961.

whether desirable or not, should necessarily be a stateless one, or in any sense more moral or prescriptively indicated than a political community organized as a state, whether or not this sustains a particular class structure.

We may conclude that the prescriptive idea of the state offers no resolution of the predicaments of international society. An assemblage of 'ideal' states, if we could conceive such a thing, each one of which would by definition according to the doctrine be wholly good and unexceptionably moral, would still be locked in the position of having to assert and defend interests, which it is hard to believe would not sometimes at least prove mutually exclusive.

The prescriptive form of the state, similarly, suggests nothing that could be regarded as offering a transformation of international society. Democratic states and authoritarian states find themselves from time to time at odds with each other. Hostile ideologies may sharpen conflict between states. Shared ideologies may not prevent conflict on other grounds. The primacy of national interests remains the compelling factor in foreign policy. Moral perceptions and prescriptive theories have always to take account of this fact or cease to be relevant considerations in seeking to understand or formulate norms of international behaviour.

To sum up: (i) We have seen that moral criteria may properly be applied to the actions of states. (ii) The condition of sovereignty in which states exist motivates many activities which find their justification under *raisons d'état*. This consideration does not, however, lift states beyond morality. It provides only the special context in which state morality operates, helping to define the area in which states may make moral choices. (iii) Such general provisos indicate the distinction that is to be made between the morality of states and that of men. (iv) Men acting on behalf of states are in their role as statesmen to be judged in relation to the opportunities and constraints which peculiarly govern state behaviour. Karl Marx's dictum that true freedom lies in the recognition of necessity will help us to assess the moral quality of state behaviour. (v) We have rejected the notion that law is only binding which issues from a supreme law-giver, and accept that in making arrangements between themselves to which they attribute the status of law states are undertaking to be bound by them. International law is thus true law. (vi) We have suggested that in international relations the moral factor may be – or may seem to be – less powerful than expediency in motivating action, while insisting that it is rarely expedient to leave moral considerations out of account. Norms of international conduct combine in practice with expediency and prudence to cause the law which states have developed among themselves to be generally observed, and to strengthen the elements both of scrupulosity and rationality which do enter into the behaviour of states. (vii) However, we recognize that the liberty of choice open to statesmen is limited and constrained in very many ways, and hence their moral scope. As Michael Howard has well said, 'Those moralists who consider the choice to be a simple one are greatly to be envied'.[19] So much is this so that the statesman is best regarded as doing the best he can in the context of an unending and commonly highly exacting predicament.

International order remains necessary. It depends partly upon the exercise of power by states and international organizations, partly upon the observance throughout international society of norms and rules of conduct. Basic to 'good' behaviour among states as among men are the recognition of legitimate mutual expectations, and a general acceptance of the duty to obey law. The 'law of nations' is not imposed from above. It is agreed between the nations themselves, who consent to be subject to it. *Pacta sunt servanda* – 'agreements are to be kept' – is not a *fiat* issued by a supreme authority. It is a legal principle, deriving from the felt expediency of a notion of reciprocity in the relations of states. Their ultimate interests are protected by the understood rider to the principle – *rebus sic stantibus* – 'while things remain the same'. The perennial difficulty is to preserve a stable order in international society while allowing for necessary (and as far as possible peaceful) change. Any given *status quo* is always under some question, and in process of some revision. However, the attribution by states to each other of rights and complementary duties remains essential if any international order is to survive and function. 'Law and order', it has been uncomfortably remarked,[20] 'rest ultimately upon a confidence trick'. While this is putting the matter strongly, it is clear that no order can persist through a general disregard either of norms or of the rules that enshrine them. Defiance and breach on a wide enough scale ensure chaos. If there is a 'common interest'

---

[19] In a footnote to the lecture cited on p. 26 – 'Morality and Force in International Politics'.

[20] Reputedly by a learned law lord in 1971.

at all among states, it lies certainly in the prevention of chaos in international society.

The moral status of men

In this chapter we have sought to delimit the nature and scope of international morality: i.e. moral relations between states. And we have tried to suggest what might seem valid distinctions to be made between international morality and moral relations between individual men. We have ventured to maintain that one of the most important of these distinctions is that between the moral obligations implicit in a man's role as a father, husband, friend, citizen, etc. and those implicit in his role as a statesman, as, that is to say, the human instrument whereby those notional persons known as states pursue their relations with each other. Morality remains socially determined, as we suggested at the beginning of this chapter, but it is no less conditioned by the roles assumed within society, whether human society or that 'metasociety', the society of states.

There is, however, one last aspect of the question upon which we must touch, although space requires that this be summarily done. What, it may fairly be asked, of the relations between states on the one side and men on the other, assuming the latter to be themselves *sources of innate rights and claims?* We cannot go here into that view of man which regards him as such a source. But clearly, if he is so regarded, then the behaviour of the state towards him, and of states towards each other in the influence of that behaviour upon him, become of critical moral significance.

In such a case, states have a moral obligation, whatever their conceived interests or political aspirations, to behave in ways that will not prevent the exercise of such innate rights and the fulfilment of such innate claims as individual men are deemed to possess. Indeed, it could properly be urged that states have an obligation to do more than merely refrain from denying men their rights and claims; rather should they seek actively to establish conditions in which the realization of human needs deriving from innate rights and claims is promoted. This consideration leads to that view of the state which sees it as discharging its moral function only in so far as it makes more possible all that may be implied in the phrase 'the Good Life'. This in turn harks back to the classic Greek philosophy of the state which regards it as in its fundamental purpose to provide means whereby human excellence may be attained. Such conceptions underlie the whole machinery of social provision characteristic, in greater or lesser degree, of all modern states laying claim to civilization.

However, we are still left with the difficulty that some of the claims made by men, which they might well regard as arising from their human status, may involve their state acting in ways inimical to the well-being of other states. And so we find ourselves back in the midst of those moral predicaments which we suggested earlier are bound up in the very fabric of international relations. If, for instance, a German Nazi considered, as indeed he appears to have done, that he had an innate right, by virtue of his innate superiority over other men, to rule Europe through conquest, the assumed innate right of non-Germans to retain their personal freedom and political autonomy became fatally compromised, and could only be defended or reasserted by a resort to force, which might result in a degree of mutual destruction (and nearly did) in which the exercise of any meaningful rights by anybody became for the time being gravely curtailed.

We may readily – and gratefully – admit that the concept of innate rights and claims inhering in individual human beings, and in human groups as well, arises from one of the most sensitive insights of both Christianity and other religions. But in the world as we observe it to be, and in so far as international society is concerned, the concept, however valuable and ultimately essential it may be to the realization of the Good Life by individual men and mankind as a whole, remains hedged about and qualified by moral ambiguities of an intractable kind.

We now pass to some discussion of that form of international relationship which has symbolized the predicaments facing statesmen most dramatically, and posed for them and their peoples the acutest moral and prudential perplexities, namely war.

7
The international relationship of war

And 'mid this tumult Kubla heard from far
Ancestral voices prophesying war! – *Samuel Taylor Coleridge.*

Wars are the physical outcome of extreme psychological tensions
involving concepts of honour and valour in approved forms and,
provided the necessary catharsis is achieved, scale is irrelevant –
Professor Stuart Piggott.

It is a good thing war is so terrible, or we should become too fond
of it – *General Robert E. Lee.*

If the people were kept in order, the official people would never
make war – *Robert, Marquess of Salisbury, British prime minister and
foreign secretary.*

History shows that there are no invincible armies – *J. V. Stalin.*

The nature of war

War is the practice of organized armed violence between human
groups. Its occurrence goes back to the dawn of history. It is not
improbable that small nomadic groups of *Homo sapiens sapiens*,
in the form of Cro-Magnon Man, in their wandering search for
food supplies, met and fought with family parties of their rugged
contemporary, *Homo sapiens neanderthalis*. Certainly the recording
of war is co-terminous with recorded history. Among non-literate
societies, too, war has been endemic. Wherever population pressure
or food scarcity have grown critical, the latter often a direct result
of the former, such societies have engaged in form of forceful
competition called war. Nor have its motives always been so
mundane, or so rational, as the desire to obtain by force needed
resources. 'Man the warrior' appears to have gloried in fighting at

least in part for the stimulus and excitement it provides, and even where a given war can be related to the defence or extension of substantive interests it has in many ages been invested with attributes of glamour and visible splendour. Only slowly, and with reluctance, did soldiers accept the necessity in conditions of modern warfare not to appear gorgeous on the field of battle. And the ceremonial and parade aspects of military capacity have largely retained the quality of visual magnificence. The will to war appears to lie deep in the collective human psyche, in fact, and we may think it deeply significant that the sacred literatures of at least three of the world's great religions, Judaism, Christianity and Islam, not to mention Graeco-Roman polytheism, are full of imagery drawn from war and combat. The Lord of Hosts smites his enemies; the Christian is enjoined to put on the whole armour of God, including the breastplate of righteousness, the helmet of salvation and the sword of the spirit; the Moslem is promised great reward if he 'fights on the path of God'; while among the Greeks, Ares, and among the Romans, Mars, were worshipped as the tutelary deities of war itself.

We stress this aspect of warfare because it is well to remember that, although war is an instrument of policy, and may in certain circumstances represent a rational option before the makers of policy, the readiness and frequency with which men have resorted to it, and the exuberance with which they have justified it, and the nostalgia with which they have sometimes recalled it, would seem to have psychological roots that go perhaps to the depths of human nature, and have their origin possibly in behavioural traits of remote hominoids that pre-date humanity by millions of years. If so, the most earnest tracts of pacifists, and the clearest apprehensions of possible catastrophe on the part of contemporary mankind, may not eradicate the willingness of men, when tension between them is critically high, and the hostility it generates sufficiently acute, to organize that generalized and ordered violence which is war. As to the actual incidence of war, it seems safe to hazard the assertion that never during the last seven thousand years has the entire world been free from war everywhere at any given time. Men, in short, have been warriors ever. We might adapt the maxim of Aristotle and say that man is a war-making animal.

Clearly there are different kinds of war. We are concerned here chiefly with warfare between states. Throughout history political communities have devoted substantial resources of manpower and productive capacity to preparing for and waging wars. Motives have varied. But constant among them have been competition for raw materials, territorial disputes, trade rivalries, the sheer desire for conquest and political aggrandizement, and the appeal of military glory. With other contingent factors arising from particular historical circumstances, these motives, severally and in varying combinations, have induced men in all ages to exercise collective armed violence against other men. Also over much of history this violence has been ordered and regulated. Moral and prudential restraints have been widely applied. Elaborate codes of military conduct have been observed in many epochs. The 'art of war' has been consciously developed. And while in many periods ordinary fighting men have been feared as the symbols and agents of social disruption, and regarded, often with justice, as no more than the 'brutal soldiery', their leaders, following the 'profession of arms', have commonly enjoyed honourable status and high social prestige.

In war the problems of tactics in relation to strategy, of the intimate, varying interplay and mutual influence of means and ends, have been a major preoccupation of statesmen and soldiers for millennia past. In ancient China, for instance, commanders played war games with each other in an endeavour to perfect their art as practitioners of war. It has had to be universally recognized that nuclear weaponry in the modern world carries a danger to the survival of organized society, indeed to the continuance of life itself on earth. Yet its effects in inducing mankind to find an alternative to war for the *ultimate* defence of collective interests remain problematical. Nearly all states are signatories of the United Nations Charter. Under this they all explicitly forego the option of force in settling their inter-state disputes. Yet wars continue to take place. And it would be idle to deny that for much of human history the destructiveness and misery of war have been gilded by an attributed glamour which has often been intensely felt. Plutarch[1] tells a story of the famous Epirot king, Pyrrhus, whose name has passed adjectively into the languages of modern Europe in the

---

[1] Plutarch, *Lives of the Noble Greeks and Romans*. A useful selection is made by Penguin Books.

phrase 'Pyrrhic victory'.[2] One of the king's counsellors, by name Cineas, asked him the purpose of his military preparations. 'To enter Italy and overthrow the power of Rome.' – 'And then?' – 'To conquer all Italy.' – 'And then?' – 'Italy fallen, we can then conquer Sicily.' – 'And after that?' – 'Why, neither Libya nor Carthage could resist us then.' – 'Indeed, my king, and following their submission you could conquer Macedon and the whole of Greece. What then?' – 'Why, my friend, then we shall sit down and feast.' – 'But', remarked Cineas, 'you could do that now, without the spending of so much blood and treasure.' Plutarch comments that Pyrrhus was troubled by such reasoning, without being able to abandon hope of what he so much desired. An element of real megalomania, similarly, seems to have infected the mind of Alexander the Great in his later career, though there was more than megalomania in his make-up. And it is said of Julius Caesar, on active service in Spain at the age of thirty-four, that he lamented that before that period of life Alexander had conquered the world.

Historically, martial delight, the desire for glory and the use of armed might by the state to protect its security or extend its presence in international society, have all combined to make of warfare as real and as regular a feature of international relations as peaceful cooperation. Hostility after all is itself a form of relationship. Diplomatic contact has customarily been ruptured between states who are on the brink of war with one another, but when the war ensues they are linked together in a relationship of peculiarly intense intimacy. Both peace and war must be seen as positive aspects of international politics. War is far more than merely the breakdown of peace, just as peace is far more than the mere absence of war.

We are forcibly reminded of this when we keep in view the fact that in addition to the misery and destruction they cause wars have always tended to become forcing-houses of social and technological change, much of which has been regarded by those subject to it as beneficial. War produces necessities of special urgency, and these mother many inventions. At no period has this function of war operated more dramatically than during the decades which have passed since the close of the Franco-Prussian war in 1871.

[2] Pyrrhus won a battle against the Romans so costly to his army that he said to his generals, 'Another victory like that and we are done for'.

Industrialization has given rise to the most momentous developments in the scale, and hence in the effects, of all wars fought in the last century between the so-called developed nations, as well as being in turn stimulated by them. Even among nations less developed, enough technological sophistication has been experienced to change the character of traditional war-making. That pleasing roseate pattern, seen from the air, of Abyssinian tribesmen scattering in all directions as Italian aircraft bombed them, which was said to have so fascinated and charmed Mussolini, may symbolize the profound impact of industrial technology on warfare everywhere in the world.

The real destructiveness of war is clearly relative to the size of population and the level of political culture and economic capacity prevailing in any given situation. In such terms, the condition of much of Germany after the thirty years' war, and of much of Italy after the second Punic war, yielded nothing in dreadfulness to the desolation of parts of Europe after each of the twentieth-century world wars. It is, however, interesting to notice that expectations this century that modern wars would be so destructive that they must needs be short have not been borne out. The second world war, far more materially destructive if perhaps less psychologically damaging than the first, lasted two years longer. Moreover, if the accessibility of many states to attack with modern weapons is in some respects greater than ever before, and the inflictable damage correspondingly huge, the capacity of industrialized societies to recover has been comparably large, as we have seen in the cases of Japan and Germany after 1945.

Two features characteristic of the modern industrial state have contributed significantly to the total character of much modern war. One is the ability of governments by virtue of their direct control of national economies to mobilize a far greater share of resources for making war than their predecessors in earlier periods could do. The other arises from mass participation in national political processes, which may be observed, in one constitutional form or another, in most of the industrially advanced countries of the world. A vital aspect of the totality possible in modern war lies in the capacity of governments by their manipulation of the mass media of communication to strengthen and sustain a collective will to fight on, and in turn to be responsive to such articulated will. It has on the whole been electorates in the present century which in wartime have denied that there was any 'substitute for victory', and which have sanctioned an insistence on unconditional surrender, as formulated for example by the allied leadership in the second world war. To be cheated by negotiation of absolute victory when it has sacrificed so much is likely to seem intolerable to the embattled nation.

Yet the situation is far from simple. It may be true that the 'general will' of the nation in arms is likely to remain strong for total victory in total war. But it is evident that for this will to sustain itself real victory must appear really attainable. Perhaps considerations of moral propriety, certainly those of political calculation, impelled the United States government to apply severe but not total military sanctions against the perpetrators of what in its eyes represented communist aggression from North Vietnam against the South. No one can doubt that the United States could, by the use of nuclear weapons, have ended at any time since 1961 with a terrible finality the capacity of the North Vietnamese to wage war of any kind. But the political risks and costs involved in some kind of nuclear obliteration of the North were unacceptably great. Even as it was, the threat of one American general that the United States air force would 'bomb North Vietnam into the Stone Age' was substantially carried out by the forces concerned. Short of a possible but inhibited total destruction of North Vietnam the war proved unwinnable in any absolute sense. Inside the United States the consensus in support of the operation steadily diminished. The Administration found itself obliged to court political advantage by seeking ways of extrication from the commitment. However, the American electorate as a whole, deeply disillusioned as it was over the outcome of the war, remained inevitably sensitive about the issue of national prestige. Hence the withdrawal of the American presence, in response to a national will expressed with varying emphasis that the war should be ended, was conducted with caution, in phases, and accompanied by the American government's assurances on all sides that the national honour was not being sacrificed, nor American objectives abandoned, but rather that the intervention of the United States had enabled the regime in South Vietnam to maintain the struggle successfully on its own for the future. The convincingness of these assurances was of less importance than the political necessity to utter them.

Attitudes to war

Because of its dramatic and forceful character, war brings up sharply the problem of morality in international relations which in general terms we discussed in the last chapter. Moral attitudes towards war can broadly be grouped, we suggest, into four.

(i) There is the view that war is a morally neutral instrument of state policy, the only considerations governing its use being prudential ones.[3]

(ii) Others hold that war is a morally ambiguous instrument of policy, to be employed as a last resort, in circumstances which can plausibly be advanced as a moral justification by reference to understood criteria defining the justice of a war. This is still the Catholic position.

(iii) Yet others maintain that war is inherently and therefore always evil, but that its outbreak is a manifestation of man's imperfection, or 'fallen' nature. War is hence to be avoided if possible, endured if not. The conception of the miseries of war as a divine judgement upon a sinful society represents a special case of this doctrine.

(iv) Lastly there are those who insist that war is indeed inherently evil, and that resort to it can never be justified in any circumstances whatever. The religious denomination within the Christian tradition which has remained most consistently close to this absolute pacifism has been the Society of Friends (the Quakers). We suggested in the last chapter that the outright pacifist option is not open to politicians charged with responsibility for foreign affairs in international society as it exists. So much the worse, perhaps, for international society. But in practice absolute pacifists are protected, possibly against their wish, by the willingness of those who are not pacifists to assume the burdens of collective self-defence.

One other attitude to war in the modern world should be noted. It may be called the 'biological' view, and it takes two main forms. The first regards war as a positive good, in that it tends to

[3] The classic statement of this view of war is in Clausewitz (*Vom Kreige*, book 1 chapter 1): 'We see, therefore, in the first place, that under all circumstances war is to be regarded not as an independent thing, but as a political instrument. . . . This is the only means of unlocking the great book and making it intelligible . . . this view shows us how wars must differ in character according to the nature of the motives and circumstances from which they proceed.'

ensure 'the survival of the fittest', the fittest in this context being, presumably, those states that prove victorious. Linked with this view, which may seem to us no more than a crude misapplication of a misunderstood Darwinism to international society, are those notions of war as 'the pruning-hook of society', cutting out dead wood, or as a bracing ordeal by fire, tempering the quality of men, etc. We may think that the evidence that those who survive war are either ennobled by it or inherently superior to those who perish in it is far to seek. Although their source eludes us, perhaps four lines of extremely unfashionable verse, with their period flavour of martial religiosity, may stand as the archetypical expression of this particular functional view of war:

> And as I note how nobly natures form
> Under the war's red rain, I deem it true
> That He who made the earthquake and the storm
> Perchance made battles too.

The other form of the biological interpretation of the significance of war is much closer to our own time. In fact it largely arises from the recognition of unique contemporary perils posed by modern war and the military technology it may employ.

A respectable body of opinion now holds that whatever the practicability and moral acceptability of war as an instrument of policy may have been in the past, the indiscriminate and potentially universal destructiveness of certain modern weapons has made war biologically maladaptive for the human species. No advantage to any party can accrue from the waging of war by anyone with such weapons. War becomes inherently irrational: victory meaningless. Certainly it seems safe to say that a tacit recognition of the force of this view of nuclear war as representing biologically maladaptive behaviour has strengthened the will of policy-makers in the superpowers to seek first for a stable mutual deterrent, and then, as notably in the Soviet-American agreement on the limitation of anti-ballistic missiles of May 1972, and the interim agreement on the mutual limitation of strategic offensive arms of the same date, for a halt in a nuclear arms race between them which was coming to have less and less conceivable military purpose. In thus grappling with the implications before mankind of the nuclearization of military capacity (and by a natural extension, of the chemical and so-called biological dimensions of warfare), statesmen draw attention with peculiar force to the coming together in 'mutual support roles', to borrow a phrase from military parlance, of ethics, caution and reason, often uneasy allies, in the conduct of international relations.

Deterrence and nuclear weapons

The development of a body of deterrence theory, in response particularly to the predicament created by the coming into existence (through human choice and decision) of nuclear weapons, has represented an important area of intellectual activity, both on the part of policy-makers in the 'nuclear club', and their advisers, professional and academic. No discussion of the role of war in contemporary society can well leave it out.

A fundamental question to which theorists and commentators have had to address themselves is whether the nuclearization of strategic weapons (and the introduction of a nuclear capacity into certain classes of so-called tactical weapons as well), which will be technically available as an option to many states in the future, perhaps to twenty or thirty by the end of the century, will have changed the nature of war. Does the unique destructiveness of thermo-nuclear missiles represent a quantitative change so great as to amount to a qualitative one? No certain answer can be given at present. Basic strategic principles are said to remain unaltered. However, if general war remains permanently inhibited it can be argued that mankind has, in effect, abandoned it. This would suggest a qualitative change in the capacity of weapons to threaten, since hitherto weapons have demonstrated their effectiveness both in deterrence and in use, or, like poison gas, been given up because they proved unreliable in the field and too big a bother to operate in proportion to their military advantage. If, however, nuclear war does occur, deterrence will obviously have failed, and men will have shown themselves willing to employ the new weapons in an operational role. What is novel in the situation since the middle 1950s is the devotion of huge amounts of national resources by the nuclear powers to the development and increase of weapons which exist *in order not to be used*. Their deployment in actual conflict would then represent not the application of a received strategy but its failure. In the past, powerful nations developed weapon systems with the intention of gaining a hoped-for decisive military advantage in the event of war. While this consideration may not have been entirely ruled out of nuclear strategy, the primary purpose of nuclear weapons has been to deter general war altogether. Associated with this aim has been the hope that wars which do occur shall remain limited in location and fought at the sub-nuclear level. It is rather as if the nuclear powers were paraphrasing the old music-hall song and saying to each other:

We don't want to fight, but by jingo! not to do
Means adding H-Bombs to the pile – we think that you will too!

We may conclude that the essence of deterrence is mutual bluff. Nuclear weapons deter so long as they are not used. Any resort to them by one nuclear power would be virtually certain to provoke a counter-strike in kind by the nuclear power attacked, provided that its delivery capability had not been destroyed. Where uncertainty is greater the role of bluff becomes more delicate while remaining equally central to the issue. The use of nuclear weapons against non-nuclear adversaries is inhibited partly no doubt by the constraint of moral scruple, as well as by the calculation of the effects on 'world opinion'. But there is also the risk – some risk – that a nuclear ally of the non-nuclear victim of nuclear attack might feel obliged to undertake a nuclear response on its behalf. The likelihood of such a response is to be assessed in the light of judgements made about the strength of the obligations assumed, and hence the credibility of the threat posed. In short, how far can the bluff be called in a given case? General de Gaulle, in the middle 1960s, evidently became convinced that the United States would not risk near annihilation for the sake of Western Europe by offering a nuclear counter-strike to the Soviet Union in response to a Soviet attack on her European allies, and publicly insisted that French safety lay ultimately in a unilateral French deterrent capability. This of course need not be, and could not be, comparable in scale to the nuclear threat it opposed. It need only be 'enough'. In effect, France declared her belief that the ability of one French missile to get through and knock out, say, Kiev or Minsk, rendered all France the safer.

This strategic doctrine had its counterpart in the British case for an 'independent nuclear deterrent'. But while the official wisdom in France maintained the doctrine in a more or less pure form, a tacit acceptance came to prevail in Britain that her nuclear armoury,

although the third greatest in the world, could only credibly discharge its deterrent role in coordination with the nuclear defence
system of the West as a whole, which meant in practice that of the
United States, although in deference to her own national *amour
propre* Britain retained a formal autonomy of decision regarding
that armoury's strategic deployment.

We notice here that strategic considerations do not stand alone
but are bound up with the factor of national prestige. For we still
live in a world in which a high military capacity, which it is hoped
of course will be used responsibly, remains prestigious. Since 1945
the two most important symbols of great power status have been
permanent membership of the United Nations Security Council
and the possession of nuclear weapons. As the late Lord Attlee[4]
made clear, Britain did not 'go nuclear' as the result of a change of
political course, or after agonized heart-searching on the part of
British policy-makers. Britain had the industrial and technological
capacity to do it: as a major power – indeed, as 'officially' a great
power – it was simply natural for her to do what she was able to do.
Her very responsibilities in the world obliged her. Such at least
was the implicit doctrine. It seems never to have occurred to the
British government of the time to take any step other than to
authorize the military expenditure involved in keeping the country
strategically 'up to date'. And when left-wing critics denounced
the British nuclear presence in the world, apparently on grounds
that it in some way endangered peace, or made international harmony less attainable, the late Aneurin Bevan justified government
policy to his fellow socialists and to anyone else who was listening
at least as much for reasons of national prestige as for strategic
desirability. 'We must not', he said, 'go naked into the conference
chamber.'[5] Together with a motive of no doubt genuine strategic
concern, French national pride found the spectacle of nuclear
status enjoyed by France's island ally while not a symbol of her
own international standing intolerable. The *force de frappe* came
into being, and *grandeur* was served.

[4] In a characteristically laconic statement to a research student at Aberystwyth
investigating the nuclear policy of the British Labour government after 1945.

[5] In 1946 the late Konni Zilliacus sent his prime minister a six-page memorandum deploring the orientation of British foreign policy. Attlee replied in three
lines: 'My dear Zilly, Thank you for sending me your memorandum which
seems to me to be based on an astonishing lack of understanding of the facts.
Yours ever, Clem.' (Attlee Papers, University College, Oxford.)

Whatever restraints upon the use or even threat of weapons of mass and indiscriminate destruction may be agreed to mutually by states, their potentiality remains. For if it were to be either explicitly or tacitly agreed all round that nuclear weapons would never be used an aggressor could proceed as if they did not exist at all. Therefore, countries or blocs of countries possessing them must ultimately, in conceivable circumstances, be prepared to use them if nuclear status is to retain any meaning. And nations have an interest in upholding and if possible enhancing their status, and do not readily relinquish it. It is true that the nuclear powers have made it generally clear that none of them will be the first to unleash nuclear bombs, but maintain them purely in a retaliatory role. Yet difficulties remain. If facing defeat in a 'conventional' war the temptation for a nuclear power to seek to retrieve the situation by calling up its ultimate weapons might become overwhelming. Moreover, a spread of nuclear weapons to other powers (which on grounds of international stability as well as their own status the members of the 'nuclear club' have been anxious to prevent) might make the tracing of an initial attack to a particular source uncertain. A misjudgement here, with a retaliatory strike at the wrong enemy, would seem likely to spread the nuclear exchange and send the consequent strategic situation out of control.

It is fair to say that a good deal of sophisticated flexibility has been built into strategic doctrines since the days when almost any act of aggression, expecially in Europe, was allegedly to be countered by 'massive retaliation'. While a would-be aggressor could never be certain this would not be forthcoming, the credibility of the threat steadily lessened. A real problem for the NATO alliance was its limited capacity to threaten anything very different. A full-scale communist ground attack across Europe had to be deterred by nuclear power since it evidently could not be defeated by conventional forces. The consequence of devoting the greater part of any country's defence resources to a costly nuclear capability was that a minor trespass might invoke the threat of 'ultimate' punishment. Now and then defence postures arising out of this dilemma – that of either acquiescence or over-reaction – approached absurdity.[6] Then slowly, with sudden falls of tempera-

[6] This was illustrated in 1953 when the Chairman of the United States Atomic Energy Commission declared: 'We will tolerate no debate as to the meaning of aggression. We'll know aggression when we see it . . . it is an

ture interspersed with gleams of wintry sunshine, the cold war in Europe began to thaw. 'Phased response' came into fashion as a part of current strategic doctrine. Not only was it accepted that there was much to be said for the European *status quo* in any case, but strategists on both sides felt their way to an understanding that limited trespass should be met by sufficient but correspondingly limited sanctions. Even in the nuclear field itself the renewed rationality was evident. Formulae were prepared suggesting ways by which a nuclear exchange could be phased on a basis of mutual understanding. Graduated response had been worked out in an *ad hoc* way in the so-called management of the Cuban missile crisis in 1962. Its general applicability became apparent. The notion basically is that a deliberately signalled pause follows each retaliatory act, in the hope that the offender will have 'had enough' and abandon his unacceptable attempt to change the *status quo*. A strategy of graduated response calls for strong nerves in those charged with carrying it out, tight political and military control, the efficient manipulation of domestic opinion, a reliable system of communication with the enemy himself, and a high level of accurate information. These are exacting specifications, and in the contingencies of the real world are not likely all to be at their optimum at one time. This may remind us that the term 'decision-maker' itself, hallowed as it is by wide usage in political science, may be at least as misleading as it is useful. It suggests a picture of wise elders, seated on the thrones of authority, gravely assessing the information placed before them, itself complete, accurate and in helpful sequence, and calmly issuing the best decisions to which their meditations give rise. Things are not like that in international politics. We need equally a word which will imply the relative ignorance, turmoil and haste amid which statesmen must discharge their harassing function. But in the taxing field of strategic theory, the doctrine of graduated response, as applied to the actual conformation of contemporary military power, and as likely to remain

aggression when a mortar or weapons carrier from the Skoda Works . . . is found next to a dead man from the Western world . . . enough when a MIG employed to assist an aggression can be traced to a Russian factory.' This sort of talk introduced the notion of indirect aggression. And all aggression, the world was informed, would be met 'by all available means'. Reduced to the ludicrous, this could have meant that the Soviet Union would be threatened by a nuclear strike if the Italian Communist Party gained seats in an election. Senator Barry Goldwater at one stage actually talked publicly in this vein. However, with the beginnings of *détente*, comparative sanity reasserted itself.

relevant for the foreseeable future, has the very great merit of a high degree of rationality, and represents a means by which a significant political dialogue can be carried on between enemies, even while they are engaged in pitting against one another their respective strengths.

Meanwhile, nuclear (and apparently various types of chemical and biological) weapons exist. They cannot be wished away or readily dismantled. Even if general nuclear disarmament became a fact, which might not in itself prove an unmixed blessing in regard to the overall stability of the international order, the technological capacity to rearm would remain. No suggested system of inspection and control succeeded in commanding the necessary assent of both the chief nuclear powers throughout the 1950s and 1960s. Wars at the sub-nuclear level, if sufficiently prolonged, are likely to prove more destructive than ever before. Nor can it be denied that modern conditions neither prevent nor perceptibly inhibit the resort to organized violence on a relatively large scale in many parts of the world. Since 1945 major wars, involving great destruction and many thousands – or hundreds of thousands – of casualties have occurred in Korea, Indo-China, North Africa, West Africa, south-east Asia, and the Indian sub-continent. There have also been serious conflicts in the Middle East, arguably the most dangerous potentially anywhere in the world, since a group of Arab states determined to prove an irresistible force, and an Israeli state resolved to be an immovable object, might bring into direct confrontation their respective champions, the United States and the Soviet Union. However, in the course of these various struggles, and in response to their implications for international peace and security, a doctrine of *limited war* has been developed, which seeks to provide political means whereby actual wars can be deliberately restricted in space and time by the caution and restraint observed by third parties, in particular the superpowers, who have long accepted the vital requirement that they should not if humanly possible become involved in situations which set them on a collision course. Thus Vietnam remained a minor threat to world peace, whatever the horrors prevailing inside Vietnam itself, because the Americans avoided using 'ultimate' weapons to defeat North Vietnam, and the Russians (and Chinese) limited their aid to the North to supplies and ideological support.

On the other hand, technical developments in weaponry now render traditional categories of arms less clear. For example, modern so-called tactical nuclear weapons, for deployment on the battlefield, have become so destructive as to assume a strategic significance. Other devices, such as the systematic defoliation of forested areas, and the widespread use of napalm, involve a degree of destructiveness at the level of tactical operations which assumes a 'total' character.

As a prominent military feature of the age the spread since the 1950s of *intra-state* violence in many parts of the world must not be overlooked. A conventional sequence traces the increasing pressure of dissident violence from terrorism, through insurgency and guerrilla warfare to full-scale civil war. Something like thirty-two major intra-state disturbances falling within that spectrum are said to have broken out, in every continent including Oceania, since 1945. Many have been prolonged, generating a degree of intractable bitterness which has made difficult to the point of impossibility any kind of viable political community embracing the sub-communities, tribes, races, sections, groups who have been locked in the most forceful defence of their evidently mutually exclusive interests. 'World peace' in our age remains at best a highly qualified, partial and incomplete thing.

One of the most notorious features of strategic doctrine as developed in the recent past has been the attempt to analyse and assess the likelihood and consequences of possible catastrophe in deliberately unemotional, coolly calculating terms. The implication seemed to be that to open our minds imaginatively to the human realities in the military possibilities would be so overwhelming psychologically as probably to induce either hysteria or despair. In any case it would cloud judgement and make less practicable the salvaging of something from chaos. So Hermann Kahn, an American scholar of strategic thought, produced a work of careful if inevitably sombre analysis and called it simply, *Thinking about the Unthinkable*.[7]

It would be unfair to assume that writers such as Mr Kahn, by adopting the technique of cool survey, were proving themselves to be callous, inhumane and merely 'cold fish'. Rather were they, with disconcerting calm, seeking to clarify strategic problems to show how statesmen, who do have to take account of political

[7] Praeger, New York, 1962.

moods and public emotions, might nevertheless shape policy on the basis of a fully articulated 'arithmetic of doom'. The propositions appeared the more terrible because removed from a direct or easy appeal to people's anxieties and sense of horror or compassion. We should bear in mind too that much of this strategic thinking was done in the acute phase of the cold war. It was a response to what then seemed an unremittingly hostile confrontation of superpowers whose national interests were closely identified with what were stridently asserted to be, by their respective believers, mutually exclusive political value-systems.

So the strategists discussed concepts such as *overkill*. This represented the formal capacity of a given stock of nuclear weapons to kill the total population of a potential enemy several times over. The suggestion came to be made by a number of academic observers[8] that the development of such a capacity was irrational. Enough was enough. There was little justification for a rigidity in the economic system or a lack of political initiative which encouraged an armaments industry to go on producing a surplus nuclear capacity that could never have any conceivable military use. Strategists also solemnly assessed the upper limits of 'acceptable damage' that might be sustained in a *nuclear exchange*, a phrase which came to stand as a euphemism for war. Could the American political community, it was asked, be expected to 'accept' casualties numbering, ten, thirty, sixty millions before complete social and political collapse ensued? Should the main effort be to create an overwhelming preemptive strike capacity, or a 'hardened', that is to say, undestroyable, counter-strike capacity? What in fact appeared to be the most credible, and therefore convincing, defence posture to adopt in the nuclear age? These were vital questions, and people who grew impatient with the whole debate, or assumed that there was (and is) a simple and readily available solution to the security dilemmas posed by the epoch-making advance of the human race in the field of military technology, merely revealed an impaired understanding of the realities of contemporary international politics.

The 'doomsday debate', in the context of a situation in which acute tension long existed and might recur between the principal nuclear powers, and in which nuclear proliferation, with its

[8] See for example, Max Lerner, *The Age of Overkill*, Simon & Schuster, New York, 1962.

destabilizing dangers, remained a probable factor in world politics, and in which existing weapons had a destructive capability global in its effects, was neither absurd nor inhuman. Both strategists and the political leaders they advised had, and have, an implicit duty laid upon them to go on trying to devise strategic concepts and dispositions that would and will safeguard substantive interests and effectively postpone doomsday itself. And while it may still be true beyond what is comfortable that 'knowledge comes but wisdom lingers', those charged with the responsibility have so far succeeded that general peace, however precariously, was maintained for a generation, and men need not yet wholly subscribe to the sentiment expressed in a London *graffiti*, 'live for today: tomorrow has been cancelled'.

War a social disease?

The Department of War Studies in the University of Manchester was placed for reasons of academic policy in the Faculty of Social Studies. It is said that the grounds were that war is to be regarded as a form of 'social aberration', to be approached accordingly. This pathological view of war is respectably argued and widely held. But in its simple form it can be challenged. Earlier in this chapter we sketched in what we suggested were the principal attitudes to war commonly held. One of these, sanctioned by the high arguments of the great Clausewitz, was the instrumental interpretation. This regarded war as a means by which states have traditionally sought to attain objectives that arise out of a participation in international politics which they cannot escape if they would. To the notion of war as an instrument of policy rather than a pathological condition of policy we must now briefly return.

We have already had occasion to repeat that to be a state is to be involved in international politics. This is a defining condition of statehood. Broadly speaking, most states seek to be as active in international politics as they can, realizing that by so doing they are likely to defend their interests best. Certainly no major state can in practice be little involved. We have noticed that in the isolationist 1920s the United States was so important to the world that its internal economic fortunes had critical effects almost everywhere else. This would have happened whether or not American political leaders wished to be isolationist. This posture was in itself a reaction to the perceived facts of international society, and so represented a policy towards the rest of the world.

Now war in modern conditions may well seem the least welcome option before a state. It is likely to represent the last policy resort. But short of a decision by international society as a whole both to 'outlaw' war and to observe the rules of outlawry, the use of war as an instrument of policy remains open to states. Rarely, it would seem, have states refrained from war on moral grounds. Invariably, when they refrain, it has been on prudential grounds. Neville Chamberlain, in seeking to appease Hitler and reach what he believed could be regarded as an honourable accommodation with the leader of the Reich, did not say, 'War is wrong in itself; therefore we must never fight Germany again'. He said, 'There are no victors in modern war'. Though this judgement may have represented an overstatement, it powerfully suggested that war had become a uniquely dangerous policy option to adopt. Yet, as the 1930s showed, it may also prove extremely difficult to avoid. Granted that in many respects the long-term interests of Europe as a whole required that 'Hitler be stopped' (and it remains highly unfashionable to argue that it would have been better for Europe if he had not been stopped), it is hard to see how this could have been done without the threat, and almost certainly the actuality, of war, given the conformation of European power at the time, the prevailing diplomatic situation and the intense, some would say demonic, quality of German political leadership.

The view that war represents a social aberration, a departure from some universal norm, is very hard to sustain in view of what we have already seen as the prevalence of war during all recorded history. Gibbon's famous dictum that history is the record of 'the vices, follies and crimes of mankind' doubtless appears much too partial a view, inspired by that tendency towards philosophic pessimism to which aristocratic ages seem to be prone. Certainly, however, warfare, with all its misery, as well perhaps as many positive achievements, has been woven closely into the fabric of human history, and has provided the dominant interest and activity of men in particular epochs. The Middle Ages in Europe may have been the 'Ages of Faith'; they were unquestionably ages of almost perpetual war. Periods of profound peace have been for most peoples an exceptional experience, precious breathing-spaces it may be, and 'times of troubles' far more frequent.

Nor is this the whole story. The *Pax Romana* from the first to the third centuries AD may seem in many respects a Golden Age, a high noon of sunny peace and prosperity throughout the civilized Mediterrannean world. But the safety of the provinces was only assured by constant vigilance along the frontiers and frequent border wars. In retrospect even the last third of the nineteenth century, in ferment as in many ways it was, by its avoidance of major war between the powers may seem to have something of a Golden Age about it. But such periods of peace are not free from acute tensions. War in Europe often seemed imminent after 1871. 'War in sight' was a phrase made notorious at one stage by Bismarck himself, whose diplomatic balancing act, superbly accomplished, just contrived to maintain peace at the price of the build-up of alliance systems which in the end did much to ensure the ultimate outbreak of war between them.

But perhaps the most serious qualification to be made about the 'social aberration' theory of war derives from the fact that Golden Ages, at least in terms of cultural achievements and an intense collective awareness of and response to life, have often *not* corresponded with general peace and plenty but rather the reverse. The Golden Age of the Greek city-states, which always existed on a relatively narrow economic margin, when their greatest attainments in literature, the visual arts and philosophy, natural and political, were reached, was characterized by a prevalence of war so constant that intervals of peace were entirely untypical.[9] On the other hand, the *Pax Romana*, majestic as it doubtless appeared, did not display a corresponding grandeur of intellectual or aesthetic endeavour. Though not negligible in these respects the age remained essentially derivative. The Roman Empire became, as it were, the custodian of a cultural heritage which it could never emulate, although this is, of course, not to deny that in the fields of jurisprudence, administration and communications it proved itself the queen of antiquity, and laid foundations on which subsequent European civilization was built. For such a stewardship succeeding ages have been grateful. But it was the Greeks, who, in the constant turmoil of their inter-state politics, erupting almost continuously into open war, established the rudiments of scientific method, scaled the heights of philosophical speculation and created tradi-

[9] See a characteristically lively discussion in A. R. Burn, *The Warring States of Greece*, Thames & Hudson, London, 1968.

tions in the arts that have quickened the perceptions of generations since. It might be argued that the Greeks did all this despite their *penchant* for war, and their ultimately disastrous failure to achieve Hellenic unity. It is true that at times exhaustion supervened, and that a decline in vitality was evident during and after the fourth century BC in most institutions of Greek life, including eminently the state itself. Yet this too was in part at least compensated for by a sharpening of the spirit of critical enquiry. But it is as easy to argue that Greek vitality was all of a piece, that the spiritual energy and intellectual restlessness which typified the Greek personality prompted not only the great art and high thought but also the tendency to quarrel, to formulate collective interests recklessly at each other's expense, and to pursue these by a ready resort to war.

Nor has a combination of high cultural attainment with a low threshold of armed violence been confined to classical antiquity. Parallels can be found in the history of Chinese and African civilizations, as well as in that of the Italian Renaissance.

However this may be, war was and remains a central theme in international politics. It highlights in a uniquely striking way the predicaments which statesmen have to face. At least as much as peace, war is a positive aspect of international relations. If peace is an interest, war has traditionally been an instrument for pursuing interests. The question, as we have seen, is whether any political interests are now so vital as to justify conflict that might seriously involve the risk of general and total war. Even the survival of the state as a basic objective may be abandoned if such war was the only means left to pursue it. Thus Tunku Abdul Rahman, the architect of federated Malaysia, in the late 1960s declared with impressive candour that his country would not attempt to resist a major attack by the People's Republic of China (which he had no special reason to fear at the time). If such a threat ensued, he would sacrifice the state for the sake of preserving the community. Resistance would only too probably involve the destruction of both. In the past war has always been difficult to control and usually full of uncertainties. Just as some of its motivations lay below the level of rational calculation, so its results were rarely if ever narrowly predictable. But it remained a not wholly irrational instrument of policy, provided offensive war was as carefully prepared as possible and defensive war was entered upon with a sound assessment of the morale and will to resist of the home community. This element of rationality still applies, where there are good reasons for believing that the war will not involve other powers, especially the superpowers, in hostilities, and where there is therefore some prospect of the situation remaining more or less under the control of the wagers of war. However, the incalculables of modern war are perhaps greater than ever before. We might then expect that the prudential constraints on potential war-makers are correspondingly stronger. On the other hand, this has not meant that fewer wars break out. The tensions which lead to war still arise, and often attain their cathartic resolution in armed strife.

On the whole, we may best regard war as a tragic predicament. It remains, perhaps for the foreseeable future, a structual element in international society. So much so that it has been said that states 'exist in order to make war'. If man is the war-making animal, the state is the war-making institution. This represents an epigrammatical distortion. States, as we have seen, exist to promote the well-being of their subjects. This condition includes their security. On behalf of the collective good of well-being the comparative evil of war may need to be invoked. If we ask what the evil of war is comparative with, we must answer that war may represent the choice of a lesser evil, lesser, that is to say, than the evil of abandoning the responsibility of defending the well-being of the national community. The Tunku defined the lesser evil, in certain conceivable circumstances, in a different way. But the point illustrates the relevance of the view adopted in the last chapter that a sound ethic in international relations may require a decision as between evils, not the choice of good in preference to evil. We note again that such a choice symbolizes the role-bound predicament of statesmen.

The role of war aims

A significant aspect of the incalculability of war lies in the ambiguous nature of what used to be known as 'war aims'.

War aims may mask each other, or they may exist in varying degrees of importance in the minds of the war-makers and their followers. The ostensible and the real may be seriously at odds. If war aims represent an end, they tend to be changed during the course of the conflict by the means used to attain them. The actual fortunes of war affect them. The grandiose attempt by Hitler to impose a New Order on Europe, itself an aim arising out of the spectacular diplomatic and military successes of the Nazi government between 1936 and 1941, changed as the second world war proceeded into an increasingly desperate effort to ensure the bare survival of the Reich. What, by way of another instance, were the British war aims between 1914 and 1918?

There was of course the obvious basic aim of defeating the German and Austro-Hungarian Empires. But the immediate *casus belli* for Britain was the violation of Belgian neutrality, to which all the great powers were pledged by treaty. Sir Edward Grey, the British foreign secretary, had no doubt that honour obliged Britain not to leave France in a position of strategic disadvantage in relation to Germany, which would have arisen in part out of naval dispositions made on the basis of staff plans established between the French and British in secret talks. Further motives for British participation in the great European war may be sought. It is widely believed that Britain fought on behalf of a traditional principle of her foreign policy, namely to prevent the hegemony of Europe passing into the hands of a single great power. In 1914 Imperial Germany seemed to be that power. Britain also fought, some suggest, to be sure of a seat at the Peace Conference which sooner or later would have to be held to re-settle the affairs of Europe when the fighting ended. Britain could not, as a great power, have allowed European destinies to be decided without her voice being heard. But participation in the peace settlement could only be earned by participation in the war.

Whatever element of *post hoc* rationalization there may be in that suggestion, there are grounds for believing that other, subrational motives helped to drive the nations into the conflict. As a superb *Punch* satire published on the very day war was declared made clear, there were not wanting those who, in Britain and elsewhere, were spoiling for a fight after so lengthy a general peace. 'A decent little scrap among the powers would do us all good', might have been said, with not too much modification, in more than one London club during that warm July of 1914. Britain too had deep internal divisions, chiefly over Ireland, and, like her *entente* partner France, over industrial relations at the time; divisions which were temporarily closed by the entry into war. All over Europe the great struggle, the death-throes of the old Europe, opened in a mood of euphoric enthusiasm. Below the level of rational calculation, justifiable causes, the defence of vital or at least legitimate interests or the honourable discharge of international obligations, there seems to have been a genuine willingness for war in the minds of the belligerent peoples. Trafalgar Square, the *Place de la Concorde, Unter den Linden* and the *Nevsky Prospekt* alike rang with cheers. This may remind us how critical a part in the course of history may be played by the irrational elements in human motivation. It may clamour for explanation but perhaps is ultimately inexplicable. In the event, a swift military decision, so nearly grasped by Germany, eluded either side. With the development of a war of attrition the exuberance of its combatants evaporated. Hopes of a negotiated peace were canvassed but denounced by government spokesmen and national publicists on both sides as little short of treasonable. War aims grew more intractable and less rational. To some extent militarily, and to a great extent psychologically, the war passed out of the control of the political leaders in all the belligerent countries. As it did so the reiteration of war aims became more strident as the aims themselves grew vaguer. Peoples had to be told over and over again why they were fighting. In Britain the sanctity of treaties, the destabilizing increase of German might in Europe, became merged in visions of a land fit for heroes, a war to end war, and a new international order to maintain perpetual peace. At the same time the German enemy was felt to be increasingly dire and evil. 'The Hun was at the gate.' There had to be a 'knock-out blow'. And in the heady exultation of final 'victory' Germany had to be squeezed till the pips squeaked. Lloyd George may not himself have pronounced this striking metaphor, but it represented well enough the mood of many in his political community.

At the level of rational policy-making too war aims changed as the circumstances of war varied. It was no interest of Britain that the Austro-Hungarian Empire should be broken up. Almost to the last months of the war the British Government diplomatically resisted the tide of Balkan and Central European nationalism, with its determination to achieve successor states on the ruins of the ancient Habsburg realms. Then came acquiescence. The postwar Europe that emerged was vastly different than anyone had clearly envisaged in 1914. Even the most prescient Bolsheviks had not anticipated so near a chance to seize power. They simply snatched their opportunity, judging shrewdly that if they had received no mandate to govern, no Russian government had any longer a mandate to continue the war. We may say that Britain's specific war aims were in fact largely attained. Belgium was restored. France was supported. Britain participated in the postwar settlement, as a major partner. The German drive to hegemony was checked. (It may well be asked in passing how conscious that drive was, or how far it was a consequence of the buoyant industrialization of the most numerous and skilled national population in Central Europe. Like British imperialism, it seems likely that the German sense of mission less inspired expansion than was inspired by it.) But these war aims were attained in a situation greatly different from what had been hoped, and from what would have given them their maximum advantage for Britain. As it was, a largely impoverished United Kingdom, in a half-ruined Europe, faced problems brought about by the war but which no war aims had envisaged.

From this example we may suggest on good grounds that it is the high degree of incalculability in its effects which makes war, in modern conditions particularly, less and less of a rational policy option. One of the most significant of these conditions is the very capacity of strong governments to mobilize practically all the collective energies of their peoples for war, so tending to ensure not only the total character of the conflict but also of its results. However, our study of international politics as a whole has already prompted the reflection that rationality is not so much a mainspring of human action, rather its limited regulator.

War, peace and pacifism

We have seen above that it is difficult on the evidence of history to regard peace as the normal human condition and war as an aberration. For some historical periods the reverse might seem to be the case. Still, peace is with reason regarded as a positive good. While it is true that great civilizations have flourished in epochs of acute and prolonged conflict, peace has provided the conditions in which the finest achievements of man's creativity have been enabled to survive and thereby to contribute, perhaps through many generations, to the quality of collective experience. Stability and prosperity are widely recognized as the 'fruits of peace'. However, any given state of peace has rarely if ever been satisfactory to all the parties to it. Any peace, however imposed, which leaves serious grievances unredressed contains within it the seeds of future conflict. (The seriousness of the grievance is of course largely a subjective matter, depending far less upon the substance of the grievance than upon the mood of the aggrieved.) Peace, like war, is an issue of politics. And as we have seen, political problems do not give rise to solutions but to settlements, which scarcely ever satisfy everybody.

In the twentieth century, an age arguably as militaristic as any in the past, *pacifism* as a reaction to the facts, and as a doctrine and an ideal, has enjoyed periods of prominence. In only one case, however, does it appear to have been erected into a principle of state policy.[10] Whatever the status of pacifism as an ideal, it evidently has never attained much standing as a policy. For this there are very significant reasons.

First, outright pacifism has rarely represented more than a relatively tiny interest group in national communities. This is not to say that the general mood of the British, for instance, between the world wars was not deeply pacific. But only for a short period in the 1930s did an intensely felt if rather vaguely defined pacifism become really fashionable in Britain. In general it is fair to say that on democratic or consensual grounds the pacifist option has had little standing. And though the total pacifist may claim to speak for absolute principles universally applicable, he has seldom if ever done so with the voice of his national community anywhere in the world.

Second, while few might deny the pacifist his right to renounce the use of force on his own account, few also would concede any claim he might make to do this on behalf of others, who would not wish the protection of available force to be withdrawn. Hence a pacifist quite properly decides for himself, and civilized states provide for conscientious objection to service in the armed forces to be respected, subject to judicial enquiry into its genuine nature. But if a pacifist were to be in a position of responsibility for the

[10] This was the case of Costa Rica in 1948, cited on p. 98. Apart from the adequate protection Costa Rica enjoyed as a member of the OAS there existed few issues facing her in which the deployment of such forces as she had could have affected such issues to her advantage. There were few wars the republic could have won. Incidentally, Costa Rica is said to have been the first country to issue rhomboid stamps: her other claim to fame.

security of his political community he would fail in his duty if, in deference to his own beliefs, he took actions which exposed its members to dangers from which it was his obligation to defend them. The pacifist George Lansbury was a popular member of the second Labour government, but would never have expected to be appointed minister for war. Governments do many things with only notional consultation with the governed, and often not even that, but a political leader who sought to implement a pacifist policy for his country without any sanction of electoral support would be generally regarded as in grave breach of his duty to nation and state. The decision to use force is admittedly always a very serious one. But those who shirk it when circumstances appear reasonably to require that they take it simply fail in their political role.

Third, we may conclude that even were an important state to embark upon unilateral disarmament by way of a moral example there is little evidence to suggest that this act would be likely to affect significantly the nature or structure of international society as it now exists in ways that would render war less probable, or even lead to a reduction in the general level of armaments. Certainly no country followed Costa Rica's lead! The sober fact is that great powers and nearly all small ones alike do not disarm unilaterally because in the world as it is their rulers cannot conceive how it could be in their interest to do so. The state, as we have had occasion to repeat, remains in being to defend the collective interests of its members, and in itself comprises one of the most vital of those interests. Clearly we may argue that states must make a start somewhere. But the most promising start is not likely to be a unilateral one. It is now hard to believe that the British Campaign for Nuclear Disarmament on a unilateral basis had any major effect in determining British defence policy. Even harder is it, perhaps, to suppose that if the campaign had succeeded the result would have been the unloading of a single Soviet warhead or the dismantling of a single American rocket. Equally we may doubt if it would have in the least deterred the French from pushing on with their nuclear military programme.[11] On the contrary a

---

[11] In June and July 1972 a new series of French nuclear tests in the atmosphere over the Pacific Ocean was widely denounced, most loudly in countries bordering the Pacific. The governments of the nuclear powers who had long since completed such tests, and had virtuously subscribed the Test Ban Treaty, for the

renunciation by Britain of her nuclear capacity would probably have made the pursuit of nuclearization by others seem all the more necessary and urgent, while merely destroying Britain's reputation as a reliable ally and pillar of the free world.

The obstinate fact remains that international society is predicated upon the possibility – and in many circumstances the likelihood – of mutual violence among its members. The violence is constrained over much of the world very effectively by the deterrent effect of armed force in a condition of tacit and often explicit confrontation, as well as by the influence of moral scruples, and by the absence, in the case of certain countries and groups of countries, of any interest in arming against each other. The 49th Parallel marking the border between Canada and the United States remains an impressive symbol of the real if rare force of that last consideration.

It is conceivable that by mutual consent on the part of its members international society may transcend the traditional expectation of inter-state violence. It might then enter upon a process of transformation in which the relationships of states would be characterized only by a competition in the practice of virtue and self-sacrifice. An entrancing prospect, we may think, but little in international experience suggests that it is other than remote. Meanwhile, against the absolutist pacifist at any rate, it can cogently be argued that in modern conditions armed forces are at least as much instruments of peace as of war. If war cannot be made without armaments peace cannot be kept without them. If the price of liberty is eternal vigilance the price of security still appears to be unremitting military preparedness. This is merely to paraphrase the hard old saying, 'If you would have peace, prepare for war', one of the earliest formulations of the principle of deterrence. To this extent armaments themselves may be regarded as serving the aim for which pacifists stand: the avoidance of armed conflict.

To say this is not in the least to impugn, even by implication, the sincerity of those holding the pacifist position, nor the validity of that position in personal terms, only to suggest that pacifists may

most part had the delicacy to remain silent. Sir Alec Douglas-Home, British foreign secretary, did suggest that it was right for the French to complete their programme, and the French asserted that their explosions were 'clean'. If their policy was justified, why did Britain not give the technical information that might have made the tests needless? If the tests were clean, why were they not carried out over French territory? (See also the Concluding note on p. 307.)

sometimes appear to be sincere rather than intellectually consistent, as in the matter of that collective security which many pacifists approved; and only to question the relevance of their position to the situation in which states actually find themselves.

Before passing on from our discussion of the pacifist option we may consider briefly its specifically Christian aspect. This is sometimes treated, at least by conventional Christians, in a distinctly superficial way. The attitude was acutely hit off by Bernard Shaw in *Major Barbara*, where he makes one character, the amiable but brainless Charles Lomax, chaff Mr Andrew Undershaft, the armaments magnate, half-seriously on the spiritual peril involved in his industrial enterprise.

Getting into heaven is not exactly in your line, is it? . . . The cannon business may be necessary and all that: we cant get on without cannons; but it isnt right, you know. On the other hand, there may be a certain amount of tosh about the Salvation Army . . . but you cant deny that it's religion; and you cant go against religion, can you? At least unless youre downright immoral, dont you know.

A little later, when Lomax cheerfully suggests that the more destructive war becomes the sooner it will be abolished (a common enough assumption in 1905 when this play first appeared), Undershaft makes the telling rejoinder that the more destructive war becomes the more fascinating we find it. But the Christian predicament goes much deeper than Cholly Lomax's vague sense of the proprieties implies. For Christians, as citizens, are not delivered from the obligation to decide on the legitimacy and morality, *in each given case*, of resort to armed violence. Was it right to 'stop Hitler'? And if in some sense it was, could it have been done by 'spiritual weapons' alone? 'Who wills the end must will the means' is as true of Christians as of anybody else. No more for Christians than for others does a necessity cease to be necessary because it is an evil necessity. Nor can the Christian allow himself to forget that his enemies too have causes to believe in and interests to defend. In the tragic perspective of history we see Christians fighting each other, not, as in the so-called wars of religion, on doctrinal issues, but as serving national causes to which they attribute legitimacy. Were German soldiers *merely* presuming when they advanced into battle with *Gott mit uns* inscribed on their belt buckles? When Queen Elizabeth I publicly thanked the

God of Battles for victory over the Spanish Armada she doubtless genuinely believed that the Divine intervention had been both real and decisive. We cannot overlook that the notion of conflict, and of its inevitability, is basic to the traditional Christian sense of a struggle against sin, or the devil, or the powers of evil, however these may be interpreted in any particular age. Christianity has been historically a highly militant religion, yielding little in this respect, at least during the 'ages of faith', to the proselytizing style and forceful expansion of Islam, and, as in the Crusades, using with enthusiasm the best military technology of the time. There were in fact actual Orders of military monks in mediaeval times, who, enrolled to defend the Christian faith by armed force, emphasized how intimately the Church was involved in mundane strife, and acquired unavoidably worldly interests. For whatever the supernatural status of the Church may be, as a human institution active in history she is both in and of the world. That this has posed and poses serious ethical perplexities for the Church few churchmen deny. At all events, in the European Middle Ages, when Christendom was so pervasive a social fact, and the Church so nearly universal an institution, warfare was a dominating activity, and the armed knight a social ideal.

The distinguished Nonconformist divine, the Reverend Lord Soper, a pacifist, has been credited, among others, with the view that Christians are called by God to witness to the Gospel by renouncing absolutely the use of armed force. At the same time, the role of forces' chaplains would suggest that God has also called Christians to witness to the working of grace within them by honourable service to their country in the armed forces of the state. The implication of these divergent views is important. For it asserts in effect the primacy of the individual conscience. A man may be evidently as good a Christian in uniform as out of it. No monopoly of virtue accrues to anyone on account of his moral intuitions whether he be uncompromising Quaker or Christian soldier. While this might seem obvious, the point is sometimes obscured in dialogue between them. C. E. M. Joad argued[12] that the claim of the Church to men's obedience was vitiated by her failure to interpret in an absolute sense the Commandment, 'Thou shalt not kill', leading her ministers to 'flounder so lamentably in

[12] In *God and Evil*, a most closely argued work published by Faber and Faber, London, 1942.

the bog of apologetics for war'. More fairly, perhaps, we may admit that the Church simply does not speak with one voice on the moral propriety of armed conflict. In any case, she tends to distinguish particular instances by reference to criteria of judgement advanced by way of general guidance. Linked with this tradition is the view commonly held by Christians that resort to war, even when justifiable, is a symptom of man's 'fallen condition'. We need not enter upon a discussion of theological statements about human sinfulness in order to recognize that the use of armed violence always poses a moral problem, and that this may well prove agonizing for certain minds. On the other hand, it must be admitted that most citizens in most states most of the time throughout history have by their acquiescence implicitly conceded the moral justification attaching to the action of their governments in embarking upon the wars which they have in fact fought. There is perhaps no instance in history in which the majority of citizens in a state have objected as *a matter of conscience* to a war that state was engaged in, as distinct from considerations of expediency or political dissent, although a minority urging moral issues in the matter might have an effect in dividing the nation and weakening the collective will to fight on. The cleavage in British opinion at the time of the Suez crisis in 1956, and of American opinion over Vietnam after 1968, illustrates this point. These are different cases from that in which governments lose their mandate to rule by leading their peoples to defeat in war. This happened in Russia in 1917. But there is no evidence that Russians generally, or communists in particular, were renouncing war as such, or the need and the right to use organized armed violence on behalf of national policy. Quite the contrary. Soviet Russia became, and remains, the second greatest military power in history.

The signal merit of the position taken up by Lord Soper and those who think like him may seem to us to be the reminder that the moral tradition of a single religion – in his case Christianity – gives rise to differing insights, and issues no absolute directive, universally applicable, about the morality of war. Instead, we all ultimately decide for ourselves, if no more than implicitly by what we actually do about it, the moral quality of warfare in general or of any particular war.

Men may irresponsibly take refuge in simplistic declarations either that violence is never justified or that justification is

225

irrelevant. Or they may try as honestly and patiently as they can to understand the issues giving rise to armed conflict or its threat, and to reach a morally coherent and consistent judgement upon them. And statesmen must perform this task, whatever may be their private wishes, with reference to their overriding moral obligation to secure the safety and well-being of their states.

It is significant that serious moral qualms about the moral admissibility of war as an instrument of policy are a comparatively modern phenomenon. It seems reasonable to assume that this is directly linked with the immediacy and breadth of impact on the whole national life of modern war. In Britain, for instance, little was heard about pacifism in the nineteenth century when British wars were fought far away and for causes whose justice was never called seriously in question. Britain's 'brave tars' and 'gallant red-coats' were the recipients of mingled admiration and sentimentality. In 1898 the Reverend W. H. Fitchett published a well-written and popular account of major British actions during the Napoleonic wars, called *Deeds that won the Empire*. He did feel it incumbent upon him to assure his readers in a preface that his tales were told, 'not to glorify war, but to nourish patriotism'. There was real danger that for the average youth 'the great names of British story' might become meaningless sounds. 'And', exclaimed the author, 'what a pallid, cold-blooded citizenship this must produce!' It would not be easy to strike quite that note now. The degree of civilian involvement in modern war and the scale of its destructiveness have both sharpened moral doubts and reinforced natural fears. It was when war became 'total' that it was found not to be glorious.

Whatever the future of pacifism as a principle and as a movement, the fact remains that the assumed 'normality' of peace is always 'somebody's peace'. It represents a *status quo* that invariably leaves some parties to it dissatisfied. When processes of peaceful change clearly fail to meet demands felt to be justified the state of peace itself is likely to appear, supremely to the aggrieved but also to others, to be both morally and politically compromised, and the option of armed violence to seem more and more warranted. Thus we see that within states of peace as well as states of war social and political dynamisms are at work, tending to lead sooner or later to an articulated challenge to the stability and the morality of any given condition of things.

War and law

Whatever moral ambiguities may persist in the waging of any actual war, an important feature historically has been the careful regulation of warfare itself. Norms of behaviour in armed conflict have been embodied in legal formulae. From ancient times a whole series of codes for the conduct of battle, the treatment of captives, the disposal of the dead in combat, cease-fires, armistices, surrenders and parleys, etc. grew up. Current practice is still sanctioned by the Hague Conventions subscribed in the early years of the present century. A real difficulty has been that the increasingly indiscriminate destructiveness of many modern weapons, and the ideological fierceness which has so often marked the mood of adversaries in twentieth-century war, tend to make the observance of the Rules of War less practicable, and therefore, it comes to be felt, less relevant.

However, the impulse to bring armed conflict between recognized enemies under regulation has an important implication. For it indicates that armed conflict has not been regarded historically as an activity which *in its nature* defies normative analysis and judgement. If war is simply inherently wrong there can be no right way of waging it. This has never been the view of civilized states. From early times they have acknowledged, in the context of their contemporary moral sensitivities, that there are right and wrong – not merely successful and unsuccessful – methods of fighting the enemy. And where the rules have been widely flouted both a sense of outrage has been as widely expressed, and, regrettably, a coarsening of moral delicacy in inter-state relations perceived. It happened, for instance, in fifth-century BC Greece, second-century BC Rome and in sixteenth- and twentieth-century Europe. As E. M. Forster characteristically observed, '. . . if people continue to kill one another as they do, the world cannot get better than it is, and that since there are more people than formerly and their means for destroying one another superior, the world may well get worse'. This highlights one of the perils of military escalation. Increasing desperation in the attempt to gain objectives presses hard on accepted restraints in the use of available means. German's unleashing of unrestricted submarine warfare in 1917 was not simply a challenge to American maritime interests; it represented to

President Woodrow Wilson a deliberate *and unnecessary* flouting of moral expectations and the laws of war which he passionately denounced. In circumstances of escalation a danger can arise of the entire conduct of a given struggle passing out of the control of those responsible for conducting it. Unpunishable atrocities may then come tacitly to represent the accepted method of waging the war. On the other hand, even in modern conditions traditions of chivalric behaviour between enemies who accord each other, so to speak, legitimate status, enshrined in laws of war, die hard, certainly among the regular forces of most states. The phrase, 'brothers of the sword', is not an empty one. To say as much is again not to glorify war but to suggest that no area of human behaviour is inherently beyond the influence of constraint, and that the relationship of armed hostility can be, and historically has been, rendered less fell and perhaps more honourable by the acknowledgement of mutual expectations about behaviour arising from the effect of accepted scruples, and the force of recognized rules.

This is not the place to enter upon a discussion of the technicalities of international law in the regulation of warfare. What matters to our present purpose is the fact that even the most forceful methods by which states have sought to work their will and gain their ends are not in their intention merely anarchic. In principle and to a large degree in practice those methods have been brought under the aegis of moral judgement and legal commitment.

Wars and the Just War

Deriving it might seem from the same social needs that led men to seek to regulate the conduct of war by reference to laws, is the endeavour made historically to establish criteria by which men could distinguish between morally justifiable wars and those that were not. Observing scrupulously all the rules of war would not justify a country engaged in an unlawful war. When is a war just? The attempt to answer this question gave rise to a whole impressive literature on the Just War, to which some of the finest minds in European jurisprudence addressed themselves. As we noticed at the beginning of this chapter, the concept remains firmly embedded in traditional Catholic teaching.

In laying down foundations of 'natural law' the great seventeenth-century jurist and political philosopher Hugo Grotius insisted that it was the nature of man which determined the existence of societies. But these could only be kept in being if certain norms of behaviour were generally observed. These norms comprised chiefly: respect for what were the rights of another over things – the concept of property; the keeping of promises and the carrying out of admitted obligations; and dealing with men according to their deserts, as far as these could fairly be judged on evidence properly collected and presented. Without such norms being accepted society would collapse and men would frustrate the fulfilment of their own nature. Among sovereign powers, likewise, comparable norms necessarily applied if international society was to survive. Peace therefore was a positive good, in that it implied that the members of international society were reasonably content with their situation in it, and were therefore presumably receiving substantial justice in so far as their expectations of good faith and fair dealing were concerned. As individuals needed to be dealt with according to their deserts, so too did states. Hence a state acting unjustly, by threatening or attacking its neighbours, or depriving them of resources or opportunities to which they had a right in terms of a reasonable expectation, deserved sanctions to be taken against it. These could include the deployment of armed force. We have reached a developed doctrine of collective security, which, rooted in seventeenth-century thought, came to rather pathetic flower in the twentieth-century international institutions of the League of Nations and the United Nations Organization.

Grotius in fact took up and elaborated theories of the Just War which had been formulated with much moral earnestness by mediaeval thinkers. Essentially the justice of a war depended on its being both defensive, and a response to a wrong inflicted. The vital extension of the doctrine into a theory of collective security implied that such a response need not be confined to the actual state injured. And from there it was a short step to teaching that it is more morally admirable for a state to fight *disinterestedly* on the side of an injured state. But in this case, the state so entering the conflict, which had not itself suffered injury, could hardly be regarded as fighting a merely defensive war. Thus in such circumstances offensive war would be 'just'. The most that could be said to preserve the defensive character of just war would be that a disinterested belligerent state was by its militant action defending the norms of the international order as a whole. The superior morality of the 'responsive defensive' was reinforced by the condemnation by Just War theorists of preventive war. States were not justified in simply anticipating wrongs. Nor indeed, the theorists argued, should war be resorted to against wrong in general. States were not morally free to embark on war merely to change a *status quo* they might happen to find inconvenient to their own interests. A Just War, it came to be felt, could only be fought in response to a *violation of peace*, such as an act of armed aggression, and *in order to restore peace*. Inasmuch as a changed situation brought about by the war initiated by an aggressor might favour interests of that aggressor, Just War tended to be regarded as one which would result in the restoration of the *status quo ante bellum*, as far as that remained possible, together with whatever grievances might have motivated the original aggressive attack. However satisfactory this might be in theory, it limited the scope of strictly Just War in practice, and probably in the seriousness with which its doctrine was treated by rulers and statesmen.

Another important norm emphasized by Grotius and others was that Just War must be waged by a properly constituted authority. Neither random violence nor conflict caused through illicit or unauthorized groups taking matters into their own hands could be justified. This doctrine, in so far as it was effective, tended to centralize responsibility for war, and to formalize the procedures by which it was started and brought to an end. It can fairly be argued that what may be called the 'ceremonializing function' of Just War doctrine has historically had a mitigating effect on the dreadfulness of actual military conflict.

Christian theorists also sought to distinguish carefully between means and intentions. There was the insistence on the moral implications of means used to attain even the best of ends. Among the unneccessary, and hence morally unacceptable, means were torture, the murder of civilians and the general intimidation of noncombatants, the wanton destruction of property and the use of inadmissible weapons. At no time, perhaps, were such restraints very rigidly enforced, or ever enforceable. Certainly the 'democratization' of war by the involvement of whole national communities in actual military violence through the use of weapons of mass destruction, and the regarding of civilian populations as military targets, has rendered these categories largely academic. However, it is noteworthy that the theory required soldiers at least to be *sad* about their bitter business. The ideal and justified soldier should be a melancholy man, saddened by the regrettable necessity to fight, and acting more in sorrow than in anger. It was evidently felt that intentions would constrain means: a man in such a mood might be expected to refrain from looting, raping and destroying, exuberances only too often associated with war 'on the ground', and, as unjust means, incompatible with the justice of the cause.

Again, while such theorizing might seem rather rarified and of little consequence in the real world of frightened and angry men and sometimes embattled states, even a mildly constraining effect is better than none, and may, by softening implacability actually promote ultimately acceptable settlement.

We must not overlook the important domestic analogue to the Just War in theories of rightful resistance to government. If international violence had to be ordered and judged in terms of moral categories of justification, so too had domestic violence. Broadly the theorists of the Grotian School held that domestic violence was justified against 'tyranny', which was defined as the violent disregard by rulers of their own duties to the ruled. Hence a ruler who stole the property of his subjects or ravished their daughters could properly be held to have committed aggressive war against his own people, and not merely might but should be resisted by force. The theoretical process was: (i) tyrannical aggression; (ii) the overthrow of the tyrant; (iii) the restoration of rightful authority. The political crisis in England during the middle decades of the seventeenth century could be taken as a historical model of the theory. The 'tyrant' Charles I is defeated and punished at the end of a 'just' civil war, and ultimately rightful authority is set up again at the Restoration.

Anti-colonial struggles from the eighteenth century onwards have sought justification on the grounds of opposing 'tyranny' which is held to be both illegal and immoral in respect of a received doctrine of 'basic universal human rights'. Now while we may not be convinced of the truth of any doctrine of *inherent* human rights, rights certainly come into existence when laws enshrine a collective agreement to recognize them. Once the rights are formulated armed struggle may be and in practice will be justified by reference to them. Just War doctrine has also been important historically in justifying the intervention of outside powers on behalf of internal rebellions. The English gave military help (not very effectively, it must be admitted) to the French Huguenots and Dutch Protestants in the first decades of the seventeenth century, and the French entered into war with England on behalf of the American rebels some century and a half later. Nor was outside help always requested by the domestic resistance forces. Scots Covenanters helped the English Parliament against King Charles under invitation, but justified their action on the ground of his unlawful rule which constituted war against his own kingdom.

What matters in this connection, as with international war, is the felt need for justification. Armed and organized violence is recognized as a form of collective action which demands to be made morally acceptable, by one justification or another, in order to remain psychologically tolerable. Although theories of the Just War are rarely invoked in a formal sense by statesmen embarking on war they insist on making as clear as possible their good reasons for doing so, reasons which are invariably dignified in practice with the seal of moral justification. The most tough-minded exponent of *realpolitik* will find it in his interest to give whatever moral countenance he can to his actions.

Holy Wars

We have been discussing theories of the Just War in which the assumption is that *peace represents the norm*, both in international and domestic society. On this view war is a disturbance of the norm. Therefore it requires moral justification, by reference to carefully formulated ethical and legal criteria of judgement. There are, in this conception, no permanent aggressors or victims: there are simply men in societies, who may be called upon from time to time to be warriors. Peace generally prevails. War erupts. Peace, all being well, is restored, and made the safer by justice being done upon those wrongdoers whose behaviour caused it to be interrupted by war. Now we must turn for a little to a fundamentally different conception of war, which sees it as in principle permanent and inescapable. This may be termed the alternative norm of the Holy War.

The assumption underlying this doctrine is precisely that peace is not the normal condition of things, occasionally and often unwarrantably shattered by the outbreak of war. It is a matter of the reverse being true. The natural state of things is a condition of struggle, of conflict. War as a generalized conception is continuous and permanent: war between the men of God and the men of the Devil, between the children of light and the children of darkness, between true believers and heretics, between good and evil. Historically this notion has resolved itself into a belief that some received good, in the form of a social or political doctrine, usually enshrined in a social or political system, is so excellent and so necessary that men and nations must be forced if need be to accept it and to adopt their existing beliefs and institutions to conformity with it. The complementary motive for crusading zeal is the belief that some other society's collective beliefs or institutional arrangements are intrinsically so evil that they must be forcibly destroyed, the more urgently as they are perceived to pose an immediate threat to the ideals and practices of one's own society. Historical instances have occasionally come close to these theoretical extremes. We noticed early in this book that to the ardent Moslem the Christian was an infidel to be resisted by force as a matter of moral duty, which if faithfully carried out till death would merit the reward of Paradise. To the Christian crusader Islam was a monstrous perversion of revealed truth, a hideous apostasy, intolerably occupying Christianity's Holy Places, and against which the principalities and powers of sacred Christendom were rightfully arrayed. In practice the ideological rigour of these motivations did not long maintain its purity. Far less exalted interests came to demand the loyalty of the warring factions. The spirit of adventure – at least relatively disinterested – and the urge of cupidity loomed large. With a decline in militant idealism came an increase of tolerance, and even some willingness to see something not wholly ignoble or wicked in the opposed values, plus a more or less rueful recognition that the adversary was there to stay. European rulers developed their interests in ways that preoccupied them heavily with each other, and Crusades became increasingly anachronistic, until in the sixteenth century the 'last Crusade' of Don John of Austria, while a success in that it administered a naval check to Islamic power in the Mediterranean, was also something of a romantic joke. On its own part the Ottoman Empire, co-existing with growing normality with the European state system, entered upon its lengthy decay. Crusade and Jehad, conceived in terms of the absolute justice of wars fought on behalf of an 'embattled righteousness', ceased to have relevance for the international politics of the seventeenth and succeeding centuries, and became large-scale historical curiosities in themselves, if always reminders of what collective passion and conviction can do in the world of men.

The cold war of our own age at its chilliest represented something comparable. The rivalry between the communist and Western blocs was less economic than doctrinal, although of course the opposed doctrines were intimately concerned with economic questions, and with beliefs not only about the 'right' way to run national economies but about the moral standing of different kinds of economic system. Each side sought to spread its own influence throughout the world and to check the spread of its opponents' influence. But for neither side was a motive of mere aggrandizement ever admitted, or on the Western side a desire merely to capture or dominate world markets, a traditional explanation of capitalist expansionism. The clash of values was understood to be the decisive factor. 'The Western way of life' (by no means a meaningless phrase) was pitted against 'the historical necessity of the triumph of communism'. The practice of statesmen in each scale of the bipolar balance proved for the most part signally cautious, but their words often enough betrayed a crusading spirit, and a highly moralizing attitude towards the 'struggle for power and peace', in Hans J. Morgenthau's phrase, which made the existing truce seem more precarious.

While, as we have seen, bipolarity was no new pattern in international politics, what distinguished it in the middle decades of the twentieth century was the correlation of intense ideological conflict with the loci of supreme world power. Thus during the presidency of General Eisenhower, and particularly under the inspiration of Secretary of State, John Foster Dulles, the United States embarked upon a series of some forty mutual defence agreements with other countries, all of whom were far less able to aid America than *vice versa*, on the ground that all were threatened, or might be threatened, by Soviet expansionism. This was the phase of what was critically called American 'pactomania'. There was even talk of 'liberating' countries already under the Soviet yoke. It was widely asserted that there could be no 'real peace' (whatever precisely this meant) until world communism had stopped plotting against the freedom-loving, democratic (and by implication in Mr Dulles's mind, distinctively Christian) West. On the other hand the Soviet leadership was prone to insist that the maintenance of peace required aggressive Western imperialism to cease from conspiring to destroy the peace-loving People's Democracies. In short, the language of both sides sounded the strident notes of an uncompromising political theology and self-righteous emotion. The conviction tended therefore to grow in the collective mind of each bloc that the other was necessarily engaged upon a sinister conspiracy against it. This may or may not have been in fact substantially true. What mattered politically was the belief that it was true.

However, it is fair to remind ourselves that considerable restraint in behaviour as between the superpowers has prevailed despite the evidently irreconcilable sets of political doctrines that have confronted one another, armed with a destructive capacity unique in history. Ideology may sharpen the clashes of other interests, but seems not to make war between the adversaries concerned necessarily more likely. It is well to remember that there was after all a shared dynastic authoritarianism, backed up by a complex of congruent social and political values held in common, between kaiser and tsar in 1914, which did not prevent 'Willi' and 'Nicky' (to borrow the friendly diminutives of their personal correspondence) from plunging into fateful war; or imperial Germany from inflicting one of the greatest defeats in modern history upon tsarist Russia.

The supreme danger of the cold war, reinforced by its 'holy' aspect, was thought to be its tendency to intensify. As the conflict of doctrines was waged with increasing bitterness, so, it was argued, peoples on each side would grow less patient with the unending compromises and accommodations inseparable from continued co-existence. Crusading zeal propagated by groups associated with the extreme expression of the basic positions of each side, would have fateful effects on policy-makers themselves, and their official publicists, who, prisoners of their own propaganda, would become less and less in control of the drift of opposing systems towards open strife.

But this has not happened. It appears therefore that a given pattern of power, however strongly drawn, need not necessarily go on intensifying until a critical point of cleavage is reached. Other aspects of political change may occur and influence the pattern in perhaps decisive ways. The emergence to world power status of revolutionary China, for instance, clearly had profound effects on relations between the United States and the Soviet Union. Even more striking was evidence in the early 1970s of a far-reaching reappraisal of the relationship between the United States and China herself. It began to appear likely that there would develop a relatively stable *tripolar* balance in international politics. And there were hopes that such a conformation of power would prevent bipolar relations between any two members of the triumvirate from reaching a critically dangerous level of mutual hostility which could be expected to rebound to the advantage of the third member.

Such considerations as these, however significant they may appear to be, do not, admittedly, dispose of a danger to which Professor Morgenthau refers[13] when he says of nuclear proliferation that if an annihilative capacity is shared by several nations, some of whom may well be governed by 'emotionalism and irresponsibility', the threat of nuclear war is intensified. The provisions of the anti-proliferation treaty have not, and perhaps cannot, alter the dangerous situation fundamentally. 'Among all the various possibilities of future development', he adds, 'this [nuclear conflict as a consequence of proliferation] is the most unpleasant to envisage, and . . . seems to be the most likely to materialize.' Yet prudence remains, and with prudence, constraint. Both may prove to be strengthened by a growth of responsible power, provided that this can be accompanied by a continuing decline among the powers of doctrinal passion.

It seems on the whole fair to regard the cold war as showing many of the characteristics of Holy War, waged not by open conflict between the principal champions of the rival systems of political dogma but by threat and counter-threat. Such confrontations are uncomfortable enough, and we may be disposed to reflect that they place in sharp focus the disagreeable aspects of living in an 'age of faith'; we may also be the more ready to welcome such evidence as appears that statesmanship among the greatest powers in the world moved during the later 1960s and after towards a more pragmatic and even creative view of the possibilities of peaceful co-existence. *Realpolitik* may indeed have its cynical side, but history, and not least the history of our own times, does not lack the suggestion that even cynical realists may contrive to keep things

[13] In *Politics among Nations: The Struggle for Power and Peace*, 3rd edn, Alfred A. Knopf, New York, 1962.

going a little longer than dedicated holy warriors are likely to do, who in their devotion and certitude are but too prone to seize the crowns of martyrdom, and to press them firmly upon the brows of other people as well as on their own.

Armaments, disarmament and arms control

Discussion of the problems of war and peace inevitably bring up the question of armaments, disarmament and arms control. No wars can be fought, or averted, without the material means to wage or deter them. But there is an essential distinction to be borne in mind between disarmament and arms control. Broadly speaking, arms control may be regarded as representing the prudential response of practical men to the given facts of military power, and to the evident reluctance of states to surrender such advantage as they believe their relative armed strength gives them in the pursuit of their international political objectives. As we have had occasion to notice several times already, states in general are not prepared to be defenceless, and continue to see in armaments one of their surest means of defence. Disarmament, on the other hand, represents on the whole an idealistic response to the facts of military power in international society by well-meaning persons who believe that armed states can be persuaded unilaterally or by mutual agreement to relinquish their armed capacities, although these require large resources of material wealth and human skill to create. Need we therefore be unduly surprised that no disarmament conference so far held has proved other than a substantial (if not quite total) failure, or that agreements about arms control have, over time, and with much difficulty as cannot be denied, proved relatively successful?

The issue of disarmament, then, is concerned with proposals to reduce the actual number of weapons which at any given time are operational throughout the world. Arms control, as the term implies, concerns ways in which existing weapons (and even weapons still in the development stage) can be used so as to attain given security objectives with the least possible actual violence and destruction. While disarmament is always concerned with lowering the level of armaments everywhere, arms control may actually provide for an increase in the number and availability of particular weapons in the interest of maintaining the stability of an arms balance, which may well be seen as offering the best guarantee of avoiding the outbreak of large-scale war.

Although much has been heard of disarmament in the present century, as a great international question it is relatively new. In earlier periods states increased or reduced their standing forces as circumstances appeared to dictate or to justify. In general most states maintained as low a level of armed force as they calculated to be compatible with national safety and dignity. Security was always desired, but for the most part as cheaply as possible. Throughout the history of the modern international system, now in existence for some four centuries, the prevailing posture of the armed forces of states was defensive. Resort to war was on behalf of interests, territorial, dynastic, economic, which were held to be legitimate and felt to be threatened. Only very rarely did states deliberately maximize their armed capacity in order to embark upon a course of unprovoked aggression and outright conquest. Even where the motive for military action was essentially national aggrandizement, it was accepted that this could not be openly admitted, and that a morally respectable justification was needed. Granted that justification was forthcoming, war remained a dangerous but legitimate instrument of national policy. Given this attitude towards warfare we might expect that during the period from around the middle of the seventeenth century to the close of the nineteenth, war in the international society of Europe should be both frequent and subject to a considerable degree of limitation, in regard at once to objectives, duration and intensity. And this is broadly what we find. The essential instrument was the relatively small professional armed service, often helped out by the use of foreign mercenaries. Even where conscription came to be practised, as in France and Prussia, the tendency was to keep the period with the colours as short as could be plausibly reconciled with military efficiency, and to create a large trained reserve for national emergencies of a major kind.

In these circumstances disarmament, except among small groups of people, such as the Quakers, who regarded war as intrinsically immoral, never became a significant issue of policy. A few voices were heard from time to time on the alleged evils of maintaining standing forces as such, but generally nations expected to be adequately defended and merely grumbled somewhat at the cost. What brought about a change was the marked increase in firepower and the technical sophistication of weapons during the second half of the nineteenth century, and in particular during its last decade. By then the existence of large rival alliance systems dividing Europe into 'armed camps', as G. P. Gooch put it,[14] and an increasing preoccupation with the danger of general war, together with a widely held if disputed belief that modern armaments represented a less and less tolerable economic burden for all nations possessing them, provoked serious discussion in political and literary circles about the possibility of reducing the level of armaments by international agreement. The two Conferences convened under the inspiration of the tsar with this object principally in view, at the Hague, one in 1899 and the second in 1907, did some useful work on the regulation of warfare, but failed to achieve any measure of disarmament at all. Nor was there any agreement on either the objective or the possible methods of 'outlawing war', to resurrect a phrase that both then and later enjoyed a certain vogue among individuals and bodies concerned with problems of maintaining international peace.

It was during the two decades between the world wars that disarmament came into its own as a moral theme in international politics. For economic and political reasons massive disarmament was carried out by the United States and Britain, while the Versailles Treaty imposed it sharply upon Germany. France, however, obsessed with the potential threat of a defeated but still immensely powerful enemy, maintained standing forces at a high level, higher than she could well stand, following her appalling losses in the first world war, and so posed for a few years as the leading military power on the Continent. A desire to keep the international peace in Europe was widespread and sincere. But political leaders were obliged to seek peace with security, and this involved measures of military readiness in a situation where international trust was limited and national grievances were numerous. Thus despite the League of Nations, and diplomatic moments such as the signing of the Kellogg-Briand Pact, the signatories to which undertook, as later the members of the United Nations Organization were to do, to forswear the use of force in settling international disputes, an arms race of sorts proceeded throughout the interwar period. Gradually, with one another's connivance and help, both

[14] In *History of Our Time 1885–1911*, Home University Library, Williams & Norgate, London.

the Soviet Union and republican Germany became – the latter clandestinely – major military powers in Europe. Even fascist Italy purported to be one, carrying a measure of conviction in many quarters which was only shattered by actual war after 1940. Britain alone among the great European powers pursued what was in effect a policy of disarmament with consistency and near disaster up until the late 1930s. Satisfied in Europe, Britain asked nothing better than that European peace should prevail, leaving her free to discharge her still existing worldwide imperial responsibilities. She sought, in fact, to maintain national security with absolutely minimum forces. One formula for establishing the margin of safety was the so-called 'ten-year rule'. This was an official expectation that there would be no major conflict involving or threatening Britain during the ensuing ten years. This calculation ceased to have any relevance after 1933, when Hitler came to power in Germany. Even so, peace as a leading British international interest largely motivated the patient attempts by British leaders to appease Hitler by condoning his open violation of the military provisions of the Versailles Treaty, and by seeking to negotiate with him a settlement of European issues on the basis of substantial territorial gains for Germany at the expense of other countries, principally Czechoslovakia. In this mood disarmament was a word constantly bruited about in Britain, and proved a recurring theme in speeches on foreign policy by successive prime ministers, in particular by Ramsay MacDonald and Stanley Baldwin.

The culmination of the search for an effective method of reducing the level of armaments during this period came in 1932 when a great Disarmament Conference was convened in Geneva. Attended by representatives of sixty nations, including the Soviet Union and the United States, neither of whom were members of the League of Nations (Russia joined in 1934), the object was to secure a general reduction of armaments throughout the world, in accordance with the League Covenant. The Conference sat intermittently for a total of thirteen months and a half over a period of two years. It completely failed. In many respects it became the classic instance of the idle nature of the disarmament dream. Almost every statesman agreed that disarmament was desirable in principle, and by attending the Conference at least implied his belief that it was not unattainable in practice. But faced with specific proposals no statesman dared jeopardize either the security, or (and discussion suggested this was scarcely less important) the prestige, of his country by actually disarming. The 'general interest in peace', which all solemnly averred existed, simply was not aligned with the particular interests of states. France, suffering serious political malaise, deeply divided and convinced that an effective system of collective security must precede disarmament, faced a Germany which insisted that any disarmament could only follow the achievement of parity by Germany with the armed might of other great powers, a concession which, if granted, would have made actual disarmament seem more than ever dangerous to her neighbours. In fact the Germans walked out of the Conference in October 1933, and the most comprehensive international negotiation of its kind ever attempted in history up to that time petered out ignominiously the following year.

The failure of this Conference, the continuing dynamism and revisionism of the Nazi and fascist regimes, and the drift towards a renewal of general conflict in Europe which could be seen in many respects as representing the 'unfinished business' of the first world war, led to a general abandonment of the objective of disarmament everywhere. First world war neutrals such as Holland and Norway began to rearm. In fact rearmament, with varying degrees of reluctance and effectiveness, was embarked upon by nearly all the European states, in response to a vaunted rearmament – actually more apparent than real at the time – on the part of Germany and Italy.

After the end of the second world war, with the creation of a new organization for the maintenance of international peace and security, interest in disarmament as a means thereto revived to some extent, though with a good deal less of the rather simple idealism and enthusiasm of the earlier period. And there was of course in the first months of peace massive and inevitable dismantling by the victor powers of the enormous war machines created during years of global strife. But the deepening rift between the Soviet Union and her erstwhile allies led in the spring of 1947 to the United States' decisive change of course. Her then nuclear monopoly was to be supported by extensive conventional forces deployed on a worldwide basis for the protection of the non-communist world. In their turn both the Soviet Union and Britain pressed ahead with the attainment of their own national nuclear armouries. The mutually destructive potential of the superpowers steadily increased, until the levels of so-called 'overkill', already referred to, were reached. 'Escalation', as applied both to military capacity and actual armed violence, became as fashionable a word as disarmament had once been. Among the non-superpowers first Britain then France and later communist China, joined what was playfully called the 'nuclear club', which it was hoped by those inside it would somehow retain a highly exclusive membership. Although the Non-proliferation Treaty, signed in 1968, may have some inhibiting effect upon the spread of nuclear weapons, it is evident that no sure *diplomatic* means exist to prevent industrially advanced nations from acquiring unilateral nuclear capacities if their strategic interest in doing so appears to them to be sufficiently pressing. On the other hand, considerable prudence in regard to the acquisition of the supreme weapons of the nuclear age, and above all in their deployment, has been a feature of the behaviour of international society ever since 1945. Despite tensions, sometimes acute, problems that defy settlement and crises that have threatened catastrophe, at the time of writing only two missiles embodying the technological triumphs of twentieth-century atomic science have been exploded in anger. And there seems to be no compelling reason to believe that the rationality of such restraint will be readily abandoned in the future.

Geneva did not in 1934 see the end of its role as a host city for conferences on disarmament. In 1954 a Standing Conference was convened there, under the joint chairmanship of the Soviet Union and Britain, to consider both disarmament proposals and actual breaches of international peace. It negotiated the end of the French colonial phase of the protracted war in Indo-China, and has been convoked from time to time since on various issues with generally little effect. However, a high water mark in the discussion of disarmament was reached in the late 1950s and beyond with the emergence of widely canvassed proposals for 'General and Complete Disarmament' – GCD. (We live in the era of initials.) GCD never came to anything very much, even as a blueprint for the preservation of international peace, chiefly because neither the West nor the communist powers had either the psychological capability, or indeed any very good reason, to trust one another's intentions sufficiently to embark upon even a limited reduction of existing force levels. The phased removal of the American military presence in Vietnam, at its peak in 1968, and signs of a growing desire to reduce the American defence commitment in Europe, evident from 1970 onwards, had less to do with any increase of international cordiality, though this was not wholly absent, than with a significant erosion of the American will to continue at the same rate the massive and worldwide containment of communism inaugurated by President Truman some twenty-two years earlier.

However this may be, it is clear that the attention given in the period roughly from 1962 to methods of arms limitation and control has proved far more useful than the pursuit of the chimera of disarmament as such. In the nuclear field the achievement of a stable balance of terror proved a genuine guarantee of armed peace, allowing ideas slowly to burgeon on ways of maintaining effective mutual deterrence without the endless escalation of military capability beyond any conceivable strategic need. It does not seem too much to say that the successful outcome of the SALT (Strategic Arms Limitation Talks) negotiations, to which reference has already been made, cautious, specific and limited as it is, represents a real triumph of rationality over suspicious fear and of arms control pragmatism over the vain fantasies of disarmament theory.

Meanwhile, great problems remain. In the sphere, for example, of nuclear proliferation, two difficulties at least prove stubborn. In the first place the existing treaty can easily be seen as an attempt by existing nuclear powers to consolidate their own preeminence. If an industrially advanced power decided to adopt the nuclear option (as India, Japan and even Israel well could) what sanctions can be taken against them which would not jeopardize the existing international order? Secondly, there is an argument, which the French have tended to favour, that 'proliferation all round' would, by maximizing the dangers, enhance international caution, and so actually contribute to security. If we can all be destroyed by each other, we are likely to behave with circumspection to everyone else. Whether this view carries much conviction or not, we need not be surprised that certain states, either junior members of the nuclear club or somewhat touchy aspirants to membership, have seen merit in the notion.

A hope sometimes expressed in regard to arms limitation is that the nuclear powers may eventually feel safe enough to enter into a Comprehensive Test Ban Treaty, in which no more nuclear devices whatever will be allowed to be tested at all. This is felt by many to be sensible and practicable, if not least because both the United States and the Soviet Union possess overkill capacity and therfore 'have enough'. However, the time for such an agreement hardly seems ripe, if only because the superpowers, even if they were willing, have no means of obliging third parties to adhere to the agreement, while voluntary adherence is unlikely to be universal for as long as questions not only of strategic calculation but national prestige remain bound up with the possession of nuclear weapons. It seems fair to say that the 1972 SALT agreements on defensive and offensive arms limitation go as far as can reasonably be hoped for in view of prevailing superpower interests in relation to contemporary international politics. Apart from any consideration of humanity or prudence, we should not forget the political importance of the nuclear and non-nuclear arms industries themselves. One of the unrealities of much disarmament advocacy has been the belief that it would be relatively easy and simple to run down a very complex and sophisticated industrial enterprise and transfer its resources, both material and human, elsewhere for other purposes. We need not postulate a full-blown 'garrison state' to recognize that arms lobbies exist, and have their political effects, or that investment in the armaments industry represents in many countries, including inevitably the most powerful as military capacity is a vital factor in international power, an extremely important aspect of the national economy.

So we may observe that though the prospect of disarmament has proved disappointingly remote, in the field of arms control solid if limited achievements stand to the credit of world statesmen and their advisers. There has been, for example, in addition to the SALT agreements the undertaking by the United States and the Soviet Union not to furnish outer space with weaponry in the form of warheaded satellites. A complementary agreement obliges the signatories not to litter the seabed with operational nuclear weapons. Such an agreement has value in showing that powers can reach one, however true it may be that agreement was the easier because the usefulness of nuclear weapons on the seabed appeared problematical. International agreements on certain restrictions upon research and development in the peculiarly sombre field of chemical and biological warfare (CBW) have, as we have noticed, been concluded. This is of particular interest, perhaps, because chemical and biological weapons remain at a relatively early stage of practicality, and restraint has been accepted *before* the powers concerned had achieved all the envisaged technological results, and not afterwards. Thus virtually to 'close the gate before entering the field' represents a self-denying ordinance rare among the defence planners of any country.

This progress in arms control has been made despite the insoluble problems associated with verification and inspection. It remains a matter of extreme difficulty for international society to be able to satisfy itself that in the area of arms control no state is violating its treaty obligations. There is the question of the sovereign integrity of national territories, and the question of practicable sanctions to be taken against offenders. All this is really an aspect of the old problem of collective security which we have already examined. States seldom perceive any advantage to themselves in taking the risks and bearing the costs of 'disciplining' other states by means of internationally agreed sanctions. The greater the number of states involved the greater the problem. As J. C. Garnett has observed of systems of collective security in general, 'the more collective they are the less security they provide'. The United Nations Organization might be thought the natural scrutineer in the matter of verification and control, but the Organization, broadly speaking, can only discharge such functions as it is endowed with by its members. Arms inspection by United Nations agents would continue to invite the criticism, often voiced by the Soviet Union, that such action derogated from the sovereignty and dignity of the state subject to it. The fact is that there is nothing in the way of an effective system of inspection and control save the will of the states concerned. We suggested in our discussion of collective security the rather depressing paradox that if collective security was successful because no state was aggressive it was not needed; if needed because states were aggressive it was unlikely to be successful. Similarly, if states were willing to open their territories freely to international arms inspection it seems safe to assume that no inspection would be necessary. The need arises precisely because states cannot be fully trusted not to attempt the pursuit of clandestine military advantage. Yet in spite of the effects of a high level of pride and a lower level of virtue among states, real progress in the limitation and control of the means of international violence has been made.

Before leaving the subject of disarmament it is only proper to notice two gestures made in recent history on its behalf. In October 1964 the fifth British labour government, led by Harold Wilson with an overall majority of four seats, created a special new section in the Foreign Office devoted to the study of means for achieving disarmament. The unit was placed under the political control of a minister of state for disarmament. The person appointed was an ex-soldier and journalist of note, Mr Alun Gwynne-Jones, defence correspondent of *The Times*. Translated to the Upper House as Lord Chalfont he set to work. Much high thinking was carried on and some important studies were prepared.[15] But there was no perceptible disarmament. Nothing Lord Chalfont or other dedicated statesmen could do availed, or was expected to avail, to change the predicament of states remaining responsible for their own safety in a world in which national security continued to depend upon military power, much of it maintained on a coordinate basis by states acting within great alliance systems. However, the commitment of a labour government in Britain to the ideal of disarmament in a context of internationalist cooperation needed, that government felt, to be symbolized, and so these values were publicly embodied in the agreeable person of Lord Chalfont.

The second instance is an international one. In 1970 the United Nations Disarmament Commission proclaimed a 'disarmament decade', in which it was intended, possibly more in wistful hope than real confidence, that the powers of the world, and in particular states members of the Organization, would address themselves with renewed zest to the search for ways by which the arms burden pressing upon nearly all of them could be reduced, and even the actual number of weapons existing on the earth made fewer, without increasing international instability or enhancing the dangers confronting states. The history of disarmament negotiations does not provoke high expectations. But if the symbolic gesture of the Disarmament Commission gives a filip to work being done in the field of arms limitation something will have been gained. It is essential not to undervalue the importance of efforts to control the distribution and use of arms because they lack the

---

[15] One of the minister's most distinguished advisers was Hedley Bull, later Professor of International Relations at Canberra, who while at the London School of Economics produced a classic work on arms control.

morally and emotionally satisfying dimension of actual and substantial disarmament, the evident beating of swords into plough-
shares.

The international community of peace

We have discussed war as a political instrumentality, and the
status, function and possible deliberate limitation of the means
used for waging or threatening war. We have noticed how
numerous wars have proved historically, and how much conflict has
raged in many parts of the world during the contemporary period.
We turn now to a consideration of the prevalence of peace, realizing that peace has probably never at any time represented a
universal condition of things since man has existed on earth, but
acknowledging that 'peace breaks out' in many places, and is
sometimes sustained for many years at a time. For our point of
departure we return to that valuable concept owed to the American
scholar, Karl Deutsch, to which we have referred previously in
these pages, the 'security community'.

We have admitted, at least implicitly, that it is in the nature of
superpowers to be in a position of rivalry with each other. In
international society as it exists interests, being worldwide but not
at all points necessarily complementary, must clash at times. The
stakes for any superpower are critically high, and the concessions
which responsible superpower leaders – responsible, that is, for the
prestige of their states – can offer each other are inevitably limited.
Throughout history it is rare, if not altogether unknown, for great
powers to be on really friendly terms over long periods. What
has been known to happen instead is for brief and precarious
truces between them to be 'dignified with the term *endless peace*',
as Gibbon somewhere comments. An instructive exception was the
relationship between the United States and Britain during the last
thirty years of the nineteenth century, when the former was emerg-
ing on the stage of world power, and the latter ruling a worldwide
Empire. A cardinal principle of British foreign policy was, as it
indeed must remain, the maintenance of good relations with
America. No British interest that could be conceived would have
been served by any serious breach with the United States. On her
own part, that country, engaged in the monumental task of opening
up, exploiting and mastering a continent, found her task facilitated

by the non-hostile presence of British sea power on both the Atlantic and Pacific littorals, while she became in turn a major supplier of food and cotton for the developed British markets. But such complementarity of interests between great powers is on the whole unusual, and made unique in the present instance by the combination of an ill-defined but undoubted common Anglo-Saxon sentiment and the bond of a more or less common language. So deeply engrained in this expectation of good relations, despite occasional divergencies of policy, that it is entirely sensible to speak of the two countries as comprising a bilateral security community, between the members of which anything approaching open conflict or even a cold war, is out of the question.

On the other hand, we have witnessed the persistence of 'peace with hostility', in as much that even clashing superpowers, when faced with the consequences of their own successful technologies, and the prospect of mutually induced non-existence, have found it both desirable and possible to explore, with fluctuating degrees of confidence and cordiality, the implications of continuing co-existence. The emergence of further superpowers will call for the exercise of great political skills on the part of all the superpower leaders, and for many delicate adjustments in the balance of power between them. But it must be hoped that four, or, with India in the remoter future, conceivably five superpowers including China and Japan, may contrive to create a superpower security community, for upon it world survival will largely depend. The arms control agreements of the 1960s and 1970s, already discussed, have undoubtedly gone some way towards bringing about such a condition of things.

Beneath the level of superpower rivalry whole areas exist where the danger of war has become so remote as to be safely disregarded, just as there are other areas where war has been more or less continuous for thirty years, as in Indo-China, or dangerously intermittent, as in the Middle East. Note here Professor Deutsch's deliberate choice of the word 'community'. Something is envisaged in his security community which is more than merely a grouping of like-minded or at least non-hostile states. The implication is that the common interest in peace with each other is linked with other interests, calculated sooner or later to bring the constituent members close enough together to transcend the notion of a peaceable society of states and to attain the level of intimacy in their inter-relationships justifying the use of the term community. We examine the prospects of such community-building in the last chapter of this book.

We have already referred to the 49th Parallel, unfortified throughout its length, as a majestic symbol of the trust that can exist between ideologically congruent sovereign states. It seems safe to assume something indeed like a 'perpetual peace' between, for instance, the countries of Scandinavia, or all the members of NATO. ('Cod wars' between British trawlers and Icelandic gunboats are serious enough, no doubt, but hardly qualify as major threats to international peace and security.) History, after all, is full of decisive developments. 'Old, unhappy, far-off things, And battles long ago' often poison present inter-state relationships. Indeed, if history is a record of decisive change, it is also a vast prison, of which all men are inmates. But it is also true that, so to speak, *plus ça même chose, plus c'est la change*! International suspicion and violence prevail in much of the international order, but it is equally the case that the Dutch and the English, so fiercely embattled at sea in the seventeenth century, now compete mainly in mutual amiability. The states of Latin America, whose armies, we noticed, have been peculiarly the instruments of internal politics, are so unlikely to go to war with each other, whatever the occasional differences between them, and between the United States and themselves, that the entire Western hemisphere may now fairly be regarded as a security community, at least at the present epoch, from the Arctic Circle to Cape Horn.

The Parliamentary Group for World Government asked plaintively in 1961;[16] 'the world is small enough for world wars; why not for world peace?' The answer seems to be that even world wars were never actually universal, and that the world evidently is not small enough, psychologically speaking, to be ready yet for world peace. (And even small countries have sometimes been racked by civil wars.) But nations have created stable conditions of peace over considerable areas. This, on a basis of pragmatic policy-making, and the mutuality of regional interests, may conceivably, if we can hardly yet say probably, represent a means by which security communities may expand, and coalesce, until something approaching a peaceable world moves within the orbit of practical policy. But authentic lessons of history are the waywardness of

[16] In *The Case for World Government.*

man, and the degree to which the interplay between his wilfulness and his environment gives rise to unexpected situations, leading in turn to quite unpredictable new things in the story of his collective life on the earth. That being understood, it still seems evident, from the history of peace-making and peace-keeping throughout the twentieth century, that we would be wise never to anticipate dramatic 'breakthroughs' to world peace, or sudden conversions of men now committed to violent means for the attainment of deeply desired ends. Nor have we good reason to expect the wide-spread transformation or abandonment of those existing interests which may need to be defended by force. Our century has been in some ways one of the most creative in history. But it has also certainly been one of the most destructive, because technical development has generalized violence. Yet despite decades of earnest theorizing by most able minds, and the development of institutional experiments on a worldwide scale intended to render it obsolete, organized force at the disposal of its individual members remains a characteristic feature of international society. The motives for rivalry between them are still enormously strong. However, it is possible to hope that, step by step, often enough no doubt with a Leninist double step back for one forward, the world *may* move towards a condition of things in which the phrase 'world peace' becomes more than an emotive abstraction and approximates to political reality. Words written by E. M. Forster in 1939 remain timely, applying as much to the age of nuclear missiles as to that of propeller-driven aircraft:

. . . the evidence of history shows us that men have always insisted on behaving creatively under the shadow of the sword; that they have done their artistic and scientific and domestic stuff for the sake of doing it, and that we had better follow their example under the shadow of the aeroplanes . . . and though Violence remains and is, indeed, the major partner in this muddled establishment, I believe that creativeness remains too and will always assume direction when violence sleeps.[17]

It is the desire to get on with 'the artistic, scientific and domestic stuff' which makes the vision of a secure world so alluring, and generates a warmth of approval towards political leaders who by a combination of flair and necessary luck have contributed to the

[17] From 'What I Believe', reprinted in *Two Cheers for Democracy*, Edward Arnold, London, 1951.

creation of those regions of stable peace which Karl Deutsch rightly held to be deeply significant for the international politics of our age.

Wars of radical dissent

In bringing our discussion of the phenomenon of war to a close we look again briefly at an aspect of armed conflict touched on earlier in this book. This is the warfare waged within and sometimes between political communities by political dissidents pledged to the radical revision of the existing order. Such struggles have of course occurred throughout history. What makes them of disturbing interest to contemporaries is the evident development during the middle decades of this century of a large body of theoretical literature devoted to an examination of the most effective means, all over the world, of achieving revolutionary change by force. This material, as studied and given practical application in many places, poses a threat not only to the constitutional norms and political structure of a number of individual countries, but to the existing international order itself. Again we are reminded of the effect of means upon ends. The international order which exists now may be in process of radical transformation in any case, and this we consider in the next chapter, but it is evident that such a transformation achieved mainly or even largely by worldwide revolutionary violence would result in a very different world order from one transformed by processes of peaceful change. Opinions obviously differ as to whether widespread radical intolerance towards established institutions reflects adversely upon the moral quality of the institutions or of those seeking their destruction. What seems clear is that the growth of such intolerance in our age, and its formalization in a body of political and strategic doctrine, represents one of the most portentous political and social developments in the modern world.

The conflict to which it gives rise runs a gamut between sporadic outbreaks of localized violence perpetrated by pockets of minority extremists, often amounting to no more than street riots, isolated acts of sabotage or single attacks on the lives and property of individuals, through a course of escalation that includes the disruption of the normal life of whole districts, and wide-ranging insurgency, up to all-out civil war, deploying large bodies of troops trained and equipped to conduct full-scale operations on the battlefield. The Irish Republican Army in Ulster after 1969 was broadly contained at the terrorist end of this spectrum of violence. The Viet-Cong, supported by the armies of North Vietnam, after 1961 or so, approached the civil war end of the spectrum. Where, as in Vietnam, external forces became actively involved, the scale and style of fighting entered the stage of *limited war*. This has some-times arisen from and retained much of the character of guerrilla war, but in itself may be defined as the waging of major campaigns between regular forces operating on one or more definable fronts, and making use of or at least threatening to use all weapons save those contained in a strategic nuclear armoury. It has been of the essence of limited war, so conceived, that it is fought at a sub-nuclear level. However, the existence and possible deployment of tactical nuclear weapons somewhat blurs the distinction. Moreover, political decisions are formally taken in the endeavour to ensure that the war does not escalate into general war. So understood, limited war represents a wide category of actual conflicts. But the Korean war, the Vietnam war and the Arab-Israeli six-day war all in their own ways offer examples of the validity of the concept. In the case of Korea, President Truman took the specific step, in dismissing General MacArthur, not only of reasserting the principle of presidential control over military policy in the United States but of ensuring that the war would not be allowed, if American policy could prevent it, from spreading beyond the Korean theatre itself. In the case of Vietnam pressure at some stages on the American Administration to use nuclear weapons to terminate North Vietnamese 'aggression' into South Vietnam was resisted, and for their part the Soviet leaders maintained a posture of carefully limited support for the Hanoi regime, thus ensuring that Vietnam would not become a precipitant of a dangerous military confrontation between the superpowers. The dramatic and remarkable six-day war also illustrated the importance attached by Russian and American policy-makers to limited war doctrine. The Soviet commitment to Egypt, and the American sympathy with Israel, were not allowed to jockey either group of leaders into a position of overt support of their respective political friends which would be likely to jeopardize freedom of manouevre, and immobilize the two superpowers in postures of unyielding hos-tility. In fact, both cooperated unostentatiously to promote a cease-fire. It is notable, too, that the Indo-Chinese war of 1962 (the 'border war'), the Indo-Pakistan war of 1965 and the conflict over-Bangladesh in 1971, though of considerable moment to international society, were not allowed by either superpower to assume a political importance which would be at the expense of continuing international stability. The notion of limited war, then, is a valuable one, providing an intellectual tool whereby the most powerful states in the world can assess their interests and commitments in relation to any actual outbreak of armed violence on a major scale, and so plan their reactions and gestures in line with their political needs at any given juncture.

Limited war of this kind is essentially international. However, large-scale civil wars, such as the Congolese war in 1960, which involved the deployment of United Nations troops in a belligerent capacity, and the Nigerian war in 1968–9, in both of which breakaway regions (Katanga and 'Biafra' respectively) were finally defeated, also evoked a positive but careful response on the part of the chief external powers. It is generally the case that a search for a cease-fire on the part of well-disposed outsiders begins at almost the very moment of the open-fire. On the other hand, disputes leading to armed violence are invariably intractable, and formulae for a truce, let alone an acceptable settlement, are not easily or quickly devised. In the case of so-called 'people's revolutionary war', where ideological considerations tend to prevail, it is often impossible to end the violence by any means short of the concession of all the main claims, however far-reaching, arbitrary and doctrinaire, with which the revolutionaries identify themselves. Communist experience, especially in China, contributed heavily to the development of both tactical and strategic concepts which form the basis of planning and execution on the part of those dedicated to the violent overthrow of the existing order in a given country.

However, it is well to bear in mind that the patterns of 'people's revolutionary war' represent techniques which can be pressed into the service of counter-revolutionary doctrine as well. It is almost certainly a misleading simplification to assume that where these methods are employed the principal forces engaged are necessarily communist, still less that their manipulators are obviously the creatures of currently ruling Soviet or Chinese political elites. The theory of an unremitting, pervasive, consistent and integrated worldwide communist conspiracy has the attraction of being a comprehensive explanation of everything that non-communists find alarming. But it seriously underestimates the weight of local grievances within disturbed states, and of particular nationalisms which have sometimes been radicalized by revolutionary groups, as well as of the readiness with which the techniques of revolutionary struggle may be utilized by movements ideologically far removed from communism.

At the same time, although 'world communism' seems to be far less of a monolithic political force than many who cling to the global conspiracy view of communist strategy tend to assume, there are good grounds for suggesting that 'competitive co-existence' as a communist formula does provide both for the Soviet Union and the People's Republic of China, as the chief if rival powers in the communist world, doctrinal means by which each can take the fullest advantage politically of serious challenges to the authority and viability of capitalist governments.

It appears, moreover, that revolutionaries of several varieties, from Marxists to anarchists, acting in what they take to be the 'historically correct' circumstances, form *de facto* coalitions in the effort to paralyse and overthrow an existing government. Even rival terrorist groups, such as the two 'wings' of the IRA, deeply divided though they may be over the finer points of their respective bodies of dogma, and the precise nature of their ultimate objectives, act both emotionally and in terms of the available means of violence, as reinforcements to one another. In Northern Ireland again militant Catholics in 1969 were joined by 'civil rightists' and various groups of radical and revolutionary dissentients in their immediate challenge to the political system, although the social values which some groups purported to represent evidently differed from the traditional Catholic ethos to the point of incompatibility.

A grave aspect of dissident or revolutionary terrorism is to be seen in the extreme difficulty the instruments of 'official' law and order have in suppressing it. (Terrorists invariably apply their own instruments of law and order pretty ruthlessly to each other.) Although the tools of social control available to modern governments far surpass anything at the hands of mediaeval rulers, it is equally true that the conditions of modern living, in urban and rural areas alike, provide virtually unlimited facilities for the perpetration of illicit violence. In many parts of the world firearms are easily procured. Once owned, they can be readily concealed and simply maintained. It is no exaggeration to say that where rebel groups have possessed themselves of a wide range of effective arms they may operate in conditions of guerrilla warfare at least as efficiently as the regular forces against whom they fight. Characteristics of such warfare are the absence of a definable front line, the high general mobility of rebel elements, the difficulty of locating and isolating them, the uninhibited use of intimidation by rebels against local populations and the unpredictability in regard to both place and time of renewed rebel attacks. Not least of the problems facing legitimate regimes so challenged is the tendency of sympathetic dissidence to spread if government measures taken in the crisis of the hour can be made to appear oppressive and arbitrary. Rebel propaganda will not fail to exploit this possibility. There is, moreover, the well-understood capacity of revolutionary movements to play a waiting game. They may suffer sometimes major reverses yet remain capable of biding their time, until they can launch new challenges to the established order perhaps months or even years after it may have seemed to gain a decisive advantage, and to have succeeded in its programme of pacification.

Indeed the supreme problem facing regular military commands fighting 'limited' wars against guerrilla-type enemy movements is how to achieve any kind of meaningful victory whatever. We have seen earlier how quickly highly industrialized states have proved able to recover after undergoing years of 'total' war. What is equally remarkable is the capacity of agrarian and industrially undeveloped countries to sustain an almost unimaginable amount of damage inflicted by an enemy armed with the most sophisticated modern weapons and overwhelming air superiority, and remain capable of maintaining the struggle. North Vietnam may have been bombed into the Stone Age, but the 'Democratic Republic of Vietnam' remained undefeated, and able to negotiate as her leaders chose, on terms which did not derogate from her national dignity, with an enemy enormously more powerful than herself, whose will to fight on had been worn down by the elusiveness of anything like comprehensive victory. On the other hand, guerrillas do not win outright either. And so the battle of bullets and rockets and bombs becomes in a very acute sense a battle of wills. In so far as these may be reinforced by a sense of mission, of the absolute demands of a cause, on behalf of which all the horror and misery are to be endured, the atmosphere of Holy War may envelop the combatants and make the ultimate truce harder to seek.

It would seem that revolutionary violence derives considerable psychological support from the mood of generalized dissidence which showed itself in many parts of the Western world from about 1960 onwards. A certain more or less explicit resentment towards and even hatred of constituted authority on the part of the young gave some countenance to the revolutionary hopes of many whose political objectives went far beyond the often relatively non-specific radicalism of disgruntled students or working-class groups. And the effect of all this dissent and challenge inside political communities upon international society is of great importance. For a stable international order, whether prevailingly 'reactionary' or 'radical' in its ethos, requires for its maintenance a general acceptance of its legitimacy, and the existence of strong national governments, whose own legitimacy is not under constant question. Communist regimes may claim to be heirs of a revolutionary tradition, but yield to no other form of political order in the sternness of their methods of maintaining their authority. International society can accommodate occasional and disparate revolutions in particular states, as it did with difficulty after 1789 and 1917, and also cope with the endurance by some states of sometimes prolonged periods of internal crisis. But a really widespread ferment of revolutionary challenge and change within many countries at once, if such developed, would have a profoundly disturbing and destabilizing effect upon international order. Indeed that order, as we have known it, would almost certainly be altered beyond recognition.

Changes in international society, whether desirable or not, are inevitable, quite apart from the possible effects of a significant increase in worldwide radical dissent and its very frequent accompanying violence. How far, it is often asked, is the sovereign state itself becoming an obsolescent instrument of international politics? What seems to be the present role and future scope of international organizations? Is world government in any real sense a policy option before the nations? To these large questions we must now address ourselves.

8
Beyond the state?
The role of international
organizations

The Purposes of the United Nations are: (1) To maintain international peace and security. . . . (2) To develop friendly relations among nations based on respect. . . . (3) To achieve international cooperation in solving international problems. . . . (4) To be a center for harmonizing the actions of nations . . . – *From chapter 1 of the United Nations Charter*.

The delegates who go to Geneva react as Frenchmen, Englishmen, Germans, never as men, world citizens, world patriots . . . pessimists . . . should remember the days when any Duke of Burgundy could laugh at the King of France, and when Hotspur shouted defiance at King Henry IV. The kings of France and England, and the quiet clerks behind them, did not lose heart. They knew that they were on the side of real progress. We, the quiet clerks behind the Invisible King of the World, do not lose heart either. We know . . . that our generation is responsible before history for her share in the Great Design – *Don Salvador de Madariaga*.

In dealing with the Russians we want more gullibility, not less. We could hardly have less . . . – *Victor Gollancz*.

Ultimately the best hope of progress towards international conciliation seems to lie along the path of economic reconstruction. . . . It stands more directly in the line of recent advance than visions of a world federation or a more perfect League of Nations. Those elegant superstructures must wait until some progress has been made in digging the foundations – *E. H. Carr*.

World Law is not something you get to and say 'Ah' – *Betty Goetz Lall*.

The United Nations perfectly embodies in institutional form the tragic paradox of our age: it has become indispensable before it has become effective – *H. G. Nicholas.*

A public authority, having worldwide power and endowed with the proper means for the efficacious pursuit of its objective, which is the universal common good in concrete form, must be set up by common accord and not imposed by force. . . . This is all the more to be hoped for since all human beings . . . are showing an increasing interest in the affairs of all peoples, and are becoming more consciously aware that they are living members of a universal family of mankind – *Pope John XXIII (from the Encyclical* Pacem in Terris, *1963).*

It is fantasy for any of us now living to expect to see a politically unified world in our life-time – *Leslie Lipson.*

Competition and cooperation among nations

International politics, we have seen, is essentially a competitive activity. But it is by no means simply a matter of the competition of each nation with each. Obviously, states cooperate with each other in all kinds of ways as well as compete. Indeed, their continued existence depends on a very complex pattern of cooperative, coordinative and complementary inter-relationships being carried on. This is the essence of interdependence in international society. States have to cooperate, as they are obliged to compete, in order to survive as states. Particular acts of competition or cooperation are matters of policy, and therefore of choice. What is not chosen is the necessity to cooperate and to compete. This arises from the nature of international society itself. It is a condition of existence in international society as at present constituted. Things change. The possibility we shall be concerned with in this chapter is of changes developing so radical as to bring about a different condition of existence, in which the characteristics of international relations as now known will prevail no longer; in other words the coming of a quantity of change so great as to have a decisive qualitative effect. To some, such a degree of change appears desirable and they await it with hope. They tend to assume that the survival of the human race as a whole depends upon it coming about. Elizabeth

258

Jay Hollins, for instance, puts the case for their view with elegance and force:[1]

Life is paradox. It is also process. . . . I wish to emphasize that a system change such as advocated by Clark and Sohn is not something distinct from the evolutionary process, but is characteristic of it. A form is developed and elaborated as far as it will go. Then something happens which is a change in fundamental structure and organization; the shift may be tiny at first but it is not mere elaboration and mere development. Indeed, *system change has carried the main thrust of life* and one can say, as does Teilhard de Chardin, that the direction of evolution has been toward greater and greater consciousness and greater and greater cephalization (heading) – i.e. organization. This is not merely an analogy with biological forms, for, just as the emergence of thought and what flows from it takes place within the evolutionary process, so does the emergence of society and what flows from it. Seen in the vast picture the change that transfers some sovereignty from the nations to the world is minute. Seen from the point of view of ourselves it is a wrench to much of our habitual thinking, a big step, carrying with it, like all system changes in the framework of evolution, new possibilities for life and growth.[2]

At the same time we have to note the persistence of forms, as well as their propensity to change. It certainly does not appear that the element of competition between members of international society, even assuming that this is somehow unfortunate, is likely to be superseded in the foreseeable future. And where states find their best interests to be served in coordinating their activity with a group of states, as for example the European Economic Community, competition prevails briskly at the group level between associations of states. Individual countries may here and there, as in NATO, pool much of their military capacity in a comprehensive and permanent alliance. But competition for security goes on between rival alliance systems at least as fiercely as between individual rival countries in the past. In effect, the members of collaborative groups of states find that their individual capacity to compete effectively in international society is enhanced by association, not that actual national competition ceases to be a fundamental aspect of their activity as states.

Inter-state cooperation, we have said, is equally intrinsic to the maintenance of international order and the life of its individual

[1] In *Peace is Possible*, Grossman, New York, 1966.
[2] My italics.

state subjects. Cooperative arrangements acknowledge the existence of areas of mutual interest between states. When the interests motivating the cooperation are fully met, or disappear, or are in some way transformed, the behaviour of the states concerned will be correspondingly modified. An existing inter-state association may well end altogether. The process may often be seen with particular clarity in the field of international cooperation for defence or for waging war. While wartime alliances will usually be dissolved, formally or tacitly, when the war is lost or won, even long-standing defensive alliances, created because the perceived threat they are intended to contain is believed to be of indefinite duration, will be subject to the strains of changing circumstances, and are virtually certain to be held up for review and possible revision from time to time. NATO and the Warsaw Pact grouping are by far the most important of the multilateral defensive alliance systems to come into being since 1945. Both are instructive, in their response to changing circumstances and in the response of member and non-member states to their continuing existence.

In the case of the fifteen members of NATO[3] the doctrine of equal sovereignty (which is of course not affected by the great inequalities of power between them) imposes upon each complementary rights and duties in respect of the undertakings written into the treaty. The most momentous of the latter is the obligation assumed by them all to regard an attack upon any one of them by an aggressor as a simultaneous attack against all. The passing of time and the changing of circumstances has made this provision seem perhaps less convincing, and also, happily, less likely to need to be invoked than it was taken to be in 1949 and for long afterwards. Not only did the enormous variation of power between the members dictate the contribution each made in absolute terms to the common resources of the Alliance. Political factors operating within individual member nations determined the proportion of their Gross National Product which could be devoted to general defence needs. Misgivings on the ground of compromised sovereignty felt by Gaullist France carried her out of her military commitments to NATO, although the French government never denounced the treaty, and France retained her membership of all

---

[3] They are: Belgium, Canada, Denmark, France, Federal Germany, Greece, Holland, Iceland, Italy, Luxembourg, Norway, Portugal, Turkey, the United Kingdom and the United States.

the constituent organs and committees except those directly concerned with the actual military command structure. By the early 1970s the Alliance was still firmly in being, and hopes were voiced that France might find her way back into participation on the side still felt to matter most – the military.

However, the gravity of the perceived Soviet threat to the independence and integrity of non-communist Europe, motivating the creation of NATO, did not prevent the eruption of serious disputes between Alliance partners. Most notably there was the extreme tension that developed between Greece and Turkey over communal relations between Greek and Turkish Cypriots and the political destiny of Cyprus. Less dangerous but still tiresome there are disputes over fishing rights in unilaterally extended territorial waters between Iceland and Britain, and to a lesser extent Federal Germany. Moreover, towards the close of the second decade of NATO's history the United States showed evidence of a desire to reduce the number of American ground forces stationed in Europe. On the other hand, European security seemed by then to be more stable than at any time since the Alliance was formed. Cautious steps were taken towards a European Security Conference, actively canvassed by the Russians, and there was talk of some kind of mutual guarantee, amounting virtually to a military partnership, between NATO and the Consultative Committee (the organizational entity) of the Warsaw Pact. While dangers and mistrust were by no means eliminated, the security problem of Europe seemed closer to long-term settlement, easing thereby the defensive rigidities of each side. But it was recognized that at any time a further period of freeze might follow the evident thaw, in particular that a highly integrated Western Europe, deriving ultimately from an enlarged Economic Community, and adopting a 'high profile' with regard to European relations with the rest of the world, could provoke a sharpening of Soviet interest, of a not reassuring kind, in Western European affairs. (See the Concluding note on p. 307.)

However that may prove to be, the success of NATO since its inception could not be denied after the first twenty years. No additional European country 'fell to communism' after 1949, either by subversion or military intervention. Of course it remains for ever uncertain how aggressive and expansionist the Soviet Union would really have been in Europe had NATO not existed as a formidable constraint. For most of the period since the absorption of Czechoslovakia into the communist bloc in February 1948 the Soviet Union has behaved very much as a *status quo* power, adopting a firm but essentially defensive stance towards the West. What mattered was the threat she was deemed to pose; that she was believed to desire the Sovietization of Europe, and that these beliefs proved strong enough, warranted by current Western views about the nature of communist doctrine and of Soviet political power, to enable fifteen fairly diverse non-communist countries to keep a burdensome military alliance permanently in being.

The preamble to the instrumental treaty of NATO expressed hopes of a growing closeness of association which approached ultimate integration. That the political and social implications of the Alliance have proved less important than its continuing military realities is significant.

Inside the area covered by the Warsaw Pact there is also to be seen evidence of dynamic change over time. The pact was negotiated because it seemed essential for Russian security against what Soviet leaders regarded, or declared that they regarded, as a direct threat by a hostile West bent on a revision of that conformation of power which arose out of the total Soviet victory, with Russia's allies, over Nazi Germany. From the inception of the pact in 1955, as a counterweight to NATO, the effective independence of its subordinate partners was compromised far beyond limits of freedom of action assumed or implied under the provisions of NATO. The looming might of the Soviet Union and the complete penetration of her allies' defence policies by Soviet military leadership were for long unchallengeable. Yet national identities vigorously persisted and internal restiveness grew. As early as 1953 serious disturbances occurred in the German Democratic Republic. The Hungarian Rising of 1956 and the Czech liberalization policy after 1967 were both crushed by sheer military strength, overwhelmingly that of the Soviet Union. But their deepest importance lay in the fact that they happened. If they were failures they were also portents. And despite the implications of the Brezhnev Doctrine the general Soviet response since the early 1960s towards the national susceptibilities of the other pact countries appears to have been notably more sensitive and flexible, although Russian leaders will clearly permit nothing that they interpret as a threat to Soviet security to develop among the political processes of the pact as a whole or of any member country. Yet it is evident that Poland, Hungary, Rumania, and even Czechoslovakia since 1968, all enjoy a measure of assertive autonomy in both domestic and foreign policy which would have been out of the question a dozen years earlier.

What emerges from this brief survey of the history of the two great European alliance systems of the post-1945 era? We may suggest it is that military alliances however far-reaching in intention and durable in time, are not particularly promising instruments for bringing about anything approaching the actual integration of the separate sovereign nations comprising them. The psychological demands of a felt nationhood appear to be very persistent. Sooner or later they are likely to modify the political complexion and perhaps even the institutional structure of a particular military bloc. In the case both of NATO and the Warsaw Pact the ideological underpinning has been strong. Yet neither the cause of the 'Atlantic community' nor that of the 'socialist camp' have been allowed to take precedence over the need of each of their constituent peoples to afirm a continuing evident separateness for each of the nation-states concerned. Above all, we are reminded that military alliances exist essentially to defend and uphold the sovereignty of their members, not to supersede it. This remains the case, however much in practice actual sovereignty may be modified by the requirements of military effectiveness, or by the preponderant power in relation to smaller partners of any one signatory.

It is necessary too to notice that military effectiveness itself may be subordinated to pressing political needs. The adjustments made from time to time in NATO, and it seems probable enough in the Warsaw Pact as well, bring sharply into focus the crucial question, referred to elsewhere in these pages, of the role of the political will. In the case of a measure of American retrenchment in Europe, in response to the realities of *détente* and the urgency of domestic issues, the allies of the United States must either undertake an extra defence effort on their own behalf, or alternatively conclude that the threat against which they seek to be prepared is less than it was, so absolving them from additional sacrifices. If that were to be the decision it would not be the first time in international politics that the wish, well-founded or not, proved father to the thought. Shall the means be enlarged, or the ends reshaped? There are always the linked problems of judging the intentions of your adversary and gauging the determination of your supporters. Particularly are shrewdness and cool nerve called for in striking this inescapable balance in countries where dissent is vocal and parties freely compete for government. A margin of national safety has to be calculated, willy-nilly, for a 'warfare state', in which all the resources of the state beyond what suffices for bare subsistence are devoted to defence, while theoretically conceivable, has no practical relevance to the making of actual policy. At the same time, no NATO member is likely to take the risks involved in the pursuit of material welfare to the exclusion of any defence capability whatever. Motives of prudence would inhibit such a decision, and even those of honour might not prove entirely negligible. Guns *and* butter must continue to be the formula while the large-scale features of international society remain as they have been. Welfare at the reckless expense of security would be precarious: security at the expense of reasonable welfare in the long run intolerable. Military alliances, in fact, represent a well-tried method of generalizing security by sharing its cost. It has indeed been forcibly argued that such alliances tend to prove assets for the weak but liabilities for the strong. On the other hand, even for the strong, who might purely in terms of resources manage to 'go it alone', membership of an alliance provides opportunities for the enlargement and intensification of political influence and thereby contributes to the real power of the strong state in the world at large.

Our conclusion has been that the road to world government is unlikely to be paved with the texts of military alliances. What of associations of states for other purposes than mutual defence? We have witnessed the spectacular increase in the mutual interpenetration of states in the modern world. And we have noted the growing inadequacy of all but the very greatest powers to provide for either the safety or the sufficient prosperity of their peoples on a unilateral basis, an inadequacy rendered the sharper by the revolution of rising expectations in many parts of the world. Such trends have motivated much of the search for satisfactory new types of international association, especially in the fields of economics and what may be broadly termed cultural and social exchange. As in the case of the European Economic Community, the supra-national potentialities of such experiements are openly admitted and institutionally provided for. To 'transcend the nation-state' becomes in these circumstances an explicit long-term objective.

There remains a paradoxical aspect in the situation. For it is evident that by and large states are still jealous for their sovereignty. But it is this very status which obliges states to be responsible for the well-being of their citizens, and this very responsibility which in modern conditions drives states more and more urgently into international agreements which, as do all treaties, limit the sovereign freedom of the states entering into them. When any sovereign country makes any treaty whatsoever, it practices the auto-limitation of its sovereignty to the extent of the obligations it assumes under the treaty. And no state in the modern world exists in complete isolation. Even without the limitations imposed by specific treaties, each state has the obligation to behave in international society in a way which fulfils the understood expectations of its fellows.

National sovereignty denotes that condition in which a state is in fact free, and is generally accepted as being free, to manage its internal affairs and conduct external relations with other states, without dictation by or intervention on the part of any other state. We call this condition one of national sovereignty, irrespective of whether the state concerned is a nation-state or a multi-nation state. Sovereignty has in modern parlance come to be virtually synonymous with independence, so that the expression 'independent sovereign state', though sonorous, is to all intents and purposes a tautology. We stress what may seem a fine point because it is important not to concede any distinction between independence and sovereignty which might suggest that independence was the status of being free from legitimate external interference and sovereignty the status of being above the law. Sovereign states are *not* free to do exactly what they like; they *are* subjects of international law, which is thus by definition above them: you cannot be subject to someone who is merely your equal in status.[4] It is true that the machinery of international law enforcement is relatively weak, and that states tend to appear in practice to be less constrained by a law they all acknowledge than by the countervailing power of other states. Yet, as we mentioned earlier, in

[4] J. L. Brierly discusses the whole doctrine of sovereignty with great authority in *The Law of Nations*, Clarendon Press, Oxford, 1955.

chapter 6, the law to which states are subject is generally observed. International society would be appallingly more disordered than it is if that were not the case. A fundamental principle of international law remains the sanctity of treaties, that is to say the understood duty of states to keep their bargains and to discharge the undertakings into which they have solemnly entered by international agreement.

Now this clearly applies in the case of agreements which specifically provide for the gradual or even the immediate modification of the sovereign status of a country, as for example in the case of countries agreeing to hand over to an instituted body representing them and acting on their behalf certain areas of responsibility for policy, and to undertake to observe certain regulations or requirements imposed upon them by such a body.

Thus while all treaties limit untrammelled sovereignty by imposing upon the parties obligations to behave in such ways as fulfilling the treaty concerned require, some treaties explicitly provide for the cession of certain sovereign rights, that is, governmental responsibility for certain areas of policy, to a duly authorized supra-national institution. The Treaty of Rome is such an instrument, and many therefore have seen in it, whether with approval or misgiving, a means by which a number of long-established sovereign European states may, through various processes of obligatory political direction and economic cooperation, gradually create at least a *confederal* structure, in which while the constituent members will maintain individual series of external relations, in important areas of policy the institution will speak and act for them all as an international person in its own right at large in international society. While it remains to be seen how far these supra-national implications and aspirations of the 'Common Market' will be worked out and fulfilled over time, the experiment does represent a striking instance of the readiness of many modern European statesmen to devote their efforts to the ultimate supercession of the nation-state as at any rate the principal and characteristic *locus* of sovereignty in world politics.

Variations on this form of regional cooperative structure may be expected to be created in other parts of the world. The EEC itself, having expanded from the original Six to the Nine, is thought by many to be capable of further enlargement, until possibly almost all non-communist Europe is bound together in an all-embracing supra-national institution. But the difficulties are very great. The history of the Six has been marked by numerous crises, of greater and lesser moment, as well as by a good deal of overall success. But the more comprehensive the institution, the more diverse its elements, the more scope there obviously will be for disagreements, disharmonies and incompatibilities.[5] Differences of political tradition and method, diversities in economic need and opportunity, and, never least, the King Charles's Head of nationalistic self-regard, ever liable to gibber in defensive anger at any evidence of the erosion of states' sovereign prerogatives, all combine to retard, perhaps render unattainable and in any case probably remote, the transformation of the society of states into 'one world', or even into a worldwide grouping of a relatively small number of large supra-national entities.

We may observe in passing that it is important to distinguish between the *exercise* of sovereignty and the *status* of sovereignty. As we have seen, states are normally engaged upon the exercise of their sovereignty in their day to day activities pursuant to the maintenance of their relations with each other. This is no less so when it takes the form of limiting by mutual agreement the areas in which they are in fact free to act. But the status of sovereignty attaches by definition to sovereign states whether they choose to exercise it or not. In the case of many small states, for instance, their freedom to act is likely to be very limited, but their sovereign status remains unimpaired. Such status may be for some states virtually the sole resource which they can deploy in the attempt to attain their objectives in international politics. It is hard not to feel that for them sovereignty becomes critically vital to their interests simply because they command practically nothing else. In the United Nations, for example, it is the status of sovereignty which gives states the right to belong to the Organization, though they may bring to it little more. Sovereign status remains an attribute, which may be accorded quite apart from whatever economic power, political prestige and accompanying diplomatic influence any particular state may enjoy.

In this connection suggestions are put forward from time to time to the effect that international society might introduce diff-

---

[5] William Pickles, a distinguished mentor of politics to generations of London School of Economics students, has long been one of the most eloquent and penetrating critics of the institutions of the EEC, and of the British decision to join it.

erent grades of membership. This might particularly apply, the suggestion goes, to membership of such a world body as the United Nations itself. In principle, the notion appears to have much to commend it, inasmuch as it endeavours to bring further institutional recognition to the inescapable fact and consequences of the inequality of power between states. Hitherto there has really been nothing between constitutional dependence and formal independence. If a colonial territory, however small, weak and insignificant it may be, ceases to be such, what can it well become except a sovereign state? Thus Fiji in 1973 becomes a sovereign state simply because it ceases to be a British protectorate. Thus the opposition party in the self-governing colony of the Sychelles demands independence, that is to say, that the responsibility for external affairs and defence shall be relinquished by Britain and assumed by the Sychelles government. In which case those delightful islands would become yet one more minuscule sovereign entity in the international system. To date, acceptable classifications of first-, second- and possibly even third-class membership of international society have not been agreed, and the existing either/or simplicity of 'subject or sovereign'[6] is of course reinforced by the prevalence of nationalistic aspirations, however much these may sometimes operate at the expense of common sense.

As we distinguish between the exercise and status of sovereignty, so we will be wise to bear in mind that so-called supra-nationality, about which so much is said and written in our day, is itself by no means a simple or even unified concept.

Supra-national elements, in the relations of states, vary very greatly in their scope and mode of operation. The notion may imply the functioning of formal institutions, endowed with a larger or narrower degree of decision-making capacity, responsible for making policy to which the members of a given group of states are subject. The object of analysis must include the defining of the legitimacy within which supra-national policy-makers may function, the determination of the areas of responsibility allotted to them and the location of their real (and not necessarily their apparent) position in whatever institutional structure accommodates them. The United Nations secretariat, for example, has

[6] The anomalous position of Byelorussia and Ukraine as 'sovereign' members of the United Nations may be noted. Who conducts Byelorussia's foreign relations?

acquired some of the attributes of international personality. It can sue states and be sued by them in international law. Its servants are expressly required to develop an exclusive executive loyalty to the Organization and not to their national states. But the UN secretariat is of course not the government of a state, nor does it govern member states. Again, some scholars have detected in the General Assembly of the United Nations actual rudiments of a world legislative function. Here the suggestion is that General Assembly recommendations over time may attain the status of 'customary law'. Thus repeated condemnation by the General Assembly of South African *apartheid* might imply, by the coming into being of something regarded as customary law, not merely the supposed immorality of *apartheid* but also its actual international illegality. This view of matters may possess some potential validity. But it seems at the present time to strain the terms of the United Nations Charter, which at no point implies that the General Assembly is to be, even in intention, an international legislature. One more example of the many nuances supra-nationality presents: where does it reside in the European Economic Community? With the Council of Ministers, who agree decisions in various fields of policy applicable to the Community, or with the High Commission, which combines advisory and executive functions? For the 'Eurocrats' are not responsible for agreeing policy, and the ministers remain ultimately answerable to their national Parliaments. Yet decisions are undoubtedly taken which are seen in practice to bind each member country. Thus a measure of supra-nationality in fact prevails, though obscured by institutional complexities and the continuing constitutional sovereignty of the national legislatures within the Community.[7]

World unity: dreams and means

Before going on to examine the experiments so far made to try to secure world peace and order by means of worldwide institutions let us consider a few of the assumptions that underlie much of the

[7] Before and after the parliamentary decision to accede to the Treaty of Rome on terms negotiated by the Conservative government in 1971, the Labour leader, Harold Wilson, insisted that nothing had been done or could be done which would derogate from the right of the sovereign British Parliament to decide to re-negotiate terms or to withdraw from the Community at some future date.

discussion about the scope and future of such institutions, and the dream, or perhaps the prospect, of a unified world.

We may notice three. The first we may call the *realist* assumption. This maintains that by their nature states are obliged unremittingly to struggle for survival and may choose to do so for dominance. On this view there is, as we suggested in an earlier chapter, a *necessary* competitive quest for power as a means to attain other objectives. Necessary, because it follows from the way that international society is in fact ordered. The nature of this society, suggest the so-called realists, gives scope for some states to achieve eminence as great powers, often of an imperial type, though not all great powers are strictly empires. It does not, they argue, provide scope for the emergence of a global political order to which all states are subject, in short, to a form of world government. The suggestion is not that world government is undesirable in principle, though some have urged serious objections to it, but that the structure of international society simply does not provide the instrumentality by which it can be brought about, at least by agreement. And a world order imposed by a state which had somehow survived all others, or defeated them, would hardly satisfy the moral sensibilities of anyone, except *faute de mieux*, as a way of preserving world peace. At present anything approaching a *Pax Sovietica* or a *Pax Americana* seems as improbable as it would appear to many of us undesirable. 'Realists' also tend to maintain that it is not (certainly as yet) within the capacity of men to ensure that might is righteous or that right is mighty. This cannot, in other words, in the real world be made the test of statecraft. If, as some sombre theorists insist, conflict and the threat of chaos are the ordained lot of mankind, the duty of statesmen is to strive to secure national survival by any available means in what would appear to be almost the worst of all possible worlds.

The second group of assumptions are held by so-called *idealists*. Such persons, in the search for ways of ensuring international harmony, have been much exercised by the possibility of transcending inter-state competition through the creation of an adjudicatory world order. Their hopes are doubtless reinforced by the suggestion that nations are not merely the prisoners of their history. The system of states can be modified by will and choice, and both the expectations and behaviour of states adjusted accordingly. Bound up with this assumption is the further one that men and their governments are not subject to any inexorable 'laws' of politics. Uncertainty about future developments is in fact thoroughly rational. If we cannot predict coming advances in the natural or social sciences it follows that we cannot predict the changes in the ordering of either domestic or international society which such advances may occasion. To believe that nothing can alter the present characteristics of the international state system is, on this view, simply to limit arbitrarily the scope of the influence of possible future developments in those areas of human endeavour and experiment which may affect international relations. Sir Karl Popper[8] has shown that there is a good deal of force in these contentions. It appears crudely dogmatic to maintain merely that what has been will be. On the other hand we have no other evidence than the past to go on. And such evidence suggests that while we may not say that men will never devise a formula that will be applied successfully to pacify and unify the world, they have aspired to do so in the past, and the institutions they have set up hitherto have not only failed to achieve global pacification but can be shown specifically to have reinforced the legitimacy of the political division of the world into independent states. Article 2 of the United Nations Charter, for instance, expressly states that 'the Organization is based on the principle of the sovereign equality of all its members'. Thus both the League of Nations and the United Nations Organization precisely did *not* attempt to put a term to the history of multiple sovereignties, or seek to transcend them. Rather did they symbolize the right of sovereign states to exist, endeavouring to guarantee their integrity by affirming their legal equality of status over against their conspicuous inequalities of power, and by placing constraints valid in international law upon their freedom to resolve disputes between them by force. Little, we might think, could be a much further cry from even implicit world government.

What may be said about international organizations in general is that they represent an especially close degree of cooperation between their constituent members which still functions within rather than beyond the traditional mode of inter-state relationship expressed in the usages of diplomatic contact and negotiation. Clearly, international organizations come into existence in order to promote the interests of the countries that agree to create them. Their basic purpose, underlying whatever specific functions they

[8] In *The Open Society and its Enemies*, cited earlier.

are designed to fulfil, remains to enable the international system as a whole to operate more satisfactorily. It has not been, at least in the crucial case of the two world organizations so far set up, fundamentally to change the nature of that system. By providing for regular consultation between member states under set conditions, and by devising machinery for implementing collective decisions, international institutions represent a movement towards *the reform and adaptation* of the international system for the benefit of those states that belong to the institutions. To imply a purpose significantly beyond that would appear unwarranted.

Yet it cannot be denied that the spectacle of the League and of UNO at large in international society has stimulated many people, especially perhaps those who have been active in such bodies as the League of Nations Union and the United Nations Association, to entertain the dynamic idea of a movement towards world government. However much the explicit purpose of the League and UNO may have been to stabilize the international order rather than transform it, such people have seen in these organizations attempts to institutionalize the ancient dream of a unified world enjoying perpetual peace. The latter aspiration indeed implies the former. While 'world peace' may never be perpetual, 'perpetual peace' is by logical necessity universal.

The belief that only a unified world can be a peaceful one has an ancient history, bound up with doctrines about the nature and status of humanity itself. The concept of a universal human brotherhood is found in certain aspects of Stoic cosmopolitanism from the third century BC. Both Buddhism and Christianity, in very different formulations, enshrine the idea of the oneness of mankind, and derive from this a moral imperative to seek the creation of universal harmony. Both religions, however, from differing standpoints, have recognized the difficulties in the way of fulfilling this obligation that arise from the obstinate self-seeking of men individually and in groups, the sometimes intractable nature of their conflicting desires, and the irreconcilability that may be a feature of their rival interests. Islam, too, has universalist pretensions. It is a measure of the depth of diversity between human beings and between their societies that no universalist religion or philosophy or political order has ever succeeded in winning the allegiance of mankind as a whole. Perhaps we would not be mistaken in concluding from this that there is a naturalness and an inevitability in the diversities that characterize the collective life of men which, if they motivate the search for universalist solutions to the predicaments of that collective life, ensure that such search will be vain.

However this may be, an important theme in history has been the repeated endeavour to regulate international politics by instruments of world order in the hope of achieving general peace and well-being. A very significant aspect of this endeavour has been the attempt to devise effectual modalities for bringing about *peaceful change* in the international order, accepting that things do not remain the same, and that the expectations and demands of the members of international society will also change correspondingly. How to accommodate inevitable and sometimes desirable change without jeopardizing desirable and always vulnerable stability: that perennial problem has become more acute as the actual rate of change has accelerated in the modern world. Certainly throughout the twentieth century it has become the increasing preoccupation of statesmanship.

From Christendom to the League of Nations

Mediaeval political thought conceived a universal spiritual order, binding on all men potentially and on all Christian men immediately. At once the symbol and institutional instrument of this order was the Papacy. This claimed an ultimate jurisdiction over the relations of rulers with each other and with their subjects. The temporal order itself, subordinate in status and function to the spiritual order, was ideally conceived in terms of the Christian Realm, of which the Holy Roman Empire was the highly un-ideal and largely ineffectual institutional expression. The emperor in theory was to guarantee the protection and well-being of all men in Christendom by virtue of his authority over kings and princes who owed to the Empire that fealty and deference due to an institution divinely ordained to make possible and to maintain such secular conditions as would enable men to practise the true faith, seek and do the will of God, and attain salvation. If this ideal influenced political theory far more impressively than it ever shaped political behaviour, this is no more than history might lead us to expect of an ideal. The elective imperial office became more and more purely honorific, the imperial authority more and more illusory, the Empire itself more and more shadowy. The Reformation fatally compromised the over-arching concept of a united Christendom. It left to European society a legacy of *national* Churches, of which secular rulers were the temporal governors. Post-Reformation settlements also provided that the religion of the ruler should be the religion of his state, to be rightfully imposed by him upon his subjects. Above all, the Reformation stimulated the development (though this was no part of any reformer's intention) of a general secularizing process. In its political aspects this largely gave rise to a characteristic system of sovereign states in Europe. Effectually in being by the middle of the sixteenth century, this system in its essentials was to be worldwide by the twentieth.

At least as urgently as in the theocratic world of mediaeval Europe, statesmen in the secularized Europe of later times acknowledged an interest in regulating relations between the political communities that comprised it. Between the eighteenth and twentieth centuries an attempt was made, more or less conscious and deliberate, to create within the continuing dynamism of international politics a measure of equilibrium among the European states. A vital aspect of this balance of power was the 'Concert of the powers'. This Concert took various forms. Never even implicitly supra-national, it did achieve a degree of institutional formality following the holocaust of the Napoleonic wars and their radical if temporary re-drawing of the political map of Europe. The Concert was embodied in the Congressional System, which might be said to have been an attempt to institutionalize it. Four Congresses of the powers were held between 1815 and 1822. Thereafter the Congressional device became stabilized as an occasional and exceptional instrument of the unstructured Concert of the powers. Congresses, convened either at the close of a major war, or in face of the danger of war, deliberated at irregular intervals throughout the nineteenth century and beyond.[9] In 1899 came the Russian tsar's initiative that resulted in the Hague Peace Conferences of that year and 1907, some of the significant aspects of which we have remarked on earlier in this book. The military

[9] They were: Paris, 1856 (the Crimean war); London, 1871 (the Franco-Prussian war); Berlin, 1878 (the Russo-Turkish war); Berlin, 1884–5 ('danger of European war'); Algeciras, 1906 (Franco-German crisis); London, 1912–13 (the Balkan wars).

backwardness of the Russian Empire in a period of European rearmament and in comparison with the advanced military capacity of the German Empire, together with the good reason the Russian government had to fear the socially disruptive effects of a new war in a land where revolution was latent, were undoubted tsarist motives in promoting the conferences. But they do not call into question the tsar's sincerity in desiring to secure peace, nor detract from the value of agreements made for the regulation of future conflict. However, neither Conference resulted in a political programme for maintaining world peace. Twenty-six nations attended the first, which was mainly European, and forty-four the second, including the Latin-American republics. This enlargement at least introduced a hint of universality. The diplomatic equality of all sovereign states was reaffirmed, and the global spread of the international system explicitly acknowledged. A proposal was canvassed, and found much favour, for holding periodical conferences to discuss problems of world peace. The seed of the League of Nations was sown.

Another achievement, of perhaps greater potential than actual importance, was the creation of the so-called Permanent Court of Arbitration. Not strictly a court, it comprises a panel of international lawyers, members of which may be convened from time to time to arbitrate on specific issues between states.

It seems fair to say that the basis of an international device for the pacific settlement of disputes was laid down at the Hague. The conferences assumed a high degree of rationality in the conduct of states. The statesmen tended to believe that men pursued rationally interests themselves rational. The implicit theory assumed that only suitable instruments were needed to ensure the success of rational endeavours. States could be expected to behave in a rationally self-restrained manner on the whole, and could confidently be invited to submit to the rational judgement of impartial arbiters chosen by mutual agreement.

But while there was some real ground for this view nothing disposed of the difficulty noted elsewhere that while every state desired peace in the abstract nearly all states have always accepted the legitimacy of war in certain circumstances. Hence international organizations having as one of their principal objectives the preservation of peace tend to be enthusiastically supported if they appear to be actively working against war, and to be resisted or disregarded when they seek to intervene in particular wars, which the combatants concerned can always find overwhelming justification for fighting.

Seven years after the Second Hague Peace Conference the first world war broke out. From the ashes of its fires arose, phoenix-like, the League of Nations.

We may then properly regard the century from 1815 to 1914 as an era of preparation for developed international organizations committed to the pursuit of international peace, and the ultimate unification of the world, perhaps, as implicitly a means to its maintenance.

Brain-child of an idealistic American president, the Covenant of the League, forming the fourteenth of Woodrow Wilson's wartime Fourteen Points for a postwar settlement, was embodied in the text of the Treaty of Versailles (10 January 1920). It thereby suffered the disadvantage of being associated with a particular peace, and therefore bound to suffer the discredit which that peace would sustain in the minds of those obliged by military defeat to subscribe to it. Of possibly even greater significance was the fact that the American Senate, in isolationist mood, failed to accord the Covenant the two-thirds majority required for ratification of the treaty. Thus the United States remained outside the League. This circumstance has generally been held to have seriously weakened both the credibility and the effectiveness of the Organization as an instrument for maintaining world peace.

The League concept, in fact, embodied elements of the old Concert of Europe and combined with them the Hague Conference notion of a standing council of states convened at regular intervals to discuss the problems of peace and security arising out of the persistence of rival sovereignties in international politics. The League was provided with a permanent secretariat (served by some very devoted men), a Permanent Court of International Justice, an International Labour Office and a Mandates Commission, which last authorized and supervised the administration of dependent territories by certain powers with a view to eventual self-government. Based at Geneva, the League acted as an umbrella to a number of international agencies, including the Postal Union and an agency for the international control of the drug traffic. Such arrangements implied faint hints of incipient supranationality. They represented useful functions that potentially at least went beyond the primary purpose of mitigating 'international anarchy' on behalf of world peace. Meanwhile the rationalist view largely prevailed in League circles that war was a horrible and avoidable accident or aberration. Linked with this doctrine was a belief that 'the peoples of the world' desired peace, irrespective of the particular grievances to which any actual condition of peace might give rise. Moreover, the liberal assumption held by many League supporters was that generally democratic political norms would prevail more or less everywhere, in a world 'made safe for democracy', and that these norms would effectively ensure that the peoples' desire for peace would be communicated to their governments, who in turn would democratically reflect in their foreign policies the pacific intentions of their citizens. The democratic ideology was carried further still. The principle of majority rule would be instituted, it was fondly hoped, in the society of states itself. Thus international society would become democratic. Sovereignty to the individual League member would then be in theory what citizenship was to the individual man within the democratic state – a means whereby he takes his part in the process of political management. States would thus discuss their international problems and vote democratically on proposed settlements. These, since they would be willingly accepted by all the League members as expressions of the general, or at least the majority, will of international society, would avail to avoid war and preserve peace.

Alas! The genuine but somewhat simple idealism infusing this conception failed to allow for, even perhaps to recognize the existence of, the tenacity with which particular states would uphold particular national interests. Equally fateful, it did not take sufficiently into account the enormous disparity of power between states. Thus League enthusiasts naively assumed that a 'transgressor' great power would meekly submit to a numerical majority of diverse small states. Hence arose the tragic fallacy of the doctrine of collective security as exemplified by the League structure and purpose. Granted that the members of the League had bound themselves by solemn Covenant, idealists might feel justified in believing that such members would honour their obligations, even if these were to operate to their disadvantage. The history of the international politics of the last three centuries, to go no further back, might have made this expectation seem unduly trustful.

But there was also the sense that a decisive and qualitative change in the nature of international relations was imminent, even in process. This simply proved not to be the case, at any rate to the degree which League supporters imagined. Lastly the League formula provided, and could provide, no means whereby sovereign states could be obliged to remain within the Organization and hence subject to the obligations of membership, against their wish. Japan left the League over the Manchurian issue in 1933, and Germany on general principles in 1935.

Indeed, with so many conceptual and structural weaknesses that the benefit of hindsight enables us to perceive so clearly, the wonder might seem to be not at the failure of the League but at the fact that it functioned at all, for some twenty years, and in its early days with some measure of success. (It achieved a stable settlement of the serious Graeco-Bulgarian border dispute of the early 1920s.) The League's most important legacy, it seems safe to say, was not the memory of failure but the persistence of an idea: the idea that an international organization for the maintenance of peace and security *could* be devised, and act as a real constraint upon the behaviour of states.

An alternative view of the League ought not to be overlooked before turning to a discussion of the role of its successor. This is that the League represented really an institutional device whereby certain European states could maintain an effective hegemony on the Continent. So doing, they would exercise an irksome constraint upon dissatisfied powers which might wish to challenge the *status quo* created by the Versailles Treaty. This interpretation regarded the League as essentially an instrument of the balance of power. That there is some considerable substance in this contention cannot be denied. France in particular, as we have seen, in her anguished search for security against a still united, powerful and probably enough *revanchist* Germany, sought in the League an instrument which would serve her national interest in a very direct way. This nervous realism of French political leaders, also evidenced by the setting up of the 'little *entente*', a *cordon sanitaire* of Central European powers round Germany, contrasted sharply with the idealism of the League of Nations Union. It is useful to remember that very different aspirations may motivate support for particular international institutions, and that such differences may well influence their effectiveness.

On the whole, however, we may be inclined to the conclusion that the League of Nations was neither a conspicuous success nor a total failure. As this would seem to be the case with very many human institutions, we may not appear to be saying much. But the achievements of the League, even in the field of international peace-keeping, were not wholly negligible, and, in relation to the mandatory system, and the work of the special agencies, were not unimpressive. That the role of the League proved more modest, and its successes more patchy, than its sponsors dreamed and perhaps genuinely expected, reflects not upon their sincerity but, we may now think, upon a certain naivety with which they were somewhat generously endowed. As with Dr Johnson's example of the men entering upon a second marriage, their efforts represented the triumph of hope over experience. And of course we can always ask the speculative question whether international relations would have been even less stable, less orderly and more disputatious between 1918 and 1939 if the League had not existed. In any case, the history of the League remains of perennial interest as it is the history of the first major attempt to implement the ancient principle of international collective security, long canvassed and even cherished by political theorists, and at the end of the first world war a fashionable notion even among statesmen. At the heart of the League's relative failure lay the illusion that the doctrine of the sovereign equality of states could prevail against the facts of international power, once one or more of the great powers had decided that the obligations of League membership were a tiresome constraint upon their freedom of action or simply irrelevent to their national needs. But failure may sometimes prove more instructive than success. In 1945 the architects of the United Nations Organization, one or two of whom, for instance Field-Marshal Smuts, had been among the leading proponents of the League, came together in a mood more practical if less idealistic. They still said, or allowed others to say on their behalf, the same large and high-minded things that had been uttered so freely at the inception of the League, but the actual political structures they fashioned at least reflected many of the realities of power and did not purport to transcend them. As for world government, much was said and written on the topic during the 1920s and 1930s, but the League of Nations remained throughout a regulative instrument in the hands of independent states. It never began to look like any kind of real world authority. We must now briefly consider the significantly different story of the United Nations.

The United Nations: potential world government?

The United Nations Charter was signed on 26 June 1945. There were several reasons for the comparatively cautious hopes of its signatories. Among them was the unprecedented physical destruction of the war just ending. Another was the shadow over future international relations cast by rumoured new weapons of unparalleled violence. There were the discouraging aspects of the League record. Not least among the new factors giving rise to sober reflections was the unconcealed dominance of the greatest of the victorious great powers, whose ascendancy was so evident as soon to suggest a new category to accommodate them, that of 'superpower'. The League of Nations, lacking the membership of the United States throughout, and of Russia before 1934 and of Germany thereafter, in effect tried to substitute collective security for any formal or *de facto* Concert of the powers. The United Nations, including the giants of East and West from the outset, had in effect to try to assimilate a Concert principle to a still loudly proclaimed principle of collective security. It was evident from the earliest days, to the growing perturbation of many medium and small powers, that any collective security that was actually achieved depended essentially upon the goodwill of the greatest powers choosing on any given issue to act in concert. Henry Fairlie[10] has quoted the joint statement agreed by President Roosevelt, Marshal Stalin and Mr Churchill announcing their determination to set up a new international organization:

'We are resolved,' declared the three great wartime leaders, 'upon the earliest possible establishment with our Allies of a general international organization to maintain peace and security. We believe that this is essential both to prevent aggression and to remove the political, economic and social causes of war through the close and continuing collaboration of all peace-loving countries.'

Mr Fairlie comments that it was like 'three gangsters announcing that they were setting up a trust to inquire into the economic,

[10] In an article in a *Daily Telegraph* weekly supplement, called 'The United Nations: Conscience or Conspiracy?'

psychological and social causes of delinquency'. He adds that having done this the three leaders turned to the 'more realistic work of carving up Europe and subjecting its peoples to their liberators'. The comments are severe, but contain more than a little uncomfortable truth. At the same time, the presence, inevitably massive, of the United States and the Soviet Union inside the infant Organization clearly made the United Nations more representative of the world's powers than the League had ever been, and as implying a recognition of political facts undoubtedly helped to keep expectations realistic and disappointments within bounds, as well as securing to the Organization a large measure of whatever actual effectiveness it might hope to deploy.

Following the signing at San Francisco sufficient ratifications had been received by 24 October in the same year to bring the Charter into force. The 24th October thus remains United Nations Day, an anniversary still widely observed, if rarely with particular jubilation.

However much a realistic appreciation of the way things really were informed the minds of the Charter-makers, moral and idealistic ends were by no means disregarded. Not merely was the Charter one of the most comprehensive and far-reaching treaties ever concluded between sovereign states. Its celebrated *Preamble* stated categorically that 'We, the Peoples of the United Nations' (so to speak) were resolved, among other high-sounding aims, to reaffirm faith in fundamental human rights, in the 'equal rights' of nations large and small as well as of men and women, and in the dignity and worth of the human person. The peoples were also held to have contracted together to practise tolerance and to live in peace as good neighbours, to restrict the use of armed force to the cause of 'the common interest', significantly left undefined, and to employ international machinery to promote the economic and social advancement of all.

What these and other ringing phrases have meant in the practice of more than a quarter of a century is the use of the Organization, by all its members, as an instrument for defending their several interests. In so far as there might, at a given juncture, develop a common interest in the maintenance of peace in a particular area, the Organization could, and occasionally did, operate with some success in the endeavour to promote it. It is apparent that the Organization was, and was intended to be, the instrument of the

collective will of its members, so far as they could agree on expressing it. The Organization therefore could do, and was meant to do,
virtually nothing save as its members directed.

This is not to deny that, largely under the inspiration (and high-
minded intriguing) of the second and perhaps to date greatest of
its secretaries-general,[11] the United Nations Organization has
acquired some of the features, and a measure of the presence, of
international personality. It is not a state, still less a superstate,
but it does now enjoy a limited degree of recognition as a subject
of international law, which is the status of sovereign countries.
But international personality is not of course supra-nationality. As
an instrument to implement the agreed will of its member states,
the United Nations Organization seems essentially *not* to be a blueprint, and most unlikely to become an embryo, of a form of world
government, to which executive capacity and supra-national
authority have been made over by states placing themselves under
its political direction. This would seem to be the answer, welcome
or not, to those who insist on seeing in the General Assembly of the
United Nations an embryo World Parliament, in the International
Court of Justice a rudimentary World Supreme Court, and in the
Universal Declaration of Human Rights a potential World Constitution.

Discussion of the *nature* of the United Nations involves matters
of doctrinal interpretation. The above notions, for example,
embody the concept of a *seed*. The United Nations is conceived of
as an entity capable of organic growth, which in its completeness
would comprise a world order as different from the present United
Nations Organization as the oak is different from the acorn, or
Jesus's famous grain of mustard seed from the unbrageous tree it
becomes, yet representing the organic fulfilment of an implicit
intention, as such an intention may be regarded as embedded, so to
speak, in the genetic structure of an actual seed. Other inter-
preters of the significance of the Organization decline to be seduced
by what they regard as a misleading analogy. They insist instead
that the United Nations represent a *construction*, without any
organic pattern of growth. The Organization was made: it can be
unmade or remade. Its future, on this view, is wholly determined

---

[11] Mr Dag Hammarskjöld, Swedish scholar and internationalist, who held
office from 1953 to 1961, dying tragically in an air crash during the course of
United Nations operations in the Congo.

by the decisions and actions of its members, both as to the form of the institution itself, and as to the issues of world politics upon which its functions may, at the express determination of its members, be brought to bear. Change in the United Nations occurs, on this view, either as a result of altered circumstances of which the members take account, or in order to meet new requirements which they envisage beforehand. Such changes take place as a result of the interplay of international politics and are not primarily determined by the nature of the Organization itself. And one of the most improbable of all changes would be that arising from an invitation by the member states to the United Nations Organization to govern them. Such an invitation seems to be, simply, but emphatically, 'not on'.

The analogy of the United Nations as essentially a *building*, which may be destroyed or drastically redesigned at the will of its users, appears at first sight to be a powerful one. It is doubtless true that in practice, where there are so many 'users', with varying ideas about desirable development of the structure, and vested interests to protect, actual agreement on a specific change may be hard to attain. Nikita Khrushchev, for instance, at the end of the 1950s, tried earnestly and at times angrily to transform the secretary-generalship into a collegiate office, a *troika* of three secretaries, each 'representing' respectively the West, the communist bloc and the 'Third World', and acting as a check upon the initiatives of the two others. The proposal was seen both by the Russians and their opponents as being in the Soviet interest. It was successfully resisted. But however difficult it may prove to introduce any particular change into the United Nations, the theorists of the *artefact*, as against the theorists of the *organism*, are able to maintain that the Organization was the deliberate creation of its members, who could have fashioned it differently if they had wished. Whatever its limitations, in conception and in function, they can argue that the United Nations, as the institution exists, is what most member states want, since it is there. If they desired something different, they could have it. The very limitations themselves are a result of decisions taken by those who created the Organization in the form in which it is found. And, the argument goes on, that form specifically excludes any implication of potential or emergent world government.

It may well seem but fair to remark that states only desire world government at all for the purpose of controlling the behaviour of other states, not their own. Whatever may be the wistful or even anguished aspirations of some individual idealists, world government might seem to tarry mainly because only states can bring it about, acting through the instrumentality of their representative statesmen, and most states in effect hold sturdily to the conviction that to do so would not be in their interest. And so it does not happen. Until and unless states change their minds on the matter it seems unlikely ever to happen. Only governments have the means to create world government, but appear to lack the will. And in this they may genuinely reflect the current prejudices of their peoples. The necessary will, which must pre-exist the wisest and most well-conceived arrangements, does not seem likely to emerge at the present juncture from the interplay of political factors inside international society, whatever might be the assumed effect of an evident external threat. If that long-delayed and it appears indescribably improbable attack from Mars ever occurred – and some rather desperate reformers urge how good it would be for us all – a global closing of the ranks under some acknowledged world executive might conceivably take place. But to be driven into invoking the possibility of interplanetary warfare as a likely motive for the creation of world government is a measure of the remoteness of the prospect.

The above may seem a rather negative approach. And indeed it is possible, and perhaps most sensible, to tackle the question from a rather different angle. Some shrewd commentators suggest that we are all too much obsessed with the prospect of world government, or its unlikelihood, conceived in the rather conventional terms of a set of legislative and executive institutions, on the familiar national pattern, simply writ enormously large, and exercising jurisdiction over the whole human community. This indeed may be exceedingly remote, and perhaps undesirable in any case. *World order*, as distinct from world government, may be far better attained by other means. World order of a kind, as we argue throughout this book, exists already. International society of any sort would be impossible – even inconceivable – without it. What appears to many to be necessary is to strengthen and reform it, in ways acceptable to mankind as a whole. This is likely to prove a hard enough task, but by virtue of the flexibility of method and pragmatism of action implied may be far nearer man's grasp than any grandiose model of world government of the kind sometimes envisaged, which may never be set up by consent, and would be widely intolerable if by some means it could be successfully imposed. It can, on this view, be strongly argued that the theory of international institutions has been bedevilled by our preoccupation with the 'governmental' model.

But whatever may be our conclusions as to the merits of 'artefactual' and 'organic' theories of the nature of the United Nations Organization it remains evident that one of its most significant functions since its beginning has been its emphatic symbolization of the national sovereignty of its members. Sovereignty remains a necessary qualification for candidacy. And although in the two cases noticed above, those of Ukraine and Byelorussia, independent statehood seems no more in reality than a diplomatic fiction, the principle has otherwise been maintained. Throughout its stormy history the Organization has continued to be widely regarded as a prestigious body, most particularly perhaps in the developing world, which almost all states desire to join, which only one state (Indonesia) has ever left, to return in a matter of months, and membership of which is highly valued, among other things, as a badge of sovereign status.[12]

Now it is certainly true that international organizations are no more static than any other political institutions. They are equally liable to change and development. These may often reflect the working of elements of evolution that go beyond the conscious choice or will of any participant in them. International organizations may simply pass into history, either, like the League of Nations, mainly because of an overall failure to sustain their explicit role, or, perhaps more commonly, like the Holy Roman Empire and the Congressional System, because the processes of historical change bring them to irrelevance. In this connection it is useful to recall the distinctions drawn by Professor Inis L. Claude, Jr.,[13] between international organization as an on-going process,

---

[12] On this point, by way of example, literature issued by the Welsh Nationalist Party (*Plaid Cymru*), to which reference was made above, p. 98, is instructive in that it reiterates a demand for Welsh state membership of the United Nations. While this doubtless reflects an internationalist strain in Welsh political thinking, as well as a thirst among a minority for an indigenous state, membership would require for Wales a sovereignty as evident and legal as that of Australia or Canada, or, for that matter, of Western Samoa or Botswana!

[13] In *Swords into Plowshares*, Random House, New York, 1959.

the increasing institutionalization of international relations, and the fortunes of particular international bodies. However, it remains hard to see how an organization specifically designed to represent and uphold state sovereignty on behalf of each of its members can have or be likely to acquire a potentially worldwide supranationality.

The insistence on the formal sovereign status of every member of the United Nations gives rise to a difficulty which has been sharply defined, for example by J. E. S. Fawcett.[14] Among a number of points meriting the closest attention, including, for example, what he sees as the evolution within the United Nations of certain functions characteristic of a 'primitive legislature', he brings out the element of absurdity in the continuance of a single-tier membership of the General Assembly in view of the disparities of power and influence between the members referred to above. The point stressed is that some of the United Nations are so weak, both in terms of resources and of the rickety condition of their political structure, as to be in no position to carry out the obligations they have assumed under the Charter. They could, for instance, make no effective contribution to any actual collective security operation in constraint of an aggressor that might be mounted, do little in an international peace-keeping role, and offer no significant support to the varied and often extremely valuable work of the Special UN Agencies. Such countries are indeed net consumers of security, welfare and international prestige, which last they do not confer upon the Organization by joining it but receive by virtue of their membership. As these 'token members' are no longer very small in number, there might seem much force in the suggestion that a separate class of United Nations membership should be devised to accommodate them, in regard to which the rights and duties of its members would be appropriately scaled down. This assumes that the general efficiency of the UN in particular and of the international system in general is likely to be enhanced if hollow pretensions on the part of certain states were to be reduced to a minimum, and the privileges granted and obligations required of states were shaped as far as practicable to their evident capacities.

While such a proposal seems sensible in principle, it may never

[14] In 'The UN and International Law', *International Relations*, vol. III, no. 10, November 1970.

be implemented within the United Nations for it appears certain to provoke the defensive emotions of the small and weak countries likely to be placed in an 'associate' or 'junior' category. We may easily imagine the clamorous lobby which such states would convene in the General Assembly. They would be losing something, whatever the Organization as a whole might ultimately gain by such a process of structural rationalization, and national pride may confidently be expected to object in the shrillest tones to the prospect of deprivation.

Meanwhile, anomalies persist. It might almost be said, not too absurdly, that while some states, such as the great powers, are, so to speak, born sovereign, and others achieve sovereignty, there remains a group which, as a result of the dismantling of Empires since 1945, have had sovereignty thrust upon them – admittedly with their eager approval. Whatever the fate of two-tier proposals, the lesson that the experience of membership of the General Assembly of the United Nations seems clearly to teach both great powers and little ones is that the viability of the institution in the future requires that the former must accept, even more whole-heartedly perhaps than in the past, real constraints on their freedom of action, and that the latter must accept real limits, prompted by common sense, to the merely automatic operation of a majoritarian principle.

An important consideration that must not be overlooked concerns the present and probably increasing value of the virtual universality of United Nations membership in relation to an improved world order. The Organization remains the most spectacular, as it is also probably actually the most important, instrument of such order. Virtually – and in the future perhaps actually – universal membership of the United Nations seems likely to confer upon it, and upon its decisions and activities, a degree of *vital legitimacy* which may conceivably go far towards reinforcing the stability and acceptability of a world order which, in one form or another, seems to be essential to the survival of mankind. We may suggest that this remains true despite the fact that in certain aspects of its role as an instrument of world order, the Organization arouses fewer hopes (and corresponding fears) than in the past. In particular, the enforcement function of the United Nations clearly declined, both in practice and in the expectation of member states, from the early 1960s onwards. But this could conceivably revive. And while the international system itself, and the United Nations within it, continues to reveal, in a well-turned phrase, those 'freaks, exceptions and irregularities'[15] inseparable from any political system, legitimacy remains, and in the prospect of its being enhanced in regard to the Organization and its multiple role lies at least some measure of hope for the better ordering of the world. That role, in its substantive aspects, we now consider.

The United Nations: the substantive role

The United Nations Organization is not, we have suggested, either in conception or in prospect a world government. What then may be said of its multi-faceted role in international society? And in what respects may we justify, by considering that role, our hint above that the UN story is 'significantly different' from that of the League?

The United Nations Organization is first, as its founders explicitly declared, an instrument for promoting international peace and security. To this end, in addition to the General Assembly of all members, a Security Council was set up. This was a standing body, and actual meetings could be convened at any time on the initiative of the secretary-general or at the request of a member nation of the UN to consider any international issue which appeared to threaten the maintenance of international peace and security. Although in dignity and intention the Security Council corresponded largely to the old Council of the League, its structure differed in important respects. There were five permanent members, each of whom possessed a right of veto over any motion, other than procedural motions, proposed by any other member of the Council. There were at first six and are now ten temporary members, who are elected by the General Assembly for two years each and are represented on the Council by one delegate. The object of this structure was to attempt to reflect, far more realistically than had been possible in the League, the realities of power in international society. It ensured that no great power (permanent membership of the Security Council, we may recall, was in effect a symbol of great power status) would in fact be over-ruled in any substantive matter to the proposed settlement of which it had an

[15] It is Mr Ieuan John's.

objection. In practice this has generally meant that in those relatively few issues coming before the Council for determination in which the policies and interests of the great powers coincide, the Security Council may take decisions involving action by the Secretariat on behalf of the Organization as a whole. Such decisions are theoretically binding in their effect upon all members of the United Nations. In practice, as we might expect, members fulfil or disregard duties arising out of these decisions in accordance with their perceived interests.[16] And it is well understood that in certain matters, notably for instance the provision of forces for assignment to United Nations peace-keeping operations, some countries, by virtue both of their available resources and of their political disinterestedness in regard to the particular case, will be in a far better position to meet the secretary-general's request for help than others. The stubborn distinction between the absolute nature of an obligation and the degree to which states find it possible or convenient to meet it in practice applies here as in every area of international politics.

In matters coming before the Security Council no specific motion may be proposed at all, as for instance if it is quite clear that any motion will invoke the veto of one or other of the permanent members. However, these members may choose to abstain on a motion: no veto arises, and the proposed action can proceed without any particular great powers abstaining being identified with it.

One thing that the Security Council veto means in effect is that the United Nations cannot act in international society against the wish in any given issue of a great power – one, that is, whose status as such is legitimized by permanent membership of the Council. This is an important if negative aspect of the function of great powers within the United Nations. Thus we see that the veto operates as a safeguard of the interests of great powers. But equally the presence of great powers in the Security Council on a special basis does not, and was never intended to, enable them merely to impose their will on smaller powers. In this respect the veto acts as a guarantee to non-great powers, since, in any particular case, it

---

[16] The case of Rhodesia is illustrative. The Security Council decreed sanctions against a rebel regime. All member states were due to observe them; most states began to do so, fewer and fewer states continued to do so. There was no question of sanctioning defectors, and the regime did not crumble.

may be – and has often been – applied by a great power on their behalf. The great powers, in short, are provided by the veto with a means to defend their own interests and those of their friends or clients by operating a check and balance to each other. The device of the veto fairly reflects the realities of international politics. The Security Council structure, after all, did not confer great power status; it recognized it.

Admittedly, the exercise of the veto has sometimes meant that swift, effective and concerted action on international problems threatening or causing breaches of peace in particular areas is frustrated. But no international organization would be likely to succeed in its purposes which ignored either the facts of power or the often deep divisions between the international interests on behalf of which power is exercised. It is probably true to say that if no institutional block on concerted great power action existed, great powers would find it no easier to act in concert than they do where interests divide them.

The value to great powers of Security Council membership was strikingly illustrated in 1950. The Russians had absented themselves from the Council in that year on general grounds that the United Nations Organization was being used primarily as an instrument of Western 'imperialism', and specifically in protest at the continuing presence in the Council of Nationalist China. Taking into account the then balance of UN membership, and allowing for the tendentious nature of the political vocabulary employed by both sides, there was some substance in Russian suspicions. However, when frontier incidents ensued along the 38th Parallel dividing the communist client, North Korea, from the Western client, South Korea, and escalated into a full-scale invasion of the South by the North, the United States and her partners in the Security Council, in the absence of the Soviet Union, carried through a motion authorizing and supporting American military action already initiated in Korea to resist aggression. There is no reasonable doubt that such action would have been vetoed by the Soviet Union had its representative been present in the Council. The veto would not, of course, have prevented American intervention, if President Truman had chosen to respond favourably to an appeal for help by President Synghman Rhee. But it would then have been a unilateral American response, not endowed with the added moral sanction of a collective security operation by the United Nations, acting in accordance with the provisions of the Charter.

It is not hard to appreciate why the Soviet Union never exposed herself to the risk of being out-manoeuvred in such a way again. Nor is it surprising that since 1950 no military enforcement action under chapter 7 of the Charter has been undertaken by the United Nations in resistance to 'aggression'.

An important aspect of the UN role, undertaken where the great powers found themselves able to act in concert, has been the occasional peace-keeping enterprises already referred to. These are essentially policing operations. For ten years UN military personnel, for example, provided by a handful of willing countries, kept Israeli and Egyptian apart in the Gaza Strip of territory disputed between the two. Sovereignty over the Strip pertained to Egypt. When in 1967, on the eve of the six-day war, Egypt demanded the withdrawal of United Nations troops, the then secretary-general, U Thant, felt bound to comply, on the ground that the United Nations had no right to a presence in any territory other than with the consent of the sovereign power concerned. Within days the Egyptians forces duly suffered a humiliating defeat at the hands of the Israelis, who proceeded to occupy not only the Gaza Strip but the entire Sinai peninsula to boot.

The interesting suggestion was made in some quarters that U Thant had not in fact been obliged to authorize the evacuation of United Nations troops from the Gaza Strip. The reasoning here is that the United Nations presence represented a contractual agreement between the country concerned, Egypt, and the Organization, which could legally only be terminated by mutual agreement, which on the UN side the secretary-general need not have given. A fine point, but one always perhaps likely to yield to the rough requirements of the current political situation. For the secretary-general to have disregarded Egyptian demands might well have had consequences, involving both the UN and the great powers, far less calculable than those which actually ensued.

United Nations contingents have helped, with considerable devotion, to keep a measure of peace between Greek and Turkish Cypriots. In Cyprus, exceptionally because of historical factors, a British component forms part of the UN force. For more than twenty years United Nations personnel patrolled a cease-fire line in Kashmir between Indian and Pakistani forces. Another United

Nations force operated extensively on behalf of internal security and cohesion in the Congo (Kinshasa) from 1960 to 1964. Another contingent supervised a change of constitutional status when West Irian was transferred under UN auspices from Dutch to Indonesian sovereignty a few years later.

These episodes may seem in themselves relatively small matters. But each, deprived of the available constraint, might have assumed the proportions of a major international crisis. Hence it seems fair to say that the UN peace-keeping function, piecemeal as it is and seems likely to remain for some time to come, represents a major justification for the existence of the United Nations machinery involved. Its limited scope, we may remind ourselves, derives from the fact, which no internationalist idealism can gainsay, that effective United Nations peace-keeping depends upon either a coincidence of great power interests, or at least the absence of any conflict of such interests in the particular case where it is proposed.

The admission of the People's Republic of China to a permanent seat on the Security Council hitherto occupied by the Kuomintang regime based on Taiwan (Formosa) in October 1971 represents a dramatic change in the conformation of power in the United Nations which may prove to be of considerable moment in international politics. Many times the General Assembly voted on the issue of Chinese membership after 1949, when Mao Tse-tung completed the communist conquest of mainland China. Until 1971 the necessary two-thirds majority was lacking. But if the ideological motives which ensured American and much non-communist hostility to the seating of Red China and the expulsion of Nationalist China were a formidable aspect of the political realities of the world, no less a reality was the growing power of communist China; and the anomaly of a worldwide international organization, purporting to represent 'We the Peoples' of the world, excluding the most populous and potentially one of the most powerful peoples on earth. A growing American interest in beginning to 'normalize' relations with mainland China, the continuing processes of bipolar *détente* and the sense of political realism, working together, made possible, then probable and at last certain the critical decision to bring the teeming myriads of Maoist China into such comity of nations as membership of the United Nations might be taken to imply.

In view of this development we may well pose the question how long the maintenance of great power status, as symbolized by permanent membership of the Security Council, on the part of France and Britain, may plausibly be supposed to conform to the facts of international power. For both these countries may find themselves fairly distanced, in the fields of economic and military capacity, in the long term, by such countries as Japan, China, and conceivably Brazil, Indonesia and India. However, for the nearer future we may feel satisfied that the composition of the Council in the 1970s reflects accurately enough the balance of power in the world.

The situation created by the admission of the People's Republic of China raises another aspect of the question of legitimacy in relation to the United Nations, touched on earlier in this chapter. How far, we may ask, may the Security Council, thus reinforced, begin more convincingly than it could in the past to act as a legitimate instrument by means of which something like a revived 'Concert of the powers' could operate as a regulative factor in world affairs? It has perhaps been implicitly assumed in this discussion that it is an occupational hazard of great powers to behave dictatorially and of small powers to behave irresponsibly. A Concert of great powers, acting within the norms provided by the functions and usages of the Security Council, and not merely as an *ad hoc* grouping of the powerful, might well contribute with enhanced effect to world stability. Subject, always, to the fact of a broad congruence of interests on the part of the great powers themselves. In such a development the role of the General Assembly could become increasingly to give the support of an acknowledged legitimacy to a great power Concert operating within the Security Council. Clearly this assumes that the measure of *détente* evident from the later 1960s will continue and even intensify. An evident requirement must be that existing issues between the great powers, and most especially between the superpowers, will not be caused by political developments generally to harden into occasions of acute confrontation. This being understood, it begins to seem reasonable to suggest that the Security Council, as constituted from 1971, and allowing for possible adjustments in size and membership at future dates to take account of possible significant changes in the conformation of international power, could provide a legitimate and prestigious institutional setting within which Concert politics might be practised in ways that would promote rather than jeopardize world stability.

Certainly the role of legitimacy in this connection is of great moment. Professor Kenneth Boulding has well said:[17]

> The *major asset* of the UN is that it is an enormous depository of legitimacy. That is, in most parts of the world it carries an aura of authority and intrinsic rightness, and that it is able to bestow this, with varying degrees of success, on the undertakings it sponsors.

If this appears to be true the Security Council of the future, its own legitimacy reinforced by the General Assembly, may – not certainly will, but may – discharge with more authority and therefore with better effect that regulative function which was central to the conceptions, and perhaps the genuine hopes, of the men who founded the Organization in the immediate aftermath of global war. At any rate the suggestion offers some corrective to what may seem the excessive contempt for the institution expressed in some quarters, of which Mr Fairlie's views, as cited, may stand as representative.

In the past occasional initiatives have been taken by the General Assembly in an attempt to bypass a Security Council whose action on behalf of a restoration of peace was stultified by the use of the veto. Most notably in November 1950 a composite 'Uniting for Peace' resolution was moved by the Assembly to meet the situation created by the return of the Soviet delegate to the Security Council, and in particular to enable the General Assembly to initiate United Nations action to deal with threats, breaches of peace or aggression, in the event of a failure of the Security Council to act. Though this had only recommendatory effect, and was not, as in the case of Security Council resolutions, concerned with enforcement, mandatory on UN members, it was significant as expressing a consensus of 'world opinion', at least in so far as the United Nations membership could be considered to embody it. The resolution could therefore be expected to influence the attitudes and actions of UN members in general, who were free, if they chose, to take action on the basis of the resolution. The undeniable fact that in practice – as distinct from legal theory – the mandatory resolutions of the Security Council were almost as 'voluntaristic' as the recommendatory

[17] In 'Population and Poverty', from *Peace is Possible*, cited at the beginning of this chapter, p. 259. My italics.

resolutions of the General Assembly, mattered really less than that the great powers might be expected to take sharp note of the latter's determination to get something done, and bestir themselves not to let the political initiative pass out of their hands into the less predictable and far more numerous hands of the United Nations membership as a whole.

At the beginning of 1972 members of the United Nations numbered 135, as against an initial membership of fifty-one states in June 1945. Thus the expansion of the Organization has closely paralleled the proliferation of independent states in the world generally. Only a handful of some ten or so states now remain outside the United Nations. This number includes the two Koreas and the two Vietnams, whose international status is still subject to controversy, Switzerland, on an assessment of the balance of her national interest as a perpetual neutral, and the tiny 'ceremonial states' of Europe. The two Germanies, Federal Germany and the GDR, lying immediately across the great East–West divide in Europe, were admitted in September 1973. We have already seen that practically the entire surface of the planet is now divided up into territorial states, with a residue of dependencies. The United Nations is practically co-extensive with this worldwide 'patchwork quilt'. Bangladesh remains outside at the time of writing, having in her application gained the somewhat daunting distinction of incurring the first veto to be cast by communist China since her own admission. (The Security Council must agree in the entry of new members.) New states may always come into existence as a result of the break-up of old ones. But there is no *terra incognita* left in the world, and no unclaimed territory either. Hence the world would appear to be nearing the upper limit of sovereign states that can be accommodated on its surface. The European state system has, in a manner of speaking, inherited the earth, however little, historically, it may have been characterized by the quality of meekness.

The United Nations, to all intents and purposes, has inherited the earth too. Again we notice how eagerly the vast majority of states beat a path to the doors of the United Nations Building in New York. And this however faulty and unsatisfactory the Organization may appear to be in the eyes of its critics, embittered or judicious. Only one member state, Indonesia, has ever resigned from it, and after a few months of self-imposed exile in 1964 (having left in a pet over Malaysia) thankfully returned. Many states it is true are in arrears of subscription, which under Article 19 qualifies them for expulsion. But the UN proves an indulgent club, and no member has been expelled for that reason. It is evidently to the net interest of the Organization to keep even bad payers in benefit of membership. Only one expulsion at all has occurred – Taiwan in 1971 – on the politically significant but logical enough ground that there is only one China in international society. The question for United Nations diplomacy was simply to determine who she was. Later the Kuomintang authorities were encouraged by their own allies and their communist adversaries to consider the proposition that they were indeed part of China, and might well embark upon the delicate political task of coming to terms with the permanence, humanly speaking, of the people's republican regime. Conceivably, if some kind of federation was agreed upon, with an appropriate formula about notional sovereignty, the Taiwan component of such a federal Chinese state might secure membership again of the General Assembly on grounds comparable with those which were permitted to apply to Ukraine and Byelorussia, and to India before 1947. But Maoist China has always been strong on unitarism, and the prospect seems remote.

Meanwhile, for the generality of states throughout the world, membership of the United Nations remains a substantial interest. In the Security Council membership confers a special distinction upon the greatest states in the form of permanent seating. In the case of the smallest and feeblest member states, membership of the General Assembly confers, we may be tempted to suggest, the sole distinction they enjoy. Majoritarian democracy prevails. The powers of the General Assembly are clearly limited, but every member shares equally in them. Upper Volta, the Soviet Union, the state of Malta, the United States and Laos, to name but five, have but one vote apiece, and no veto applies.

Article 13 of the Charter spells out the purposes of the General Assembly. These are first, to study and propose recommendations for the promotion of international cooperation – a wide brief. Second, the General Assembly is to encourage the development of International Law and its codification. Third, the Assembly is to consider and approve the budget of the Organization. Fourth, it is to exercise a general oversight in respect to the Special Agencies, and to the Organization's subordinate councils and other bodies. On the whole the General Assembly, unwieldy as it might appear, has carried out these functions with reasonable effectiveness, although during the 1960s the United Nations as a whole moved deeper into debt.

On a broader consideration the uses of the United Nations can perhaps be summarized under the following functions. These are not formally stated in the Charter. They arise out of the day to day and session to session activity of the Organization as the years go by.

The United Nations undoubtedly provides a valuable – and highly valued – *forum for debate* over a very wide range of issues all affecting more or less the stability, and indeed the viability, of the international order itself. Resolutions and recommendations arising out of such debate, as well as particular debates, comprise what may be regarded as a register of world opinion. But of course this must be understood in a qualified sense. However grandiloquently the Preamble to the Charter opens by claiming to echo the voice of 'We the Peoples', the world opinion expressed in the United Nations can only be at best a majoritarian view on a particular issue held at a given time by the governments of the countries whose representatives are present and voting. Such world opinion is a very partial thing, and cannot be otherwise. The canvassing of world opinion by holding global plebiscites is obviously the idlest of dreams. Nor does such world opinion as a vote in the General Assembly represents often affect issues directly. World opinion, so identified, overwhelmingly disapproves of *apartheid* in South Africa, but the policy continues, modified if at all far less by general expressions of condemnation than by the specific needs of particular interests, in the fields of sport or commerce, perhaps, which become apparent to the authorities through the ordinary processes of political representation inside the country. However, it can plausibly be argued that it is on balance more useful to have *some* register of opinion held by a majority of governments on some particular issues than not. So this aspect of the United Nations function need not be merely disregarded.

Perhaps more importantly, the Organization provides a means for the pursuit of multilateral diplomacy by a large number of small states who would be in no position, and would probably be aware of no compelling need, to maintain any kind of worldwide diplomatic representation. A great deal of exchanging of views and generally useful horse-trading takes place, it is authoritatively stated, in the washrooms at Lake Success. 'Diplomacy on the cheap' is by no means the least of the benefits conferred by membership of the United Nations who could not afford very much of the conventional – and expensive – article.

Where major interests of the superpowers are not directly involved, as we have seen, the organizing of peace-keeping missions in various parts of the world has proved to be a valuable service which the United Nations has from time to time offered international society. In addition to the operations mentioned above, and also the maintenance of a truce line between North and South Korea, United Nations 'presences' have also been suggested from time to time for Malaysia, Vietnam and Northern Ireland. In this last case the propriety of any United Nations involvement is vitiated by the undeniable fact that legally the crisis in Ulster has always been an internal question for the United Kingdom. It is no doubt a powerful emotional and political concern of the government of the Irish Republic, but not a legal one. Any invitation by the British government to the Irish government to participate in talks over the future of the province would be a matter of political convenience, not of legal obligation. A number of member states have had occasion to invoke Article 2 paragraph 7 of the Charter, in their own interests, which specifically forbids the United Nations from intervening in matters 'essentially within the domestic jurisdiction of any state'.

Lastly, there is the very important 'umbrella' function discharged by the United Nations in providing an institutional context in which the various international agencies can operate. Among them is the Trusteeship Council, intended to supervise the gradual preparation of non-independent territories, mainly the residues of the old European Empires overseas, for self-government. We may notice once again, in this connection, how consistently the movement of the United Nations is *directed towards the spread of new sovereignties around the world* rather than towards supra-national coalescence and integration. The World Health Organization (WHO) has undoubtedly done a great amount of most valuable work, much of it of a particularly patient and unspectacular kind, in reducing the incidence of endemic diseases in many parts of the world, and increasing the average expectation of life in some countries where it has been conspicuously low in comparison with the rich lands of the globe. (The effects of such achievements on the global population explosion are of great significance, and WHO must ultimately be no less concerned with them.) The Food and Agricultural Organization (FAO) has grappled as manfully as it can with what appear to be fairly intractable problems of the production of sufficient foodstuffs for the growing needs of mankind, and the efficient (and equitable) distribution of what is produced. The ponderously named but intellectually lively United Nations Educational, Social and Cultural Organization has for a quarter of a century promoted often highly stimulating ventures in popular education of the kinds designed primarily to explain to different human groups the nature of some of their more obtrusive distinctions from each other. UNESCO publicists and writers have also, while respecting the psychological imperatives of national identity, tried hard, if with limited success, to encourage a 'common humanity' view of the predicaments and prospects facing the world's peoples, and to transcend undue preoccupation inside national educational systems with the more self-absorbed sagas of national history. An uphill task. Less glamorous but perhaps not less useful at the practical level of keeping an international system going has been the work of the International Postal Union and the International Labour Office, both functioning under the aegis of the United Nations.

All these bodies count for much in their respective fields. They represent the devoted work of a corps of international public servants who, within often severe limits imposed by political considerations and budgetary restrictions, cope as best they can with constantly increasing problems of natural resource exhaustion, environmental pollution, increasing population pressure, educational need, and in many places political turmoil. Deep disillusionment over the general functioning of the United Nations, we may think, will probably not be felt except by those who may have entertained exaggerated hopes about the practical scope of the Organization in the international system which actually exists. In any case, the gap such persons may painfully perceive between their own hopes and the realities of the world around them should not blind them to the practical achievements attained by the subordinate agencies of the UNO, whose activities, on the whole, comprise one of the more reassuring aspects of the entire United Nations experiment.

In view of the foregoing considerations it seems clear that however unenthusiastic many people have come to feel about the United Nations it remains a salient structural feature of international politics. There seems to be no prospect that it will be wound up. Some perceptive observers have insisted that its functions are necessary in the modern world. 'If the United Nations did not already exist, we should have to invent it.' We have concluded that it is not an embryo world government. In only a partial and idiosyncratic sense is it a world parliament. Elements of a legislative role can be detected, but only at a very rudimentary stage. But the UNO is not to be dismissed because it does not begin to discharge certain rather arbitrarily conceived functions. We should never blame the pear tree for not bearing plums. International politics might well be less stable and manageable if the instrument of the United Nations were not at the hand of statesmen. Even as an international propaganda sounding-board the General Assembly appears to fulfil a somewhat ameliorative role in enabling pent-up frustrations to be released by the internationally aggrieved. The secret of coming to terms with the Organization as it exists and functions, and with the disappointments it may sometimes impose upon idealism, seems to be not to expect too much of it. No international organization can be expected to do more than reflect the current norms of international behaviour or the moral sensibilities of the statesmen, delegates and officials who direct and man it. There is scanty evidence that any international body created to maintain international peace and promote the general welfare of mankind will in itself generate enhanced moral expectations in those who created it, or transcend the norms by which they justify their political acts. Similarly, no international organization on a global scale has so far transformed the balance of power. It has provided instead a further political context in which the balance of power can be seen to operate. But none of this is to say that the United Nations type of international institution, as a regulatory and administrative device at work within the society of states, is not an important, indeed vital, component of the international order. UNO is still, we may conclude, the best United Nations we have.

'How it strikes a contemporary'

What, then, of the foreseeable future of the society of states? We should never forget that the present worldwide international system is a comparatively modern phenomenon. While there are suggestive parallels to be made, as we noticed in chapter 2, between contemporary international society and other sets of relations between autonomous political units in the past, the present complex of sovereign states, differing so widely in size and power yet formally equal in diplomatic theory and international law, had its origin in the European state system which developed from the mediaeval world. A phenomenon that has developed over a period of some four centuries we need not suppose to be eternal. We have had occasion to bear in mind more than once in the course of our discussion in this book the effects of the vastly increased mutual inter-penetration of states in the modern world, diplomatically, economically, industrially, even militarily, as well as – not least significant – in the field of communications. This inescapable intimacy prevails at practically all social levels, and involves closely not only government policy and non-governmental enterprise but also the need for governments to intervene actively in all aspects of group relationships between their peoples, extending from the regulation of trade and commerce to the areas of sport and artistic activity. So far does this rocess go that the question is raised of the continuing capacity of any but a small handful of the very greatest states to retain control, in more than a formal sense, of internal development and prosperity. As in the case of the Brezhnev Doctrine, explicit constraints upon sovereignty may be formally articulated in respect to a given group of countries. We have also seen how the auto-limitation of sovereignty which is implicit in the obligations arising out of any international agreement carries in the case of such treaties as those of Rome, the Warsaw Pact and NATO far-reaching implications of a conceivable supercession of sovereignty.

Yet we would be rash to conclude that the nation-state is obsolete, or even obsolescent. The collective psychological needs which it meets appear to be as urgent as ever. The very processes of inter-penetration and integration which we have seen at work provoke strong defensive reactions. The French will not suffer too close and comprehensive an Anglo-Saxon embrace. Many Englishmen insist, in the words of James Callaghan, that they are Europeans but not continentals. The Icelanders, unilaterally extending their home waters to fifty miles from their coasts to conserve for their own exploitation fish stocks which they regard as vital, proclaim, in the words of one of them, that 'our national survival is not negotiable'. However much regional groupings may evolve which might assume some of the traditional functions of the single state, they will have to reckon, in their institutional arrangements and their political style, with the persistence. and in many cases probably the passionate reassertion, of national feeling within their constituent political communities. While the European Economic Community, for a notable example, may achieve over time a highly developed supra-nationality, and even looser-bound sets of arrangements, such as the Organization of American States, may develop into a kind of hemispheric 'co-prosperity sphere', to borrow a formula associated with a particular dynamic phase in Japan's international relations during the 1930s, they seem most unlikely to erode the need for a felt national identity on the part of the peoples concerned, or to avoid the necessity of providing political and cultural means for its continued expression. The centripetal forces that make for 'One World' themselves provoke the centrifugal forces that make for its persistent division.

It is of course not inconceivable that a transformation of the present forms of international politics may take place sooner than anyone might now suppose. The development of a 'security community' in Western Europe within some ten years of the end of the most destructive and one of the most ideologically inspired conflicts of European history in 1945 affords striking evidence of the speed and apparent completeness with which deep changes in certain areas of international society can take place. Moreover, as we have seen, both the prestige and relevance of many traditional institutions of the state have been subjected to radical and often extraordinarily bitter question by groups of doctrinaire dissidents, mostly young, who are apparently searching for quite other forms of political community. This mood of hostile rejection, if pervasive enough, might well endanger the viability of the sovereign state in many parts of the world.

On the other hand, security communities, thankful as we will be for them, represent at least as much guarantees of the continuity and safety of their member states as any potentiality for making them obsolete. France and Federal Germany, through the instrumentality of General de Gaulle and Dr Adenauer, pledged their historic reconciliation in the Treaty of 1962 not in order vaguely to merge but to go on bring French and German in peace and safety *vis-à-vis* one another. And as for the forces of revolutionary change, so often committed to the uncompromising formulae of revolutionary violence, there is no guarantee that the new political forms urged by many fashionable radicals would not, if achieved, rigidify sooner or later into institutional structures quite as hard and demanding in their claims upon their members as those of any traditional sovereign state. History suggests indeed that the likelihood is all the other way. Napoleonic France and Soviet Russia became far more tightly integrated and efficiently administered (liberals would say oppressively so) than either the *ancien régime* or the tsarist Empire. Again, the People's Republic of China, despite an inherited tradition that rejects the division of the world into a multiplicity of formally equal sovereign entities,[18] has largely taken her 'natural' place as a major state in an international system whose credentials offend her traditional norms. Chinese interests remain paramount in the minds of China's leaders. And those interests have dictated that, as in the case of Bolshevist Russia after about 1922, an international system that cannot be beaten had better be joined.

The sovereign state, it would seem, whatever modifications may come to be introduced into its condition of sovereignty over time and through inevitable change, continues to represent both a convenient and a customary means by which nations may conduct their collective affairs in the world.

It also seems evident that nationalism is as powerful an ideology in the last third of the twentieth century as at any time previously. It continues, in many places with painful urgency and even destructive force, to politicize the psychological force of nationhood, and to formulate demands on its behalf which are, so to speak, thrust before the attention of international society. Although some forms of nationalism tolerate, and may even press for, highly institutionalized kinds of international cooperation, in general nationalist

[18] For a useful brief discussion of this traditional attitude, see Arthur Huck, *The Security of China*, Institute of Strategic Studies, London, 1968.

doctrines emphasize the divisive elements in international society, and tend to articulate strong reactions to the integrative implications of the technological shrinkage of the modern world. Statesmen discount the fervour and force of contemporary nationalisms at their peril. With hardly less peril, perhaps, do they embrace them, identify with them and fashion policy in their lurid light.

At this sub-national level, apart from specific doctrines of revolution, ferment and change manifest themselves. A vociferous complaint heard in some quarters is that the nation-state itself is too large, too bewildering in its institutional structure, too impersonal, to satisy the psychological needs of its citizens. The call then is for decentralization, for regionalism within the state, even for a revived parochialism. Not only nations within multi-national states but local communities within nations are tending to demand a greater share in the processes of politics, and in the taking of the decisions which directly affect the lives of their members. These demands are often unexceptionably moderate and reasonable in their formulation, and are expressed entirely within the norms of constitutional debate. Sometimes, however, they too evince the kind of angry impatience which can link them only too readily with those forces of radical dissent which proclaim their resolve to end the state itself. For them the state is not to wither away but to be smashed. It is to end, not with a whimper, but a bang. The coalescence of certain forms of sub-national particularism with this sort of revolutionism may greatly complicate the tasks of national governments as they seek to maintain an overall political cohesion that will accommodate what may have become a real need in the community for the devolution of power and function. Political systems inevitably vary in their adaptability and their capacity to entertain and introduce revised structures of authority and methods of administration. But governments will resist if they can. They will deem that they have a duty to resist what may be in effect no more than a furious, and perhaps indiscriminately violent, demand to abdicate responsibility. Such challenges where they arise have to be contained and if possible ended as a plain obligation to the great majority of citizens who, whatever grumbles they they may have, play the game by the rules. And this has to be attempted even while many of the energies of government are absorbed in the pursuit of conventional diplomatic relations with the rest of the world, on behalf of a complex of national interests which the immediacy of a given crisis cannot allow political leaders to neglect.

In fact the tasks of statesmanship have perhaps never been more onerous than in the twentieth century. As that century ages, the unremitting duty of making policy, taking decisions, keeping the *res publica* – the 'public thing' – going, itself burdensome enough, is made the heavier by the pitiless glare of publicity in which so much of the function of governing has to be carried on. The statesman will be constantly called upon for the instant response, the immediate statement, the spontaneous explanation. When Palestinian terrorists murdered two members of the Israeli Olympics team in Munich in September 1972 (to be killed or captured later themselves, with the death of nine other Israeli athletes in a holocaust of shooting at a military airfield) the Federal German chancellor, Herr Willy Brandt, was immediately obliged to face a press interview, and to attempt, in the midst of the horror, shock and profound embarrassment of the episode, a considered analysis of the situation, of terrorist motivations, and of the current international politics of the Middle East. It has been said of the United States presidency that in modern times it has become a job which must be done by one man and which no one man can do. Even allowing for the appeal of office and the stimulus of power, it seems surprising that the zest of political chiefs in international society remains as buoyant, the judgement as sound and even the physical health as good, as on the whole they appear to be.

One of the wisest of living British historians[19] wrote some twenty years ago:

... if in one age aggression is more terrible and violent than in another age, it is not to be explained on the argument that human nature is being produced on the earth in baser forms than ever before. It reflects a failure in that whole system of safeguards which has to exist in time of stability – safeguards against the cupidity of states, preventing men from feeling that circumstances give them the opening for a high gamble or a colossal design. . . . There are vast numbers of people who can be regarded as neither absolutely vicious nor utterly unselfish, neither criminals nor saints. And some show a fine face to the world while they live in a conventional society. . . . Many will be reasonably virtuous if the conditions are not too hostile and the price is not too high; and things

[19] Sir Herbert Butterfield, *Christianity, Diplomacy and War* (3rd edn), Wyvern Books, London, 1962.

are so disposed that all the arrangements of a stable, healthy society tend to keep these people on the rails. Once there is a police strike, or a revolution, or a terrible dilemma, we are astonished to see how ugly this ordinary human nature can be; and it is then that we learn how greatly respectability has been buttressed by institutions.

The buttressing institutions both of international society and of the sovereign state within it are in many respects under uniquely heavy strain. Yet it is incumbent upon those who urge that the state is obsolete or that the international society of states should be superseded to make clear what can be put in their place. Airy assertions that the sovereign state as such, irrespective of particular regimes within states, is inimical to the human personality, or vague declarations to the effect that 'the world is for people, not systems', carry us nowhere. States and the society of states exist because it is not easy to substitute anything else for them. Nostrums offered by some would-be world-changers imply a breakdown of legitimacy, a degree of disruption and a prevalence of violence that seem in prospect, and in actuality where they are in process already, far less humane and far more problematical in any ultimate benefits they are purported to bring, than the devices, institutions, compromises and moral ambiguities to which the political world is subject at present.

Despite all that may be urged against it, and accepting those elements of transformation which may indeed be already at work in our essentially dynamic world, nation-states in all their variety remain the most stable and viable means by which peoples can maintain collective relationships with each other, and stake claims upon each other's consideration. The international system in which states function, subject as it is to a propensity to change, still provides essential elements of balance and equilibrium between its constituent political units. In a seemingly rough and ready but in reality subtle and complex way it adjudicates the rival claims of nations. It offers indeed the essential framework for a world order. Such an order, by the acknowledgment on the part of states of the need to maintain delicate diplomatic usages, by the practice of custom, the exercise of prudence, the general observance of law and the promptings of moral norms, provides a necessary means whereby all states may contrive to co-exist, whether rivals or partners, hostile or well-disposed; differing greatly as they do in power, style, and even in the expectations of their citizens. National identity, integrity and general well-being remain high political values. To the upholding of them states remain the chief means. In turn, states themselves need to be upheld by an international order. Admittedly, this can never offer absolute guarantees. But the undermining of it will always jeopardize the society of states and the values it embodies.

Sir Winston Churchill made famous as the title of one of his finest works the phrase, *The World Crisis*. It is said that the Chinese word for crisis comprises two characters. One means 'danger', and the other, 'opportunity'. The society of states subsists in the midst of a perpetual crisis; for danger is never eliminated, nor are opportunities ever absent. But while world government may hover, like Robert Browning's heaven, closer to our reach than our grasp, *order* remains. If states are to survive, and to go on fulfilling their instrumental role in the lives of their peoples, the international order needs to be defended, even cherished. For the likely alternative to it still appears to be, not a cooperative global society under a benevolent world authority, but anarchy and chaos.

Concluding note

As this book went to press, two events occurred illustrating in the one case the disturbing effects of national pride on international stability and goodwill, and in the other the grounds for hope of greater international harmony. In July 1973, against a storm of world protest in which the governments of France's nuclear allies discreetly did not join, France proceeded to a further testing of nuclear weapons in the Pacific. It was generally agreed outside France that such a test would do nothing to stabilize further the existing military balance, nor to enhance actual French security. But it presumably satisfied French *amour-propre*. Meanwhile, in Helsinki in the same month, representatives of thirty-five countries met in the first European Security Conference, with the hope of moving towards a settlement of outstanding problems, not least in relation to post-second world war frontiers, and the establishment of a generally accepted *status quo* in Europe, on the basis, naturally, of continued and unquestioned state sovereignty. Both events, in their different ways, reaffirmed once more the central role of the *state* in international politics.

Appendix: the contemporary society of states

This is a table of the society of states as it exists in the 1970s. Only fully sovereign members appear; thus a small group of states, self-governing save for the crucial responsibility for external relations and defence, discharged by another power on their behalf, is excluded. The table sets out the latest known approximate population, size of territory in square miles, and type of regime, and membership of the United Nations and of the Commonwealth where applicable. The order is alphabetical.

STATE	APPROXIMATE POPULATION	SIZE (sq m)	REGIME	UN	CW
AFGHANISTAN	16,516,000	250,000	Republic	Yes	
ALBANIA	2,079,000	10,700	People's Republic	Yes	
ALGERIA	13,547,000	855,000	Republic	Yes	
ANDORRA	20,550	180	Republic		
ARGENTINA	23,360,000	1,079,965	Republic	Yes	
AUSTRALIA	12,881,100	2,967,909	Commonwealth	Yes	Yes
AUSTRIA	7,391,000	32,376	Republic	Yes	
BAHRAIN	216,000	500	Emirate	Yes	
BANGLADESH	52,000,000	55,126	Republic		Yes
BARBADOS	253,700	166	Monarchy	Yes	Yes
BELGIUM	9,691,000	11,775	Kingdom	Yes	
BHUTAN	1,010,000	18,000	Kingdom	Yes	
BOLIVIA	415,000	4,658,000	Republic	Yes	
BOTSWANA	620,000	220,000	Republic	Yes	Yes
BRAZIL	93,215,400	3,289,440	Republic	Yes	
BULGARIA	8,524,000	43,000	People's Republic	Yes	
BURMA	27,584,000	262,000	Republic	Yes	
BURUNDI	3,475,000	10,747	Republic	Yes	

STATE	APPROXIMATE POPULATION	SIZE (sq m)	REGIME	UN	CW
CAMEROON	5,836,000	183,381	Republic	Yes	
CANADA	21,689,578	3,851,809	Dominion	Yes	Yes
CENTRAL AFRICAN REPUBLIC	2,255,600	234,000	Republic	Yes	
CHAD	3,510,000	487,920	Republic	Yes	
CHILE	10,000,000	290,000	Republic	Yes	
CHINA	730,000,000	4,300,000	People's Republic	Yes	
COLOMBIA	22,000,000	440,000	Republic	Yes	
CONGO	915,000	129,960	Popular Republic	Yes	
COSTA RICA	1,800,000	19,653	Republic	Yes	
CUBA	8,553,450	44,178	Republic	Yes	
CYPRUS	633,000	3,572	Republic	Yes	Yes
CZECHOSLOVAKIA	14,361,600	49,700	Socialist Republic	Yes	
DAHOMEY	2,640,000	47,000	Republic	Yes	
DENMARK	4,879,400	17,000	Kingdom	Yes	
DOMINICAN REPUBLIC	4,012,000	19,322	Republic	Yes	
ECUADOR	5,890,000	226,000	Republic	Yes	
EGYPT	34,000,000	385,100	Republic	Yes	
EL SALVADOR	3,390,000	7,722	Republic	Yes	
EQUATORIAL GUINEA	286,000	11,000	Republic	Yes	
ETHIOPIA	26,000,000	400,000	Empire	Yes	
FIJI	524,800	7,083	Monarchy	Yes	Yes
FINLAND	4,706,000	130,165	Republic	Yes	
FRANCE	50,770,000	210,038	Republic	Yes	
GABOON	500,000	101,400	Republic	Yes	
GAMBIA	374,000	4,003	Monarchy	Yes	Yes
GERMANY (Democratic Republic)	16,000,000	41,380	People's Republic	Yes	
GERMANY (Federal)	61,503,000	95,980	Republic	Yes	
GHANA	8,600,000	92,100	Republic	Yes	Yes
GREECE	8,768,650	51,182	Republic	Yes	
GUATEMALA	5,014,000	42,042	Republic	Yes	
GUINEA	3,890,000	96,865	Republic	Yes	

STATE	APPROXIMATE POPULATION	SIZE (sq m)	REGIME	UN	CW
GUYANA	714,250	83,000	Cooperative Republic	Yes	Yes
HAITI	4,770,000	10,700	Republic	Yes	
HONDURAS	1,890,000	43,278	Republic	Yes	
HUNGARY	10,344,000	36,000	People's Republic	Yes	
ICELAND	206,750	40,500	Republic	Yes	
INDIA	559,000,000	1,261,816	Republic	Yes	Yes
INDONESIA	120,000,000	735,000	Republic	Yes	
IRAN	26,800,000	628,000	Empire	Yes	
IRAQ	9,466,000	168,000	Republic	Yes	
IRISH REPUBLIC (Eire)	2,971,230	26,600	Republic	Yes	
ISRAEL	3,034,000	7,992	Republic	Yes	
ITALY	54,684,000	131,000	Republic	Yes	
IVORY COAST	5,100,000	127,000	Republic	Yes	
JAMAICA	1,973,000	4,411	Monarchy	Yes	Yes
JAPAN	103,730,000	142,812	Empire	Yes	
JORDAN	2,300,000	39,730	Kingdom	Yes	
KENYA	10,890,000	224,460	Republic	Yes	Yes
KHMER REPUBLIC	7,100,000	70,000	Republic	Yes	
KOREA (Democratic Republic)	13,300,000	46,814	People's Republic		
KOREA (Republic)	31,470,000	38,452	Republic		
KUWAIT	733,000	7,500	Emirate	Yes	
LAOS	2,700,000	90,000	Kingdom	Yes	
LEBANON	2,645,000	4,300	Republic	Yes	
LESOTHO	975,000	11,116	Kingdom	Yes	Yes
LIBERIA	1,500,000	43,000	Republic	Yes	
LIBYA	1,700,000	810,000	Republic	Yes	
LIECHTENSTEIN	22,000	65	Principality		
LUXEMBOURG	339,900	1,000	Grand Duchy	Yes	
MALAGASY	7,000,000	228,000	Republic	Yes	
MALAWI	4,600,000	45,411	Republic	Yes	Yes
MALAYSIA	10,500,000	27,581	Federal Kingdom	Yes	Yes
THE MALDIVES	114,500	115	Republic	Yes	
MALI	5,000,000	465,000	Republic	Yes	

311

STATE	APPROXIMATE POPULATION	SIZE (sq m)	REGIME	UN	CW
MALTA, GC	322,190	120	State	Yes	Yes
MAURITANIA	1,145,000	419,000	Republic	Yes	
MAURITIUS	855,290	805	Monarchy	Yes	Yes
MEXICO	48,313,000	758,000	Republic	Yes	
MONACO	24,000	2½	Principality		
(OUTER) MONGOLIA	1,240,000	600,000	People's Republic	Yes	
MOROCCO	15,530,000	180,000	Kingdom	Yes	
NAURU	7,000	8¼	Republic	Yes	
NEPAL	11,290,000	54,362	Kingdom	Yes	
NETHERLANDS	13,250,000	13,500	Kingdom	Yes	
NEW ZEALAND	2,869,250	103,939	Dominion	Yes	Yes
NIGER	4,020,000	459,000	Republic	Yes	
NIGERIA	66,176,000	356,669	Republic	Yes	Yes
NORWAY	3,990,000	125,016	Kingdom	Yes	
OMAN	750,000	82,000	Sultanate	Yes	
PAKISTAN	57,000,000	310,403	Republic	Yes	
PANAMA	1,428,150	31,890	Republic	Yes	
PARAGUAY	2,396,000	157,000	Republic	Yes	
PERU	13,600,000	531,000	Republic	Yes	
THE PHILIPPINES	39,102,000	114,834	Republic	Yes	
POLAND	32,595,000	121,000	People's Republic	Yes	
PORTUGAL	8,670,000	34,500	Republic	Yes	
QATAR	170,000	4,000	Emirate	Yes	
RUMANIA	20,250,000	91,600	Socialist Republic	Yes	
RWANDA	3,500,000	10,169	Republic	Yes	
SAN MARINO	17,000	23	Republic		
SAUDI ARABIA	7,300,000	927,000	Kingdom	Yes	
SENEGAL	3,800,000	77,814	Republic	Yes	
SIERRA LEONE	2,250,000	27,925	Monarchy	Yes	Yes
SINGAPORE	2,080,000	224½	Republic	Yes	Yes
SOMALIA	2,730,000	246,000	Republic	Yes	
SOUTH AFRICA	21,285,000	472,359	Republic	Yes	
SPAIN	34,100,000	196,700	Republic*	Yes	
SRI LANKA	12,800,000	25,352	Republic	Yes	Yes
SUDAN	15,312,000	976,750	Republic	Yes	

* Officially designated to become a Monarchy again upon the departure of the Caudillo, General Franco.

STATE	APPROXIMATE POPULATION	SIZE (sq m)	REGIME	UN	CW
SWAZILAND	465,000	6,704	Kingdom	Yes	Yes
SWEDEN	8,015,000	173,436	Kingdom	Yes	Yes
SWITZERLAND	6,170,000	15,950	Confederal Republic		
SYRIA	6,300,000	70,800	Republic	Yes	
TAIWAN	14,800,000	13,800	Republic		
TANZANIA	12,940,000	362,820	Republic	Yes	Yes
THAILAND	36,000,000	198,247	Kingdom	Yes	
TOGO	1,860,000	21,000	Republic	Yes	
TONGA	87,000	270	Kingdom		Yes
TRINIDAD AND TOBAGO	1,044,000	1,980	Monarchy	Yes	Yes
TUNISIA	5,200,000	45,000	Republic	Yes	
TURKEY	36,000,000	301,302	Republic	Yes	
UGANDA	9,770,000	91,000	Republic	Yes	Yes
UNION OF SOVIET SOCIALIST REPUBLICS	244,000,000	8,599,806	Federal Republic	Yes	
UNITED ARAB EMIRATES	240,000	32,000	Federation	Yes	
UNITED KINGDOM	55,347,000	93,026	Kingdom	Yes	Yes
UNITED STATES OF AMERICA	203,410,000	3,633,675	Federal Republic	Yes	
UPPER VOLTA	5,340,000	100,000	Republic	Yes	
URUGUAY	2,500,000	72,172	Republic	Yes	
VATICAN CITY STATE	1,000	109 acres	Sovereign Pontificate		
VENEZUALA	10,800,000	352,150	Republic	Yes	
VIETNAM (Democratic Republic of)	21,340,000	63,000	People's Republic		
VIETNAM (Republic of)	17,867,000	66,281	Republic		
WESTERN SAMOA	141,000	435	Principality		Yes
YEMEN (Arab Republic of)	6,000,000	75,000	Republic	Yes	
YEMEN (People's Republic of)	1,250,000	117,000	People's Republic	Yes	

STATE	APPROXIMATE POPULATION	SIZE (sq m)	REGIME	UN	CW
YUGOSLAVIA	21,500,000	98,725	Federal Socialist Republic	Yes	
ZAIRE	17,100,000	905,582	Republic	Yes	
ZAMBIA	4,054,000	290,587	Republic	Yes	Yes
RHODESIA	5,190,000	150,829	*De jure* Self-governing British colony; *de facto* Independent Republic		Yes

Addendum

In July 1973 the Bahamas attained their independence after being a British colony for some 250 years.

BAHAMALAND	170,000	5,380	State		Yes

Suggestions for further reading

The literature of international politics is extensive. A full bibliography in English alone would fill a volume the length of this one, and comprise a major work of reference in its own right. The interested general reader to whom these suggestions are addressed might well be daunted rather than stimulated by a lengthy list of books. And I have no wish to attempt to reflect any academic credit on the compiler at the expense of the interest of the reader. So the list which follows is deliberately selective and confined to some of the works which are to my mind crucial to a study of the subject. They should be readily available. In many cases the books listed themselves contain valuable bibliographies which will lead the interested reader deeper into the field. The general works listed under chapter 1 are relevant to every aspect of international politics touched on in this book. But I have added short sections of less general books appropriate to the theme of each chapter.

Chapter 1 : The nature of international politics: the centrality of interests

John W. Burton, *International Relations: A General Theory*, 1967.
A somewhat controversial but valuable work which suggests under the name of 'steering' what the author regards as a desirable enrichment of the conventional notions of power politics, and as a useful conceptual means in the attempt to resolve international conflict.

Ivo D. Duchacek, *Nations and Men: An Introduction to International Politics*, 2nd edn 1971.
A full-scale and racily written survey of the subject by an American scholar whose pages are sprinkled with apt quotations from statesmen and commentators and enlivened by the use of relevant cartoons, etc. A first-class study.

Nigel Forward, *The Field of Nations: An Account of Some New Approaches to International Relations*, 1971.
A fairly difficult treatment, using current techniques of quasi-mathematical model-making, but having considerable value and insight.

315

Joseph Frankel, *International Politics: Conflict and Harmony*, revised edn 1973.
Professor Frankel always writes with economy and insight. Here are useful chapters dealing with fundamental theoretical concepts and their historical application in the modern world.

Joseph Frankel, *International Relations*, 1964.
A crisp short study which manages to cover a great deal of ground.

C. A. W. Manning, *The Nature of International Society*, 1962.
An extremely subtle, idiosyncratic and at the same time genuinely profound work, which richly repays the attentive reading it demands. Professor Manning's reflections upon the status of the state and the nature of law and its relationship to morality in international politics are brilliantly illuminating.

J. D. B. Miller, *The Nature of Politics*, 1962.
Though primarily concerned with domestic politics Professor Miller's arguments and insights have an equally acute application to the international sphere.

Hans J. Morgenthau, *Politics Among Nations*, 3rd edn 1962.
A massively comprehensive and authoritative text, frequently revised to accommodate later data. The book's underlying insistence on power politics as universal and inescapable attains the quality of a tragic vision. Indispensable reading for the serious student of the subject. There is a very full bibliography.

Brian Porter (ed.), *The Aberystwyth Papers*, 1972.
A valuable symposium by leading scholars on the history and methodology of the subject of international relations.

Philip J. Reynolds, *An Introduction to International Politics*, 1971.
A characteristically assured and lucid treatment. Professor Reynolds gives much weight to systems analysis.

Chapter 2 : Some international systems in history

Adda B. Boseman, *Politics and Culture in International History*, 1960.
An ambitious work, ranging over the whole of the near east. Much valuable material if no real theoretical framework.

A. R. Burn, *The Warring States of Greece*, 1968.
Sparkling short history of the ancient Greek inter-state system.

J. B. Bury, *A History of Greece to the death of Alexander the Great*, 3rd edn 1951. Concise yet detailed standard text.

M. Cary, *A History of Rome*, 2nd edn 1954.
A standard history by a major scholar.

Peter Fliess, *Thucydides and the Politics of Bipolarity*, 1966.
An illuminating commentary which draws many suggestive parallels between the rivalry of Athens and Sparta and the post-second world war relationship of competitive hostility between the United States and the Soviet Union.

Michael Grant, *Ancient History*, 1952.
A relatively early work by this great scholar which contains an illuminating discussion of ancient nationhood and the 'international anarchy' as it existed in antiquity.

Mario Atillio Levi, *Political Power in the Ancient World*, 1955, Eng. trans. 1965.
A study of political legitimacy in ancient society and of the causes of conflict between political units. Excellent on the political role of ancient religion.

Charles A. M. McClelland, *Theory and the International System*, 1966.
An introduction to the techniques of systems analysis in the study of international relations past and present.

Colin McEvedy, *The Penguin Atlas of Ancient History*, 1967.
Colin McEvedy, *The Penguin Atlas of Mediaeval History*, n.d.
Two short reference works, in which a concise but very informative text supplements a sequence of admirably clear maps.

Thucydides, *The History of the Peloponnesian War*, 405 BC.
A good modern version is in Penguin Classics.

Chapter 3: All states great and small: some diversities in the contemporary world

Ronald Barston, 'The External Relations of Small States', *Nobel Symposium 17; Small States in International Relations*, 1971.
A useful article which seeks to clarify the classification of states as well as to discuss the role of small states.

Ronald P. Barston (ed.), *The Other Powers: Studies in the Foreign Policies of Small States*, 1973.
A valuable symposium in which a number of political scientists contribute analyses of the foreign policies of nine small countries, ranging in importance from the Netherlands and Israel to Cyprus and Singapore. A timely corrective to the neglect of the role of small states in the study of international politics.

Joseph Frankel, *The Making of Foreign Policy*, 1963.
A lucid treatment in which 'decision-making' in international politics represents the organizing idea.

David Vital, *The Inequality of States*, 1966.
An important study of the disparateness of power in international society, with special emphasis on small state behaviour.

Chapter 4: The notion of the nation: some images and myths

Kenneth Boulding, *The Image*, 1st paperback edn 1961.
An exhilarating discussion of the nature of perception, including men's perceptions of what are taken to be the realities of international politics, reminding the reader that whatever may be the objective truth of a thing, even such a thing as a nation, our knowledge of that truth cannot be other than subjective: there is reality, and 'reality-as-perceived' which is all we can ever know.

Sylvia G. Haim (ed.), *Arab Nationalism – An Anthology*, 1965.
A symposium strikingly setting forth what one major contemporary example of nationalist ideology is believed by its adherents to represent.

Hans Kohn, *The Idea of Nationalism*, 1945.
Hans Kohn, *Nationalism*, 2nd edn 1965.
Two learned studies in depth by a major scholar.

K. R. Minogue, *Nationalism*, 1967.
A brilliant discussion weaving strands of history and political theory together in a tight pattern of close argument.

Elie Kedourie, *Nationalism*, 2nd (revised) edn 1961.
Another short book of comparable merit, containing an elucidation of that body of ideas which was developed in the writings of the great European theorists of nationhood. Very useful bibliography.

Chapter 5: The instrumentality of power

Bertrand de Jouvenal, *On Power*, 3rd edn 1962.
A fundamental work dealing mainly with the relations of the state to the citizen but in its verve and profundity offering invaluable insights into the nature – and the pathology – of political power. A book full of intellectual excitement.

Leslie Lipson, *The Great Issues of Politics*, 3rd edn 1965.
A comprehensive study, all of it deserving attention, especially in relation to power in international politics, sections 12 and 13.

Sir Charles Grant Robertson, *Religion and the Totalitarian State*, 1937.
A mature discussion shedding light on the nature of 'totalitarian' power, and examining its pretensions as against those of Christianity as a faith claiming a universal validity.

Bertrand Russell, *Power*, Basis Books edn 1940.
Written with all the late Lord Russell's elegance and cogency of style, this book analyses power as a social phenomenon with all its international as well as intra-state implications.

Three works may be noted from the growing literature on civil-military relations which are of such critical importance in regard to the legitimacy, stability and power of governmental institutions.

S. E. Finer, *The Man on Horseback*, 1962,
Analyses the phenomenon of military intervention in government in terms of the level of 'political culture' prevailing in a state.

Samuel P. Huntington, *The Soldier and the State*, 1957.
A sound, closely argued discussion by a leading American scholar.

Morris Janowitz, *The Military in the Political Development of New Nations*, 2nd imp. 1965.
Explores civil-military relations in the highly dynamic context of the post-imperial phase of nation-building, mainly in the 'Third World'.

Chapter 6 : Morality and law in international politics

Bernard Bosanquet, *The Philosophical Theory of the State*, New York edn 1899.
A classic treatment which remains after three-quarters of a century valuable for the guidance of anyone wrestling with problems of the relations of the 'is' of state power to the 'ought' of political behaviour. Bosanquet's conception of the attributed self-hood of states may be profitably examined in the light of Professor Manning's thought in the work cited above.

Sir Herbert Butterfield, *Christianity, Diplomacy and War*, 3rd edn 1962
Sir Herbert Butterfield, *Christianity in European History*, 1952.
As with all Sir Herbert's writings, these short books provoke long reflection. No brief annotation can do any justice to the quality of his thinking, or its timeliness in regard to the current predicaments of international society.

E. H. Carr, *The 20 Years' Crisis, 1919–1939*, 1939.
A work set in an historical context which has proved by the depths of its analysis to be of continuing value. A most important discussion, on

the fundamental problems of international order, its norms and its prospects, by one who is arguably the greatest living English historian.

E. F. Carritt, *Ethical and Political Thinking*, 1947.
Covers much the ground of T. D. Weldon's work cited below, and with a comparable authority.

R. S. Downie, *Government Action and Morality*, 1964.
A useful enquiry of which Part Two is particularly relevant.

D. M. MacKinnon (ed.), *Making Moral Decisions*, 1969.
A distinguished collection of lectures, of which Mr Michael Howard's on 'Morality and Force in International Politics' is essential reading for anyone studying the subject-matter of this book.

Reinhold Niebuhr, *Moral Man and Immoral Society*, 1932.
A seminal work which in its exploration of the moral ambiguities embodied in international relations remains dateless.

T. D. Weldon, *States and Morals*, 5th imp. 1962.
An acute discussion, agreeably mordant in places, which examines the nature of obligation at once of citizens towards their states, of states towards their citizens and of states towards each other.

Chapter 7 : The international relationship of war

Raymond Aron, *The Century of Total War*, Eng. edn 1954.
An impressive survey of the predicaments facing statesmen and their publics in the period of world wars, and the cold war that followed the second, from the standpoint of the prospects for Western Europe.

Alastair Buchan, *War in Modern Society*, 2nd edn 1968.
A sharply conceived, smoothly written study bringing into focus the basic problems arising out of the scale and destructive potentiality of international armed conflict in the twentieth century.

Robin Clarke, *The Science of War and Peace*, 1971.
A critical examination of many assumptions prevalent among governmental and military establishments about the desirability of modifying the human environment and even human beings themselves in the interests of current strategic objectives.

John C. Garnett (ed.), *Theories of Peace and Security: A Reader in Contemporary Strategic Thought*, 1970.
A wide-ranging symposium contributed to by writers of great authority. There is a very closely reasoned Introduction by the editor.

Victor Gollancz, *The Devil's Repertoire, or Nuclear Bombing and the Life of Man*, 1958.
The response of a humane and sensitive observer to the actualities and possibilities arising from the existence of nuclear weapons. A *cri de coeur* against the danger of what Gollancz saw as an undue obsession with the power-political orientation of international society, the case he passionately advocated enjoined non-violence as a technique and trust as a necessary risk if mankind was to survive. That the prescriptions have not been taken does not of course in itself invalidate them, but few serious 'thinkers about the unthinkable' seem so far to be convinced by them.

J. W. Herz, *International Politics in the Atomic Age*, 1959.
Discusses the problem of the territorial viability of states in the light of their total permeability by strategic nuclear weapons.

Max Lerner, *The Age of Overkill*, 1962.
A discussion of the strategic implications of the nuclear balance during the period of the cold war.

Anatol Rapoport, *Fights, Games and Debates*, 1961.
A brilliant critique of the assumptions of power politics, offering a conceptualization of conflict as consisting of fights, in which opponents attempt to destroy one another, games, in which they seek to outwit one another and debates, in which they try to persuade one another. Rapoport's prescription is to change fights into games and games into debates.

Kenneth N. Waltz, *Man, the State and War*, 1959.
Another endeavour to analyse the prospect opened before international society by the advent of weaponry capable of destroying it. Sombrely wise.

Chapter 8 : Beyond the state? The role of international organizations

John Bowle, *World Order or Catastrophe?*, 1963.
Examines concisely the current world crisis in terms of a clash of ideologies, including assertive nationalism as well as universalist doctrines, which he deems to threaten the continuance of a necessary international order.

Inis L. Claude, Jr, *Swords into Plowshares*, 1956.
Enjoying a very wide reputation, this fine study remains essential to a developed understanding of the role and possible potential of the United Nations in regard to a collective security function.

Alfred Cobban. *The Nation-State and National Self-Determination*, revised edn 1969.
A treatment of classic authority. The late Professor Cobban's discussion of the status and role of the doctrine of self-determination in modern international history sparkles with critical intelligence.

Carold Ann Cosgrove and Kenneth J. Twitchett (eds), *The New International Actors*, 1970.
A helpful study of the role of the United Nations and the European Economic Community as multi-national actors in the international system of sovereign states. The implication that this system may be transformed by the functioning of such new components deserves to be carefully pondered.

Maurice Cranston, *Human Rights Today*, 1962.
A short but useful discussion of the development of the notion of human rights as properly the subject of attempted guarantee by international organizations.

W. B. Curry, *The Case for Federal Union*, 1939.
An eloquently argued case for world unity by consent, no less endearing for not having achieved acceptance.

Elizabeth Jay Hollins (ed.), *Peace is Possible*, 1968.
A series of readings characterized by urgency and compassion. The plentiful prescriptions are well balanced by a recognition of the difficulties.

Fred R. von der Mehlen, *Comparative Political Violence*, 1973.
A case-by-case study of political violence in many parts of the world other than in relation to war between states. The generalizing of violence as a technique by which dissident groups seek to gain their ends, and as characteristic of polarized communities within states, is coolly analysed. The implications of its theme for the well-being of any effectual world order make this book especially timely.

Jack C. Plano and Robert E. Riggs, *Forging World Order : the Politics of International Organization*, 1967.
A magisterial work in the tradition of American comprehensive texts. Factual and authoritative.

F. P. Walters, *A History of the League of Nations*, 2nd edn 1960.
A comprehensive standard history by a former deputy secretary-general of the League.

Index

M